PRENTICE-HALL SERIES IN SPEECH COMMUNICATION
Larry L. Barker and Robert J. Kibler, Consulting Editors

ARGUMENTATION

Inquiry
and
Advocacy, 1975.

GEORGE W. ZIEGELMUELLER,
Wayne State University

CHARLES A. DAUSE
University of Detroit

PRENTICE-HALL, INC., ENGLEWOOD CLIFFS, NEW JERSEY

Library of Congress Cataloging in Publication Data

Ziegelmueller, George W.
    Argumentation: inquiry and advocacy.

    (Prentice-Hall series in speech communication)
    Includes bibliographical references.
    1. Debates and debating.   I. Dause, Charles A.,
joint author.   II. Title.
PN4181.Z5   808.85'3   74–7358
ISBN: 0–13–046029–X

To Elenore and Marilyn

PN
4181
Z5

© 1975 by PRENTICE-HALL, INC., *Englewood Cliffs, New Jersey*

Printed in the United States of America

10 9 8 7 6 5 4 3 2 1

Prentice-Hall International, Inc., *London*
Prentice-Hall of Australia, Pty. Ltd., *Sydney*
Prentice-Hall of Canada, Ltd., *Toronto*
Prentice-Hall of India Private Limited, *New Delhi*
Prentice-Hall of Japan, Inc., *Tokyo*

Contents

241544

Preface

Argumentation: Inquiry and Advocacy has been written with four primary objectives in mind. The first is to place the study of argumentation in a broad philosophical framework. The introductory section of the book is devoted to an examination of the philosophical and logical assumptions underlying the processes of argumentation. In Chapter 1 the relationships between argumentation and truth and between argumentation and social action are considered. In Chapter 2 the logical and legalistic premises of argumentation are explained and justified. Throughout the remainder of the book philosophical assumptions continue to be emphasized. In Chapter 4, for example, the concept of agreement is seen as basic to the use of supporting data, and in Chapter 6 the assumption of uniformity is identified as basic to the reasoning process.

The book's second objective is to identify a wide range of practical application for argumentation theory. Most argumentation texts discuss the uses of argument primarily in the context of academic debate. While this book accepts the validity and desirability of academic debate as a training vehicle for argumentation, it recognizes that argumentation training ought to be immediately applicable to the whole range of an individual's mental activities. Thus, the book looks at the inquiry phase of argumentation from the perspective of personal inquiry and personal truth determination, and the discussion of the advocacy phase of argumentation considers the application of argumentation to a wide range of advocacy situations. Chapter 10, for instance, discusses various advocacy situations in terms of an argumentation-propaganda continuum, and Chapter 13 suggests how communication strategies can be developed to help make arguments more persuasive.

The third objective of the book is to clarify, reinterpret, and extend argumentation theory. Chapter 3 introduces the systems approach to analysis as a complement to the standard stock issues methodology. Chapter 4 broadens the concept of data to include perceptual and value premises, and Chapter 5 suggests ways in which these premises may be tested. Chapter 7 presents a reformulation of the forms of argument and attempts to explain the unique aspects of each of these forms. Chapter 9 offers the logical outline as a way of structuring arguments and of testing their relationships to one another. Chapter 11 presents the first theoretical description of the effect-oriented and on-balance cases, and Chapters 11 and 12 provide a discussion of affirmative and negative case approaches to propositions of judgment. Chapter 13 attempts to clarify the concept of communication strategies and to suggest a rationale for the use of strategies consistent with the philosophy of argument.

Finally, the book provides illustrative material in an effort to make the concepts of argumentation practical and interesting. In most instances the illustrations deal with topics of contemporary concern and have been selected to demonstrate the application of argumentation in a variety of contexts (political campaigns, investigative committees, courts of law, newspaper editorials, etc.). The use of contemporary topics does not, of course, assure that the illustrations will remain relevant beyond the date of this writing. We believe, however, that illustrations drawn from recent controversies are more likely to be of interest and value than hypothetical examples. An effort has also been made to present the material concisely and in a clearly organized manner. Initial chapter outlines and final chapter summaries are provided to help the reader perceive relationships and identify major concepts.

1 Introduction

1 The Philosophical Framework of Argument

In order to function effectively in life, one must attempt to discover what is appropriate behavior and to act on the basis of his conclusions. The responsibility for making such decisions is one which none of us can avoid. Each day we make a variety of relatively simple decisions concerning the places where we will go, the activities in which we will engage, the people with whom we will associate, and so on. Most of these decisions require little conscious effort because of their simplicity and because they are determined largely by the patterns of our every-day lives.

Many of the decisions which we are called upon to make, however, are much more complex and much more vital to our lives than these routine decisions. Should I attend a school near my home or should I go away to school? Should I experiment with drugs? Should I participate in the boycott of classes planned for tomorrow? Should we get married before graduation? Should we rent an apartment or buy a home? Should I accept the new job or stay where I am? Such decisions fall outside of the routines of everyday life and force us to think before we act. Moreover, since so many of these decisions affect, and are affected by, how others behave, it is frequently impossible for us to act without the aid and approval of others. The nature of decision making in the society within which we live, then, forces us not only to discover what is appropriate and to act on that discovery, but it also frequently demands that we be advocates of our conclusions.

THE NATURE OF ARGUMENTATION

In studying argumentation we are studying ways individuals can be assisted in their efforts to make important decisions and in their efforts to convince others of the wisdom of those decisions. More specifically, argumentation is defined as *the study of the logical principles which underlie the examination and presentation of persuasive claims.*

This definition suggests that the central concern of argumentation is with logical principles. It is this focus on logical processes which distinguishes the study of argumentation from the study of persuasion, group communication, and other specialized aspects of communication theory. However, while argumentation emphasizes the logical bases of decision making and communication, it cannot and should not be isolated from the "nonlogical." Thus, as the above definition recognizes, the immediate focus of argumentation is on *logical principles,* but its ultimate concern is with *persuasive claims.*

This definition also suggests that the study of argumentation is concerned both with inquiry and advocacy. As an investigative study, argumentation is concerned with discovering what is probably true in any controversy. In directing the student to such discovery, the inquiry phase of the study of argumentation includes consideration of research methods, the nature and evaluation of data, the nature and testing of argument, and the synthesis of ideas. As a study of advocacy, argumentation is concerned with the individual's ability to convince others of the validity of the conclusion which he has discovered. The advocacy phase of argumentation involves an understanding of advocacy situations, of case structuring, of refutation skills, and of strategic concepts. Through the study of argumentation, then, an individual should be able to achieve a stronger logical foundation for the decisions he reaches and should become more effective in advocating those decisions.

THE NEED FOR ARGUMENTATION

Why study argumentation? The answers should be obvious in a democratic society, but as one looks at the events of the past decade perhaps the question is legitimate. We live in a society which appears to be becoming less reliant upon its powers of reason and more dependent upon force and power confrontations. Riots, demonstrations, sit-ins, and boycotts all testify to a breakdown in societal communication. Many groups in our society have adopted power-confrontation tactics on the assumption that they are more "effective" means of achieving the objectives of the group than are rational discussion and debate. Why, then, should one study argumentation? The continued relevance of the argumentation process may be demonstrated in terms of two considerations.

MAKING INDIVIDUAL DECISIONS

The skills of argumentative inquiry are needed to help us in making personal decisions. What power confrontation is possible in the question whether or not to buy a new car or to take a different job? Questions such as "How far should I go in premarital love making?" and "What do I want out of life?" are personal problems which demand reasoned examination. Many people find problems like these difficult to deal with because they do not know how to analyze the facts of the situation or how to evaluate conflicting values. This inability to analyze and evaluate is not confined simply to intimate personal problems but extends as well to social attitudes and beliefs. As young children we acquire many of our ideas from our parents. Later on, peer groups exert an important influence on our attitudes and perspectives. Still later in life, our judgments become heavily influenced by the political and economic institutions with which we are associated and by the magazines and newspapers which we read. If we are to avoid being mere sponges simply absorbing what we are exposed to, we must learn how to evaluate critically the ideas and influences of others. Thus, to be able to arrive at satisfactory answers to intimate personal problems and to achieve intellectual independence requires the application of the skills of reasoned inquiry.

EFFECTING SOCIAL CHANGE

We believe that the methods of reasoned advocacy provide the only viable means of effecting social change. Public demonstrations and mass confrontations may effect change either through force or through the arousal of public sentiment. To the extent that mass confrontations are intended to *force* change, they are philosophically unacceptable. Force assumes, rather than tests, the rightness of a position, and, as a result, it suppresses opposition and denies the freedom and integrity of all who oppose it. To the extent that demonstrations and marches seek to effect change through the arousal of public sentiment, they are ultimately dependent upon reasoned advocacy. The original civil rights marches were effective in drawing public attention to the social plight of black men and in creating sentiment in their behalf. But the resulting civil rights legislation which attempted to respond to these grievances was the culmination of months of careful study, analysis, and debate. Where protests have gained public attention but have not been reinforced with reasoned inquiry and advocacy, they have been ineffective in bringing about change. Thus, if we are to avoid the disruption and suppression of force, and yet be effective in implementing social changes, we must ultimately rely upon the methods of argumentation.

TRUTH AND PROBABILITY

Whether we are concerned with finding answers for our personal problems or those of society, we inevitably have great difficulty in knowing what is true. The study of argumentation provides a variety of tests based upon the principles of completeness and consistency which are helpful in examining both the means and materials used in arriving at conclusions. But helpful as these tests are, they cannot provide us with absolute assurance of the certainty of our conclusions.

LIMITATIONS ON ABILITY TO KNOW TRUTH

To the extent that the mathematician and the scientist deal in controlled, measurable phenomena, they can provide answers which appear to be certain. Even these answers, however, are subject to the limitations of measurement devices, formulas, and perception. When we move out of the realm of science into the fields of human relations, politics, and ethics, our ability to be certain of the truth of a position becomes even more restricted. We are unable to reach certainty because of the limitations of knowledge, perspective, and time.

First of all, our knowledge is limited. Because man is human he can never know all there is to know about anything, even himself. Biographers have been studying the life of Lincoln for decades, and yet there remain many uncertain and unexplained aspects of his life history. After centuries of study, historians are still not certain about the real causes behind the decline and fall of the Roman Empire or the factors which produced the American Revolution.

But even if we could have all of the pertinent facts regarding any situation, we would still be limited by our perceptions. Inevitably, man tends to perceive events from the perspective of his own previous experiences and values. Thus, even given a complete body of data, a white American historian and a black American historian might come to considerably different conclusions concerning the motivations behind and effects of the Emancipation Proclamation.

When we consider contemporary problems, the third limitation, that of time, becomes of major importance. The world and relationships between phenomena are constantly changing so that it becomes impossible for anyone to keep completely up-to-date on any current situation. It may take decades and even centuries to discover enough of the facts concerning the United States' involvement in Vietnam before a proper understanding of that issue can be achieved. Such an understanding is denied to a contemporary citizen, politician, or historian. Thus, while we are obliged to seek to discover what is true, the limitations of knowledge, perspective, and time prevent us from ever being certain that we have achieved that goal.

If the certainty of a position can never be fully established, why should we be concerned with attempting to discover what is "true"? To say that one cannot know with *certainty* the truth about a particular problem or situation is not to deny the existence of true facts or true perspectives. Clearly, Lee Harvey Oswald either killed John F. Kennedy or he did not. In spite of months of extensive investigation by the Warren Commission we cannot be *absolutely certain* that Oswald fired the shots which killed Kennedy. Our lack of certainty, however, does not mean that there is no objective truth in the specific situation. Clearly, the indefinite continuation of present rates of increase in air pollution will either make the earth uninhabitable for mankind or it will not. Our present inability to achieve absolute certainty concerning this statement does not mean that no truth exists in this situation. Ultimate truth in any situation does exist, even if man is incapable of knowing that truth with certainty.

IMPLICATIONS OF PROBABILITY OF PERCEPTION

The fact that even the most conscientious application of argumentation cannot lead to *certainty* of knowledge has important implications. First, it implies that man can and must operate in society on the basis of less-than-certain conclusions. To refuse to make a judgment or to take a stand until one is certain of his conclusion is to cease to function in any meaningful way. Man is not free to avoid making decisions because he cannot make them with certainty. He must operate on probabilities.

It is helpful to think of our ability to know truth as though it exists on a continuum. At one end is complete uncertainty and at the other complete certainty. As we investigate a question, the degree of our commitment to a given answer may progress from uncertainty, to possibility, to probability, to high probability. Since we can never achieve certainty, we must be satisfied to act on the basis of high probability.

A second implication of our inability to know the truth of a situation with certainty concerns our degree of emotional commitment to a position. If we can only know truth probably, then dogmatism must be considered an inappropriate attitude. It is possible for a person to have deep convictions without becoming dogmatically committed to them. Intelligent advocacy requires that we be willing to set forth and defend our commitments, but it also requires that we be willing to listen to and to learn from others. Dogmatic advocacy, on the other hand, assumes such certainty of truth that it precludes the possibility of new knowledge or additional insights. In short, an intelligent person should never let the advocacy of his beliefs override his search for more certain truth.

The third implication of our limited ability to know ultimate truth concerns our attitudes toward those who differ with us. Once we understand that limitations exist on our own ability to know truth, it becomes more difficult for us to view our opponents as liars and distorters of truth. The public sometimes finds it difficult to understand how some political leaders can oppose each other in so many controversies and still have warm and genuine respect for one another. The explanation can be found in the fact that such leaders, like all intelligent advocates, have come to look upon their opponents as partners in a joint search for wise decisions. Thus, our opponents in committee meetings, parliamentary assemblies, or public debates ought not be viewed as barriers to wise action but as testers of our own wisdom.

ARGUMENTATION AND HUMAN NATURE

Inquiry and advocacy rarely, if ever, take place in a purely logical atmosphere. Self-interest, ignorance, and group pressures impose considerable limitations upon reasoned investigation and decision making. Intellectually, most Americans have come to accept the equality of all races, but self-concerns regarding property values and job competition have precluded more rapid civil rights action. The needs of local governments for greater tax revenues have been clearly documented, but self-concerns about higher taxes and ignorance of the real impact of lower spending have stood in the way of tax increases. In spite of the increase in violent crimes, the assassination of public figures, and the greater restrictions on firearms in almost all other countries, the efforts of powerful lobbies have succeeded in limiting gun control legislation.

Situations like these are often discouraging to believers in the viability of the argumentation process. But in spite of such human restraints, changes do occur, and solutions are worked out. The skilled advocate learns how to construct his arguments upon self-interest or to relate the self-interest to a higher motive or to refute the appeal to self-interest. Low audience knowledge levels may require more simplified arguments and education through a variety of media, but man is capable of learning, and reasoned advocacy can succeed. The efforts of pressure groups require equal efforts from contrary groups, and if the arguments of the opposing pressure group are invalid, they cannot be sustained for long.

The nonrational dimensions of mankind will control human behavior only so long as evidence is not explored, reasoning is not tested, and communication is ineffective. If we believe that logical factors should prevail in individual and social decisions, then we must have a commitment to training in argumentation. The more we produce individuals trained in reasoned inquiry and committed to the belief that reasoned advocacy should prevail, the more likely we are to end with decision making which is based on a sound logical framework.

SUMMARY

Argumentation is the study of the logical principles which underlie the examination and presentation of persuasive claims. Its immediate focus is on logical principles but its ultimate concern is with persuasive claims. It is concerned with the processes of inquiry and advocacy.

The study of argumentation is justified both as a means of making personal decisions and as a means of effecting public change. Satisfactory answers to intimate personal problems and the achievement of intellectual independence require the skills of reasoned inquiry. The effective implementation of social change without the use of force is dependent upon reasoned advocacy.

Our ability to know what is true is limited. We cannot be certain about the truth of our decisions because of limitations of knowledge, perspective, and time. Although we can never be certain of our answers, ultimate truth in any situation does exist. The fact that we cannot be certain of our conclusions suggests that we must act on the basis of probabilities, that we should avoid dogmatism, and that we should welcome opposition.

Human self-interests, ignorance, and pressure groups often limit the effectiveness of argumentation processes. Such limitations, however, do not negate the viability of argumentation. Rather, they require more effective application of, and more widespread training in, argumentation.

STUDY QUESTIONS

1. Does the organization of power blocs, such as labor unions and lobbying groups, in any way compromise the principles upon which the study of argumentation is based?
2. Can the concept of *probability* be applied to the religious beliefs of an individual or group?
3. Does the concept of unnegotiable demands clash with the philosophical framework of argument as outlined in this chapter?
4. The chapter asserts that "logical factors should prevail in individual and social decisions." Are there any conditions under which this conclusion should be modified?

2 The Logical Framework of Argument

All of us, at one time or another, have had the experience of participating in informal "bull sessions." Such sessions usually involve heated dispute concerning one or more controversial topics of interest to the participants. While most of us enjoy the free give and take involved in such exchanges, we frequently come away from such sessions confused, with the feeling that nothing has been accomplished. Why is it that discussion, involving intelligent people freely expressing their views, so frequently ends in confusion and misunderstanding? The answer, in part, is that such sessions rarely operate within a *logical framework.* These sessions are characterized by a lack of ground rules. Rarely does anyone bother to make a clear statement of the question being discussed or debated. Seldom do the participants fully understand the logical responsibilities inherent in the arguments they are forwarding. Arguments tend to occur in isolation rather than as part of a total analysis of the question at hand. The result is an interesting session which usually falls short of being a thorough analysis of the topic under consideration. While few of us would advocate imposing strict ground rules on informal sessions such as this, adherence to a logical framework is essential when real decisions are to be made.

To see the importance of such a logical framework we need only look to our American legal system. When an individual is accused of a crime, we demand a clear statement of the indictment against that individual; we prescribe that the individual is not guilty until proven otherwise; and we carefully outline what the prosecution must prove before we conclude guilt. Few of us would approve of a legal system which operated as an informal bull session with no ground rules. In short, because we believe that our courts of law are making decisions vital to all of us, we demand a carefully devised system of logical ground rules which controls the argumentation in those courts.

The purpose of this chapter will be to show that a similar logical framework is vital in order to ensure clear and reasonable analysis of all problems requiring personal or public decisions. While the concepts to be discussed in this chapter have their roots in the American legal system, they are just as vital to nonlegal argumentation. When used in general argumentation they cannot always be applied with the preciseness that is possible in a court of law, but they are none-the-less essential concepts in directing the student of argumentation to his logical responsibilities as an advocate. The remainder of this chapter, then, will be devoted to a discussion of the classification and phrasing of debate propositions and to a discussion of the basic logical concepts that constitute the framework within which argumentation takes place.

PROPOSITIONS

The first step in assuring a sufficient logical framework for debate or discussion is a careful phrasing of the question to be considered. Clear phrasing of a question can provide a meaningful basis for argument, whereas vague phrasing or no phrasing at all will inevitably lead to misunderstandings and to superficial analysis. A student forum concerned with students' rights, for instance, can drag on for hours and end in frustration for all if a clear resolution is not phrased and defined. A block club concerned with local real estate practices may never reach the action stage if it doesn't stop to state its objectives. A debate over United States foreign policy can wander off onto tangents if the direction and nature of the change being proposed are not clearly defined by the advocates. In short, the prerequisite for adequate analysis of any question is the careful phrasing of a statement expressing the basis of the controversy. In argumentation we call such a statement a proposition.

The proposition for discussion or debate can appear in a variety of different forms depending upon the situation. In academic debate it is usually phrased as a resolution: *Resolved: That the private ownership of handguns should be illegal.* In discussion it is usually phrased in question form: *What can be done to improve the freshman orientation program at X University?* In business meetings it is phrased as a motion: *Mr. Chairman, I move that the report of the budget committee be approved.* In legislative assemblies it is frequently phrased as a bill: *Be it enacted by the Common Council of the City of Detroit that. . . .* No matter what form it takes, the proposition's primary function remains constant: to make clear to all what is being proposed or examined—to isolate the essence of the controversy.

A considerable amount of preliminary investigation usually must occur before a final statement of a proposition for discussion or debate evolves. In legal cases, the prosecuting attorney or plaintiff's lawyer will study the facts of the situation carefully and the nature of the relevant laws before deciding upon a formal statement of charges. In legislative assemblies, proposed bills are usually sent to committees for consideration, appraisal, and rewriting, if necessary. Only after a proposal has gone through this process is it brought before the entire assembly for debate. In parliamentary debate a resolution may be reworded by amendments or by general consensus several times during the course of its consideration. Even in committee meetings considerable preliminary discussion may have to occur before the group can decide on the exact nature of its problem area. Inexperienced advocates sometimes become frustrated by the processes involved in the phrasing of bills, resolutions, and other forms of propositions, but the effort expended in working out an acceptable phrasing is necessary if a clear clash of issues and a thorough analysis are to follow.

Before we consider guidelines for phrasing propositions for debate and discussion we must first understand that there are different types of propositions. All propositions—questions, resolutions, motions, etc.—may be classified according to two categories: *propositions of judgment or propositions of policy.* This classification of propositions is based upon the assumption that these two types of propositions demand essentially different analytical procedures. These analytical approaches are discussed in detail in a later chapter. Our purpose here is simply to identify the twofold classification.

Propositions of judgment. *Propositions of judgment are descriptive, predictive, or evaluative statements which assert the existence or worth of something.* While propositions of judgment take several different forms, all require the same analytical approach. In dissecting our definition we find that propositions of judgment can appear in three different forms: descriptive judgments, predictive judgments, and evaluative judgments.

The *descriptive proposition of judgment* asserts the existence of past or present events or relationships. As in all propositions of judgment, the claim of the proposition is not an established fact, but rather is an alleged fact. The following are examples of descriptive propositions of judgment:

Lee Harvey Oswald fired the shots that killed President Kennedy.
Existing federal laws against industrial pollution have not been enforced.
A teaching certificate is no longer a guarantee of employment.
Smoking causes lung cancer.

Predictive propositions of judgment assert claims concerning future events or relationships. The added dimension of prediction makes such judgments more complex than most descriptive propositions of judgment. The following are examples of predictive propositions of judgment:

The cost of new housing will increase substantially in the next year.
The stock market will begin a steady increase which will last until the end of the year.
The Mets will win the pennant this year.
The cost of the new domed stadium will exceed $100 million.

Evaluative propositions of judgment go beyond the assertion of past, present, or future existence in that they assert the worth of something. While sometimes difficult to distinguish from descriptive judgments, evaluative judgments are usually characterized by an evaluative term which suggests goodness, badness, desirability, undesirability, etc.

A Chevrolet is a better value than a Ford.
Freedom of speech is the most important of all of our rights.
Professor X is a poor teacher.
Restaurant A serves better meals than restaurant B.

Propositions of policy. A proposition of policy is a statement which asserts that a course of action should be taken. Every time a discussion participant questions the desirability of a course of action, every time an advocate claims that "something should be done," and every time a legislator calls for the passage of a pending bill, a question of policy is under consideration. Propositions of policy are considerably more complex than propositions of judgment and demand, as will be explained in Chapter 3, a different analytical approach. Propositions of policy are the type usually used in academic debate, and the examples below are stated in resolution form as they would be phrased in a college or high school debate proposition.

Resolved: That the federal government should establish a system of compulsory wage and price controls.
Resolved: That X University should adopt a "pass–no credit" grading system.
Resolved: That future moon exploration should be discontinued.
Resolved: That we should buy a new automobile this year.

PHRASING PROPOSITIONS

To this point we have seen how propositions are classified. It is now necessary to examine some guidelines for phrasing propositions since a poorly phrased proposition can be as detrimental to the conduct of debate or discussion as no proposition at all. If the proposition is to serve its intended function of isolating the essence of the controversy, then we must take great care in working out its phrasing. Four simple guidelines can assist us considerably in working out the phrasing of propositions.

The proposition should be phrased to indicate a change from the present policy or belief. There is no reason to debate or discuss if everyone is content with existing belief or policies. Therefore, propositions should be phrased in terms of change in order to provide a general idea of the "felt difficulty." Moreover, since propositions are the starting point for any controversy, it is important to word them in consistent ways so that other related concepts can have a fixed point of reference. In a court of criminal law, for instance, the statement of indictment is always phrased in terms of alleged guilt. This phrasing never varies since part of its function is to properly identify the prosecution and the defense and to outline the prosecution's specific burden of proof. In general argumentation, if the proposition is phrased as a clear, specific statement of what the affirmative wants, and if it clearly identifies the affirmative as the person who is advocating change in belief or action, then we have a proposition which correctly places presumption and burden of proof. These two concepts will be discussed in more detail in the last half of this chapter.

The statement of the proposition should clearly indicate both the nature and direction of the change desired. A proposition should identify the essence of the change in belief or action being proposed and should indicate the philosophical or political movement away from the present belief or action. The proposition, *Resolved: That our present welfare system should be abolished,* indicates neither the nature nor the direction of the change being proposed. Many alternatives, from total elimination of welfare payments to a proposal for a guaranteed annual income, are within the range of this negatively worded proposition. The proposition, *Resolved: That the United States should substantially reduce its foreign policy commitments,* clearly indicates the direction of the action being proposed but fails to identify its nature. The proposition leaves the affirmative free to pick and choose among foreign policy commitments and to develop his own definition of a *substantial reduction.* The assertion that *history has inaccurately judged the literary worth of Mark Twain's writings* suggests the nature of the change desired (a more accurate judgment), but it fails to reveal the direction of the change in judgment desired.

The more open-ended wording of propositions may allow for greater latitude in the development of advocates' cases, but in so doing it places the defender of the present system at a real disadvantage. When the defense cannot anticipate the nature or direction of the attack, the task of providing a thorough response becomes extremely difficult. Obviously, prosecuting attorneys would find it easier to charge defendants simply with *wrongdoing,* but our legal system requires that the specific nature of the crime be spelled out so that the defendant can more adequately respond. The more specifically a proposition prescribes both the nature and the direction of the change being advocated, the more clearly drawn will be the line between the defender and the advocate of change, and the less likely we are to have definitional arguments and confusion. A clear clash of ideas can only occur when the participants in a controversy agree on both the nature and the direction of the change being proposed.

The statement of the proposition should contain one central idea.
As much as possible, advocates should attempt to debate one question at a time. The whole process of analysis is one of breaking down propositions into smaller units, and this process is made extremely difficult if the statement of the proposition contains multiple ideas. To argue, for instance, that X University should expand its student union recreational facilities and grant greater student representation in its governing councils invites analytical confusion. While both questions have to do with desires of the students of X University, they have to be analyzed and debated separately because they deal with separate and distinct problems. Further justification for this guideline is found in the fact that an individual might favor only half of a dually worded proposition such as the one above. One might favor, for instance, granting greater student representation in university governing councils but at the same time might question the financial feasibility of a proposed expansion of the recreational facilities of the student union.

Propositions of judgment may also be improperly phrased so that they ask for the acceptance of dual concepts. The statement that *Harvard is the best and most prestigious university in America* involves two judgments. In effect, this statement offers two propositions for analysis and debate.

In legislative and business sessions our rules of parliamentary procedure encourage wording propositions as single ideas. If someone proposes a motion with a dual idea, parliamentary procedure permits the division of the motion so that separate and distinct ideas can be considered separately. When an amendment to a motion is proposed, parliamentary procedure prescribes that the amendment must be considered and acted upon first before moving to the main motion. Such rules are certainly not arbitrary. They simply recognize that we can debate profitably only one idea at a time.

The proposition should be phrased in neutral terminology. This final guideline suggests that the phrasing of the proposition should not favor either side in the controversy. Frequently, advocates of change are tempted to add colorful terminology to the proposition for debate. The judgment that *the writings of foul-mouthed, sex-crazed authors are an unhealthy influence on American youth* is expressed in colorful language, but such language implies an unfair affirmative bias. A more neutral phraseology such as, *authors who use explicit sexual language are an unhealthy influence on American youth,* encourages a fairer appraisal. The proposition, *Resolved: That our antiquated and psychologically destructive grading system should be abolished,* begs the question as a phrasing of a proposition. The advocate here has attempted to incorporate some of his value judgments into the statement of a proposition of policy. If such phrasing is allowed to stand as the basis for debate, fair consideration of both sides of the question becomes impossible. Every attempt should be made, then, to phrase debate propositions in a way that the phrasing itself gives no advantage to either side.

The proposition, then, should be phrased in order to indicate a change from the present policy or belief. Both the nature and the direction of the change should be clearly indicated. The statement should contain only one central idea, and it should be phrased in neutral terminology.

BASIC LOGICAL CONCEPTS

In any argumentative situation, be it a court of law, a legislative chamber, or a committee meeting, there are certain logical constants which operate to allow for fair and reasonable consideration of the question at hand. It will be the purpose of this section to discuss these logical constants and to demonstrate their importance to the student of argumentation.[1]

[1]During the inquiry phase of argumentation these concepts should be thought of as logical absolutes. This will help to assure more thorough analysis. Chapter 10 will, however, demonstrate how the importance of these concepts and the logical obligations imposed by them vary according to the nature of the advocacy situation.

Presumption is the logical advantage inherent in defending exist-ing beliefs or policies. This concept recognizes that in every argumen-tative situation the person who is defending *things as they are* will win if nothing is done. Presumption makes no judgment concerning the wisdom of present policies or beliefs; it simply recognizes that what exists will continue to exist if nothing is done. An example of presump-tion in a legal context is the presumption of innocence. In the American legal system an individual who is accused of a crime is presumed not guilty until proven otherwise. This presumption requires acquittal unless guilt is established by sufficient evidence. If the prosecuting attorney fails to present a case against the accused individual or presents an insufficient case, the presumption of innocence requires that the man be freed. If a legislator proposes a bill to replace existing sales taxes with a general income tax, the existing sales tax system has presumption. Such presumption makes no judgment concerning the wisdom of the sales tax system; it simply describes a state of existence. The sales tax system will continue to exist until someone raises a reasonable case against it and proposes a viable alternative. The concept of presumption, then, simply recognizes that something now stands on the argumentative ground that the advocate of change wishes to oc-cupy.

The student of argumentation might question this use of the con-cept of presumption by asking, "In an era of rapid change, why should we give an advantage to existing policies and institutions?" The answer to that question is twofold. First, the concept of presumption doesn't *give* an advantage; it simply recognizes an advantage which is *inher-ent* in any decision-making situation. The concept does not make a value judgment concerning the policies or beliefs in question; it merely describes a state of inertia. It recognizes the simple fact that the failure to make a decision is a decision in itself—a decision in favor of existing beliefs or practices. If a family is deciding whether or not to purchase a new car, failure to decide means that the family will continue to ride in the old car. If a university governing body tables a proposal for its reorganization, the failure to decide has sustained the existing orga-nizational structure. The concept of presumption, then, simply states that in case of a tie in any argumentative situation, someone wins, and that someone is always the individual defending present beliefs or policies.

Second, the concept of presumption is justified in argumentation because change is always costly. Any change, even ultimately desir-able change, involves disruptive effects. A decision to buy a new car involves obvious costs. The concept of presumption suggests that significant reasons for incurring that cost must be present. To change from a sales tax base to an income tax base involves administrative reorganization and cost. The concept of presumption suggests that someone must first demonstrate serious deficiencies in the sales tax system before such administrative reorganization will take place. The acceptance of a previously discredited style of art as a significant form of self-expression requires redefinition of certain artistic principles and adjustments in perception. Presumption requires that the mental efforts involved in making these adjustments be warranted. The application of the concept of presumption to argumentation, then, is justified by the fact that existing policies and beliefs will continue to exist unless challenged and by the fact that all changes involve real or psychological costs.

BURDEN OF PROOF

The concept of burden of proof is the logical opposite of the concept of presumption. It is *the inherent obligation of those advocating change to raise arguments logically sufficient to remove the presumption of existing beliefs or policies.* In our legal system it is the duty of the prosecution in a criminal case "to establish the truth of the claim by preponderance of the evidence." If a man is charged with murder, the prosecutor has the burden of proof to produce a "preponderance of evidence" to establish guilt and remove the presumption of innocence. The faculty member advocating a change in the grading system has the logical obligation to demonstrate the inadequacies of the present grading system which could be removed by changing to the proposed system. In short, anyone advocating change from existing beliefs or policies has the responsibility for initiating and supporting action against those beliefs or policies. The obligation of the burden of proof is an important safeguard. By requiring that those who attack existing reputations, policies, or institutions be prepared to justify their attacks, we help to prevent irresponsible charges and actions. The knowledge that our accusations must be supported encourages responsibility.

It should be noted that the burden of proof always rests with the advocate of change; it never shifts during the controversy. While both sides in a dispute have an obligation to go forward with the debate, to engage in refutation, and to produce evidence as the debate progresses, the advocate of change always has the obligation to produce a preponderance of evidence and arguments. Unlike the man who defends existing beliefs or policies, the advocate of change cannot be satisfied with a standoff.

ISSUES

The word *issue* has a variety of meanings in everyday usage. It can mean anything from a controversial question to an isolated argument. In argumentation, however, this term has an important and very specific meaning. In argumentation, *issues are inherent questions vital to the advocate's cause.* One can better understand this concept by dissecting the definition.

First, issues are *inherent* in the proposition for debate or discussion. This means that issues are not created by the participants in the dispute, but rather exist within the statement and historic context of the resolution. In our legal system one discovers the issues through analyzing the specific indictment in the light of the written law and legal precedents. In argumentation one must analyze in depth the statement and context of the debate proposition in order to discover these crucial potential areas of clash.

Second, issues are *vital to the advocate's cause.* For the advocate of change this means that to lose an issue is to lose a debate. An issue, then, is something more than an argument or a contention. An advocate may lose an argument but still win his case. An issue, on the other hand, is vital to the logical sufficiency of that case. A prosecutor in a murder case, for instance, may not be able to establish the *argument* that the defendant owned the murder weapon. If he has sufficient evidence, however, he may be able to carry the *issue* that the defendant was the individual who fired that weapon. The question of ownership of the gun is an argument rather than an issue because it is not vital to the prosecution's case. But the question of who fired the gun is an issue because the failure to carry it will lead to the defeat of the case. The number of issues may vary among propositions, but the important thing to remember is that they are vital to the advocate's case.

Finally, we note that issues are *questions.* This formal consideration is contained within the definition for the sake of clarity. Issues should be phrased in question form so that the advocate of change must answer "yes" and the defender of existing beliefs or policies may answer "no." In the issue noted above, an appropriate phrasing would be "Did the defendant fire the shot which killed Mr. X?"[2]

The concept of issues is not an arbitrary concept. Rather it is the logical outgrowth of the concepts of presumption and burden of proof.

---

[2]A distinction is sometimes made between real and potential issues. *Potential issues* are all of the issues which exist within a given proposition, while *real issues* are the vital, inherent points which actually become a basis of clash. The process of logical analysis is concerned with the identification of potential issues. The nature of advocacy situations, case patterns, and strategic considerations determine which of the potential issues will, in fact, become real issues.

The concept of issues helps to define the specific limits of the burden of proof. Only by providing a positive answer to each of the issues can an advocate overcome the presumption and meet his burden of proof. Furthermore, this concept helps the student of argumentation to distinguish what is important, what is vital to his case, from comparatively unimportant arguments. The ability to discover the real issues is what distinguishes the successful lawyer from the hack, what causes one member of a committee to seem more insightful than the others, and what allows one person to make important personal decisions confidently while others hesitate over even small decisions. To be able to isolate the vital considerations in a proposition is the essence of the inquiry phase of argumentation.

PRIMA FACIE CASE

The advocate of change, in order to overcome the presumption of the present belief or policy, is obligated to present a prima facie case against that belief or policy. The term prima facie, literally defined, means "at first sight" or "on the face of it" or "before further examination." In legal terms, a prima facie case is a case "which will suffice until contradicted and overcome by other evidence." For our purposes, *a prima facie case can be defined as a case which is logically sufficient to overcome the presumption of the present belief or policy and to force the defender of that belief or policy to respond.*

The concept of the prima facie case allows us to relate the concepts of presumption, burden of proof, and issues. Because of the presumption of existing beliefs or policies, the advocate of change must assume his burden of proof to present a prima facie case. Whether or not that case is logically sufficient to overcome the presumption of the present belief or policy will depend upon whether or not the case provides a positive answer to each of the issues inherent in the proposition.

SUMMARY

There are two basic types of propositions: propositions of judgment and propositions of policy. Each of these types requires a different analytical procedure. Propositions of judgment are descriptive, predictive, or evaluative statements which assert the existence or worth of something. Propositions of policy are statements which assert that a course of action should be taken.

Careful phrasing of propositions is necessary for adequate analysis. There are four guidelines which should be followed in phrasing topics for discussion or debate: (1) The proposition should be phrased to indicate a change from the present system or belief. (2) The statement of the proposition should clearly indicate both the nature and the direction of the change desired. (3) The statement of the proposition should contain one central idea. (4) The proposition should be phrased in neutral terminology.

The concepts of presumption, burden of proof, issues, and prima facie case provide certain logical touchstones which operate to allow for fair and reasonable consideration of the question at hand. Presumption is the logical advantage inherent in defending "things as they are." It makes no judgment regarding the wisdom of present policies or beliefs; it simply recognizes that what exists will continue to exist if nothing is done. Burden of proof is the logical opposite of presumption. It is the inherent obligation of those advocating change to raise arguments logically sufficient to remove the presumption of existing beliefs or policies. The burden of proof always rests with the advocate of change and never shifts during the debate. Issues are inherent questions vital to the advocate's cause. Only by providing a positive answer to each of the issues can an advocate of change overcome the presumption and meet his burden of proof. The term prima facie means, literally, "on the face of it." A prima facie case may be defined as a case which is logically sufficient to overcome the presumption of the present belief or policy and to force the defender of that belief or policy to respond. The presentation of a prima facie case initially meets the advocate's burden of proof and initially provides a positive answer to each of the issues.

STUDY QUESTIONS

1. What is the rationale behind the statement, "In case of a tie, the defender of existing beliefs and policies wins"?
2. What happens when the parties involved in an argumentative setting cannot agree on the statement of a proposition?
3. Are there any unique problems in determining presumption in propositions of judgment, particularly evaluative propositions of judgment?

EXERCISES

1. Identify each of the propositions below as either a descriptive proposition of judgment, a predictive proposition of judgment, an evaluative proposition of judgment, or a proposition of policy.
   a. Resolved: That it is more important for colleges to teach students how to think than to prepare them for specific jobs.

    b. Resolved: That the United States should withdraw all of its troops from foreign soil.

    c. Resolved: That the single-family automobile will be nonexistent by 1990.

    d. Resolved: That X University has a better graduate program in history than Y University.

    e. Resolved: That the history program at X University is more flexible than the program at Y University.

    f. Resolved: That tuition will have to be increased next fall.

    g. Resolved: That the tuition increase planned for next fall is unjustified.

    h. Resolved: That the planned tuition increase should be rolled back.

2. Each of the propositions below has some weakness in its phrasing. Identify the weaknesses and rephrase each proposition so that it correctly isolates the essence of the controversy.

    a. Resolved: That our laws concerning abortion should be changed significantly.

    b. Resolved: That domestic automobile producers should be subject to federal safety and pollution standards.

    c. Resolved: That the United States should reduce its military expenditures and use the money to revitalize urban areas.

    d. Resolved: That the Supreme Court has unjustifiably relaxed controls against abusive and unnecessary police practices.

    e. Resolved: That our system of funding public elementary and secondary education should be overhauled.

3. Identify the side which has presumption and the side which has the burden of proof in each of the propositions listed under exercise 1 above.

II Argumentation as Inquiry

3 The Process of Analysis

In Chapter 2 we discussed the importance of being able to discover the issues in any proposition. It is one thing, however, to know that it is important to discover issues; it is another thing to be able to find them. When faced with a complex controversy, how does one search out the issues? This chapter will answer this question. The chapter will focus first on the nature of logical analysis and then will consider the methods of analysis.

THE NATURE OF ANALYSIS

Inquiry into the nature of logical analysis requires that the process of analysis be defined and that several basic assumptions which underlie the process be examined.

DEFINITION OF ANALYSIS

Analysis may be defined as *the process of breaking down a controversy into component parts in order to discover the issues.* The definition indicates that analysis is an attempt to understand a complexity by examining its constituent parts. The definition also identifies the ultimate goal of analysis: the discovery of issues. This suggests that the breaking down of controversies is not an arbitrary process, but rather a systematic search for the inherent questions which are vital to the advocate's cause. Since issues will emerge most clearly in those situations where the controversy is specifically focused, the definition implies that a clearly worded indictment, resolution, or proposition greatly facilitates the process of analysis.

ASSUMPTIONS BASIC
TO THE PROCESS OF ANALYSIS

In examining the nature of analysis it is wise to go beyond the specific definition to consider several basic assumptions which underlie the entire process. The first assumption is that *the process of analysis is essentially a search for appropriate methodologies—for appropriate tools of analysis.* In much the same way that a chemist needs methods and tools in order to do chemical analysis, the advocate needs to find the appropriate tools to enable him to discover the issues which inhere within controversies. Analysis is a discovery process, and discovery processes require systematic methodologies if they are to become more than unrepeatable accidents.

A second assumption is that *no one tool or methodology provides a complete system for analysis.* The process of analysis of propositions is extremely complex, and no single tool or combination of tools will provide a magic formula for analysis. The process of analysis utimately involves personal judgments at critical points. The student should be constantly aware that the methods of analysis, no matter how useful, are means to an end and not ends in themselves. The methods, which will be outlined in this chapter, will assist the student in making analysis more systematic, but they are not molds which can be rigidly imposed upon propositions. Analysis methodologies are appropriate only to the extent that they can be adapted to the uniqueness of each individual controversy.

The final assumption is that *the process of analysis involves in-depth investigation into the subject matter of the proposition.* Our focus on methods of analysis should not obscure the fact that analysis is rooted in the substance of the controversy. The entire discussion of analysis assumes that the advocate is engaged in intensive research in the subject matter which he is analyzing. While analytical methods provide the advocate with a systematic approach to the discovery of issues, the issues utimately grow out of the subject matter of the proposition under consideration. Analysis and research cannot be separated.

METHODS OF ANALYSIS

In outlining methods to be used in the process of analysis, one central question must always be asked: "Do these methods of analysis contribute to the discovery of the inherent questions which are vital to the advocate's cause?" With this question in mind, a twofold classification of analysis methodologies has been developed: (1) analysis of the background of the controversy and (2) application of the analytical formulas to the controversy.

ANALYSIS OF THE BACKGROUND
OF THE CONTROVERSY

Before you can begin to apply analytical formulas you must have an understanding of the context in which the controversy exists. A study of the background of the controversy can provide the definitional and historical perspectives which are the necessary starting points for the discovery of issues. The study of the background of a controversy is a four-step process which includes consideration of the immediate causes for discussion, examination of the nature and history of present policies or beliefs, examination of the nature and history of the proposed policy or belief, and discovery of common ground.

CONSIDERATION OF THE IMMEDIATE CAUSES FOR DISCUSSION

The first question to ask when beginning analysis of any controversy is, "Why has this particular controversy become important at this point in time?" An answer to this question will provide the advocate with an initial view of the contemporary events and values which have raised a specific controversy to a level of personal or social significance. It is not at all uncommon for a single event or series of events to raise a controversy from obscurity to the forefront of our thoughts. The assassination of a major political figure rekindles debate over more effective gun control legislation. An armed invasion lifts a minor border dispute between two small countries into a military conflict of international significance. A major airplane disaster stimulates debate over the control of air traffic lanes. A sudden increase in oil consumption by the family automobile leads to consideration of the purchase of a new car. While the analysis of any controversy must go much deeper than the consideration of the immediate causes for discussion, such a consideration will lead the advocate to discover the events and values which are of immediate concern.

EXAMINATION OF THE NATURE AND HISTORY
OF PRESENT POLICY OR BELIEF

One of the most dangerous temptations involved in analyzing any controversy is to consider *only* the contemporary circumstances which give rise to proposals for change. Every controversy, no matter how contemporary, is rooted in the past. In order to gain insight into the nature of any existing policy or belief the advocate must place the controversy into perspective by considering its origins and its historical development. An analysis of the contemporary problems in the Middle East, for instance, would be impossible without an understanding of the historical events leading up to the creation of the State of Israel and of the significant events from that time until the present. Likewise, a court, in attempting to determine whether or not a school system is illegally segregated, must consider the development of housing patterns and past policy decisions of the board of education as well as the current practices in the educational system. Only through an examination of the specific rationale for these policies and beliefs at different points in time can one evaluate their relevance to contemporary circumstances.

EXAMINATION OF THE NATURE AND HISTORY OF THE PROPOSED POLICY OR BELIEF

Analysis of nature and historical development is important not only when examining *existing* policies and beliefs but also when examining *proposed* policies and beliefs. Few proposals for change are really new. Most have been considered and even implemented in one form or another in the past. Examination of past controversies over proposals currently being considered can provide insights into the potential strengths and weaknesses of such proposals. Proposals for the withdrawal of U.S. troops from Europe, for instance, have been debated many times since the end of World War II. Examination of those debates is a vital part of the analysis of a contemporary proposal in this area. In much the same manner, our courts of law turn to legal precedent in evaluating propositions of judgment. Cases similar to the proposed change in legal interpretation are sought out, and opinions of the courts in such cases are carefully examined. If historical analysis can provide an understanding of the strengths and limitations of policies or beliefs similar to those currently proposed, the advocate can better begin the process of discovering possible arguments for and against the proposal under consideration.

DISCOVERY OF COMMON GROUND

A final element of the study of the background of a controversy is the discovery of common ground. Common ground is composed of those facts or arguments or values on which both sides in the controversy agree. In many questions of policy or judgment, large areas of common ground may be discovered. In a debate over revisions in the national welfare system, for instance, both sides may be in agreement as to the minimum level of income necessary for subsistence and as to the desirability of training programs to enable poor people to work their way off the welfare roles. Likewise, in a murder trial, both prosecution and defense may be in agreement as to the time and place of a murder and as to the specific weapon used in the crime. The identification of common ground in any controversy serves to narrow the potential issues and to save time which would have been spent researching and analyzing areas which will not become important clashes in the controversy.

APPLICATION OF ANALYTICAL FORMULAS

The in-depth study of the background of a controversy should provide needed insight into the substance of a proposition. The application of analytical formulas helps to carry the analysis process a step further by relating that substance to the specific requirements of the resolution. The formulas provide a means of categorizing arguments and of viewing the crucial relationships within a controversy.

The three formulas described below respond to the unique characteristics of three different argumentative situations. The *stock issues formula* provides a systematic approach to questions of policy which can be focused into a clear statement of the specific course of action being advocated. The *systems formula* is adapted to policy controversies which are not yet focused on a specific policy proposal. The *status formula* provides a systematic approach to the analysis of propositions of judgment.

STOCK ISSUES ANALYSIS
FOR PROPOSITIONS OF POLICY

While the four-step process suggested for the study of the background of a controversy provides vital insights into the nature of the policy proposition under examination, it does not really constitute a systematic methodology for breaking the proposition down into its vital component parts. In searching for such a methodology it is imperative that we examine more closely the logical obligations of those who advocate change in policy. Any methodology for breaking down propositions of policy must grow out of the nature of policy propositions in order to be universally applicable. In Chapter 2 it was observed that the advocate of policy change has an inherent obligation to raise arguments logically sufficient to remove the presumption of existing policies. A more careful examination of the nature of policy propositions reveals that certain specific logical obligations exist in the advocacy of any change of policy. The identification of these specific logical obligations provides a methodology for approaching the analysis of propositions of policy called the "stock issues."

Stock issues, very simply, are hunting grounds for arguments. They provide general phrasing of potential issues which correspond to the inherent logical obligations of the advocate of change. Since each of the stock issue categories corresponds to a logical obligation of the advocate of policy change, each of these categories constitutes a vital area of concern—an area in which the advocate of change may logically lose his case. While there are several ways of structuring these logical obligations into an analytical system, the fourfold classification of ill, blame, cure, and cost seems to be the clearest. The *stock issue of ill* grows out of the logical obligation of advocates of change to show a significant past, present, or future problem or harm. The *stock issue of blame* grows out of the logical obligation of advocates of change to be prepared to causally relate that ill to the basic structure or philosophy of the present policy. The *stock issue of cure* grows out of the logical obligation of advocates of change to be prepared to outline a specific plan of action and demonstrate how it will solve the problem of the ill. The *stock issue of cost* grows out of the logical obligation of advocates of change to be prepared to respond to disadvantages in their proposals. In developing these stock issues concepts, the proposal to substitute a guaranteed annual cash income for the present welfare system will be used as an illustrative case study.

The stock issue of ill. The stock issue of ill asks the question, "Are there significant harms or ills within the present system?" There must be a *felt difficulty* with the present policy. For the advocate of change, the stock issue of ill becomes a hunting ground for arguments that suggest the existing way of doing things results in serious internal problems or does not achieve certain important goals. For the defender of the present system, the ill issue becomes a place to look for arguments to deny the existence of harms or to minimize their significance.

Advocates of a guaranteed annual cash income as a replacement for the welfare system argue a variety of *felt difficulties* with the existing system. Many argue, for instance, that the existing welfare system fails to provide a subsistence income for a large proportion of its recipients. It is further argued that many individuals who live in poverty receive no assistance at all from the existing system. Still others argue that racial discrimination exists in the determination of eligibility for assistance. If the failure to provide subsistence income, the exclusion of poor individuals from any assistance, and the problem of racial discrimination can be proven to be widespread and significant harms, the advocate has met his first logical obligation by establishing the ill issue.

A decision to make a change in a course of action may not only be motivated by internal problems within the existing system, but may also be considered because of the present system's failure to satisfy certain external goals. Many advocates of a guaranteed annual cash income believe that government aid to the needy should be administered so as to protect the dignity and self-respect of the poor. They argue that the present structure demeans the poor by requiring inspections of their expenditures and by providing direct goods and services. If the goal of avoidance of degrading practices can be established as a significant consideration in analyzing the welfare structure, the advocate may have found a ground for establishing the system's failure to meet a desirable objective.

The stock issue of ill, then, identifies a vital area of analysis because no change in policy will be made unless it can be demonstrated that the existing system is failing to achieve its own primary goals or unless it can be demonstrated that the system is not achieving other desirable objectives.

The stock issue of blame. The stock issue of blame asks the question, "Is the present system inherently responsible for the existence of the ills?" The existence of certain problems or the failure to achieve certain goals does not necessarily mean that present policies have failed or that a new course of action is required. A totally new policy approach is warranted only if it can be shown that *by its very nature* the present system *cannot* overcome the problems or achieve the goals. Unless the *inherent structure or philosophy* of the present system is the cause of the continued existence of the ill, then minor adjustments or repairs within the present system can be made to alleviate the harm.

The identification of the inherent structural or philosophical characteristics of a policy cannot be completely accomplished without establishing some reference point and that reference point is an opposing policy system. In other words, to determine the inherent nature of an existing system it is necessary to examine the basic values (philosophy) and major components (structure) of that system in relation to the basic values and major components of an opposing policy.

By comparing the values and structural components of public assistance with those of a guaranteed annual income three inherent differences in the nature of the two systems may be identified. First, a goal of public assistance is to provide minimum necessities to the poor. To assure that these necessities are provided the welfare system gives aid in the form of services (medical care, public housing) and controlled spending (food stamps, clothing allowances). In contrast, a value of the guaranteed income is freedom of choice, and this value is realized through the provision of unsupervised cash payments. A second value of the system of public assistance is local responsibility and control, and this value is realized by placing the administration of welfare in the hands of state and local governments. The guaranteed income, on the other hand, values uniform protection above local responsibility and seeks to implement this value through federal administration. A third value or philosophical conflict exists between the two systems. Whereas the goal of public assistance is to aid the deserving poor, the guaranteed income seeks to help all poor. The public assistance goal is realized by the use of nonfinancial, as well as financial, criteria to determine which poor are deserving. The guaranteed annual income imposes only a financial criterion for assistance. Thus, the two systems are inherently different: the guaranteed annual income provides federal cash assistance to all poor; public welfare provides state and locally controlled services and vendor payments for the deserving poor.

The identification of the inherent characteristics of the present system is only part of the analytical responsibility imposed by the blame issue. To complete the blame analysis, the inherent characteristics of the present system must be causally linked to the continued existence of the ills. An affirmative might argue, for example, that state and local control is the inherent feature of public assistance which is responsible for (causes) inadequate benefit levels and racial discrimination. Welfare's philosophical commitment to assist only the deserving poor could be identified as the reason why large numbers of poor families receive no assistance at all. And the present system's philosophical and structural preference for services and vendor payments could be said to cause the poor to feel demeaned.

Within the stock issue of blame, then, the advocate of change is obligated to identify characteristics of the present policy which are inherent to its structure or philosophy and to demonstrate the ways in which they are causally related to the ills of that policy. The opponent of change may seek to deny that the alleged inherent characteristics are, in fact, fundamental to the present system and suggest minor, nonstructural repairs or he may accept the characteristics as inherent and deny the causal link to the ill. This area of analysis is crucial to the advocate since it is generally less costly to repair an existing system than it is to junk it for a completely new one.

The stock issue of cure. The stock issue of cure asks the question, "Will the affirmative proposal remove the ills of the present system?" The cure issue shifts the focus of the analysis from a consideration of the existing policy to a consideration of the action proposed in the statement of the proposition. This stock issue identifies a hunting ground for arguments growing out of the advocate's obligation to outline a specific plan of action and to demonstrate how it will solve the specific ills and deal with the specific causal factors under consideration. Even if it can be demonstrated that a significant ill exists which is causally related to inherent features of the existing policies, a course of action which fails to guarantee a solution to the problem is not likely to be adopted.

Advocates of a guaranteed annual income generally outline proposals which involve total federal financing and administration of a guarantee to all U. S. citizens of a minimum annual cash income. The proposals generally stipulate a specific minimum income level based on family size and location, a procedure for determining income levels and for distributing funds, and a mechanism for raising the necessary money to finance the program. Advocates argue that by substituting a totally federal program for a program committed to state and local administration, racial discrimination can be eliminated. They further argue that a program of total federal financing will permit the raising of benefits to a subsistence level. By guaranteeing this level of subsistence to all citizens, the program is said to eliminate the problem of poor families who receive no welfare assistance at all. Finally, by providing the assistance in cash, it is argued that the program eliminates the "demeaning" control over spending which characterizes the present welfare system.

Within the cure issue opponents of a guaranteed annual income seek to demonstrate that the adoption of such a program would not alleviate the alleged ills. They claim, for example, that federal administration will not insure an end to racial discrimination in programs for the poor. It is argued that federal employees have racial biases and that these biases can affect indirect aid programs such as public housing and medical services. Opponents of a guaranteed income also argue that a blanket guarantee of cash will not necessarily assure a subsistence standard of living because many of the poor are incapable of spending the money wisely. Finally, they maintain that the poor will feel no less demeaned under a guaranteed annual income because it is the dependency on public support, and not the controls on that support, which creates the feeling of inferiority.

The cure stock issue, therefore, provides a hunting ground for arguments that suggest the change in policy will or will not achieve its stated or implied objectives. Such considerations are crucial to the advocate of change since a course of action which fails to solve the problems of existing policies provides no solution at all. The action proposed must be matched precisely to the ill and blame analysis.

The stock issue of cost. The stock issue of cost asks the question, "Are the disadvantages of the affirmative proposal insignificant?" Any change in policy will incur some cost, some disruption, some social or material burden. The advocate of change is under a logical obligation to be prepared to demonstrate that the disadvantages of the proposed change are not so great as to outweigh any benefits. Frequently a course of action clearly cures a problem inherent in the present system but must be rejected because of its excessive social or material cost.

Opponents of a guaranteed annual income program forward a variety of cost arguments. First, they raise the sheer monetary cost of guaranteeing a minimum level of income to all U. S. citizens. Estimates of this cost range from $15 billion to $50 billion depending upon the minimum income level set by the proposal. Loss of work incentive is also argued as a cost of such a proposal on the grounds that many people will simply not work if a comfortable standard of living is guaranteed by the government. A related cost argument is the claim that such a guarantee will reduce retraining incentives thereby eliminating the mechanism by which many poor people work their way off the welfare roles.

By focusing on the noncure effects of the proposed action, the cost issue provides another hunting ground for arguments. The advocate of change in policy is logically obligated to respond to such arguments by denying their existence or by minimizing their importance. The case for a proposed course of action can be lost if it can be demonstrated that the cost of that action is more significant than the ill it is designed to cure.

The stock issues of ill, blame, cure, and cost, therefore, constitute a systematic approach for breaking a proposition of policy down into its component parts. The framework of each of the stock issues concepts constitutes a crucial area of concern since each corresponds to an inherent logical obligation of the advocate of change. While the real issues must be discovered through an in-depth investigation of the subject matter under consideration, the system of stock issues provides a tool for the categorization of arguments and for the viewing of relationships based on an advocate's logical responsibilities. The real issues may be more specifically worded and differently structured, but the stock issues concepts will be contained within them.

As indicated earlier, the system of stock issues operates best in argumentative situations where a clear statement of a proposed course of action can be phrased. Such a phrasing focuses the controversy on the comparative merits of an existing system and a single alternate course of action. This focusing clearly separates the advocate of change from the individual who will defend the existing system or minor repairs of that system and permits the use of an analysis system based on the logical obligations of an advocate of change.

Frequently, however, controversies are not sufficiently focused to permit the statement of a proposition in terms of a single proposed course of action. Such controversies may center around relatively open-ended questions, and the participants in argumentative inquiry are initially uncommitted to a specific policy. A university, for instance, may be motivated to analyze the functioning of its freshman advising system. When this analysis begins, however, it may be impossible to phrase a clear statement of policy change. Rather, the controversy may be no more clearly focused than the general question, "What can be done to improve our freshman advising system?" Everyone involved in such an analysis is concerned with the functioning of an existing system, but policy alternatives are multidimensional rather than two-dimensional as in the clearly phrased proposition of policy. The analysis situation, therefore, is more open-ended as compared to the highly structured situation created by a clearly focused statement of a proposition of policy.

While the stock issues comprise a logically complete analysis system and while a modified form of this system could be applied to the analysis of open-ended controversies, a more inductive analysis approach becomes useful in such situations. The approach, known as systems analysis, has been borrowed from the behavioral sciences.[1] In order to achieve a general understanding of systems analysis, two initial definitions are necessary. A *system* can be defined as *a whole which functions as a whole by virtue of the interdependence of its parts.* *Systems analysis,* in its simplest form, is *an attempt to study interacting components as a whole.*

A simple illustration may help to clarify these concepts. The U.S. federal government can be considered a system which functions as a

[1] For a different perspective on the application of systems analysis to argumentation see Bernard L. Brock, James W. Chesebro, John F. Cragan, and James F. Klumpp, *Public Policy Decision-Making: Systems Analysis and Comparative Advantages Debate* (New York: Harper & Row, Publishers, 1973).

whole by virtue of the interdependence of its parts (the executive, legislative, and judicial branches). A systems analysis of the federal government would be an analysis of these interacting components as they relate to each other to comprise what we call the federal government. While systems analysis does involve breaking a whole down into its parts or components, those components are not analyzed independently, but rather as they interact within the framework of the whole system.

In argumentative situations where a controversy has not yet focused on a single specific course of action, there generally exists a focus sufficient to identify the *system* which is being analyzed. While those considering the question of freshman advising may not have settled on policy alternatives, they have at least agreed upon the present advising system as a focal point for analysis. If the controversy is focused enough to identify a system which is being analyzed, then systems analysis may be used to bring some degree of order to the process of analysis.

A variety of models and formulas exist which could be used in attempting a systems analysis of policy controversies. The five-step model outlined below is forwarded for purposes of clarity, but it is recognized that other systems formulas are equally appropriate. This model involves (1) system selection, (2) component selection, (3) relationship assessment, (4) goal determination, and (5) effect assessment and input experimentation. It is important to note that these five steps are not necessarily sequential in nature. While system selection generally precedes component selection and component selection generally precedes relationship assessment, it would not be unreasonable to begin the entire process with goal determination.

System selection. In many controversies the selection of the system to be analyzed may be almost automatic. If the Senate Judiciary Committee is considering reorganizing the federal judiciary, then the structure of the federal judiciary system will provide the limits for the analysis. It is important to realize, however, that every entity which can be designated as a *system* is also a component part of some larger system. The freshman advising structure of a university, for instance, constitutes a system. It is, however, also a component part of the total university advising system. That advising system, in turn, is a component part of the system which we call "the university." Since all systems constitute component parts of larger systems, the process of system selection is crucial to the total systems analysis. It may be impossible, for instance, to study the system of freshman advising separately from the framework of the total university advising system. System selection always involves personal judgment, and he who makes the judgment should be prepared to defend his choices.

Component selection. Once a system has been selected, analysis of that system begins with the identification of its major components. Every system contains an infinite number of potential components. The task of the investigator is to determine which of these elements comprise the most stable, the most vital components within the system. This can only be accomplished after the investigator has thoroughly researched the nature of the system which is being analyzed.

In the example of the analysis of the functioning of the freshman advising system, one might identify as components the freshman student, the advising staff, the university administration, and the freshman curriculum. Another individual, on the other hand, might argue that the advising philosophy under which the system operates ought to be considered a component. Someone else might argue that the university administration is not really a vital component within these system limitations. Whoever identifies components within a system, therefore, is exercising personal judgment based on his investigation of the system.

Relationship assessment. When one considers our definitions of *system* and *systems analysis* with their emphasis on interdependence of components, one realizes that the assessment of relationships between the components of a system is one of the most important steps in systems analysis. In such analysis, components are not important so much for what they *are* as for what they *do.* The focus is on the nature of the activity that exists among the components as they operate within the system. In systems analysis components are selected or identified, but the analysis focuses on the nature of their relationships.

In the example of the analysis of a freshman advising system the components of freshman students, advising staff, curriculum, etc. are not important for what they *are* but for *how they relate to each other* in the total system. Questions of the ratio of students to advisors or of the methods by which advisors explain curriculum to students are questions of relationships. If one were to draw a diagram of the process by which students are advised from their admission to the university until the end of their freshman year, one would be drawing a diagram of relationships. Such a diagram must contain all of the vital components, but its emphasis is on how these components relate to each other within the framework of the total freshman advising system.

Goal determination. This step in the process of systems analysis assumes that every system is purpose-oriented, that every system functions to achieve certain goals. For an evaluation of a system to take place the goals or objectives of that system must be determined and placed in some sort of priority order. Nothing is more difficult in the process of systems analysis than to make the value judgments which underlie goal determination and priority setting. The process of determining system goals has two aspects: (1) the discovery of the stated or implied goals of the existing system and (2) the determination of optimum system goals.

The discovery of the goals of the existing system involves an in-depth investigation into the stated goals of those who designed the system and of those who operate the system. Frequently, stated goals and real goals may differ, so the process of assessing existing objectives may involve exhaustive research. If a system is to be evaluated fairly, however, it must first be evaluated in terms of its own goals.

The determination of optimum system goals involves a greater degree of personal judgment on the part of the systems analyst. It may well be that a malfunctioning within a system is a result of inappropriate goals. Student unhappiness with a university's freshman advising system, for instance, may grow out of the fact that the system does not place enough emphasis on personalized advising of each individual student or on the objective of publishing clear explanations of curriculum options. Often the search for optimum system goals may lead the systems analyst to an examination of the larger systems of which the system under examination is only a part. Optimum system goals for a freshman advising system, for example, may have to be found in an examination of the goals of the total university advising system.

Effect assessment and input experimentation. While this part of the systems analysis process could really be divided into two separate steps, the interrelationship of these elements justifies a unified discussion. Once existing and optimum goals have been determined, the components and their relationships must be assessed in terms of the achievement of these goals. If there are deficiencies in reaching system goals, then available resources must be examined to determine possible new inputs into the system. Those new inputs, in turn, must be assessed in terms of their effect on the various component relationships within the system and in terms of their ability to achieve system goals.

Once the systems analyst has arrived at input experimentation, the analysis narrows to cure and cost considerations. Assuming that the system goals have been predetermined, each individual input suggestion becomes a policy alternative which must be evaluated in terms of its ability to achieve system goals in the areas in which the existing system is deficient. Assuming also that component relationships have been predetermined, each input suggestion must be evaluated in terms of its impact on the other system goals. Ultimate input choices will be made on the basis of which inputs best achieve system goals with minimum disruption to the vital component relationships within the system.

In the freshman advising example it may have been determined that the need to save money in the freshman advising system is an optimum goal imposed upon that system by the larger system within which it exists (the financial priorities of the university as a whole). One possible input into the system might be to reduce the number of advisors on the freshman advising staff. While this input might achieve the primary objective of saving money, it might also increase the student/advisor ratio to such an extent that it would be deemed undesirable in terms of other system goals. A possible alternative input would be to reduce the professional advising staff while at the same time training faculty members to assume some role in freshman advising. The entrance of faculty members into the advising system again changes the pattern of relationships within the system, but this input may be capable of achieving the primary goal of saving money while at the same time maintaining an adequate ratio of advisors to students.

In sum, the systems approach provides an inductive model which is optimally useful for the analysis of controversies which have not yet been focused on a specific course of action. As a tool for the analysis of policy controversies it should be thought of as complementing the stock issues formula rather than as an alternative to stock issues. It is possible, and frequently desirable, to use the two formulas together. While the stock issues approach has its primary usefulness in policy controversies which are clearly focused on a specific course of action, stock issues concepts are also useful during the input experimentation stage of systems analysis. Likewise, systems analysis, with its focus on the relationships of interdependent components within a system, can provide useful insights into the nature of an existing system even within the framework of a stock issues analysis.

STATUS ANALYSIS
FOR PROPOSITIONS OF JUDGMENT

The analytical formula which is used in discovering issues in propositions of judgment is known as the *status system of analysis.* This approach provides three frames of reference which may be used to direct an advocate to the issues in any statement of fact or value.

These three reference points are the frames of definition, existence of fact, and quality.

It should be noted that the status system is not limited in its usefulness to propositions of judgment. Since every proposition of policy is composed of several layers of statements of judgment, every argument advanced in a policy debate is subject to analysis in terms of the status formula. In the policy debate over the guaranteed annual income, the ill arguments that the public welfare system fails to provide minimum subsistence for many of its recipients, that it excludes needy poor, and that it discriminates against racial minorities should each be examined in terms of the status formula in order to discover their specific proof requirements (issues).

The frame of definition. Before the existence of an alleged fact or the validity of a value judgment can be established, the nature of that fact or value must be identified. An employee cannot be shown to be competent until some standards of competence are identified. An engine cannot be judged efficient except in relation to certain standards of efficiency. In a court of law a man cannot be found to have committed manslaughter until the jury understands what the term "manslaughter" means. Whatever the field of study—be it law, philosophy, science, or literary criticism—it is impossible to establish a judgment without first determining the aspects of that judgment.

The criteria or definitions which are used as a basis for further analysis are generally derived from the specific subject matter area of the controversy. Legislative acts and previous court decisions generally provide a fairly precise body of standards to guide lawyers in the development of legal definitions. In controversies involving moral judgments, religious and philosophical sources will be helpful in suggesting criteria. In the field of science, previous experimentation provides useful guidelines. In situations involving personal value judgments, the criteria may have to be derived, in part, from the audience's values. The criteria, however, must be relevant to the specific subject matter under consideration.

If an advocate wished to argue the predictive judgment that the Detroit Tigers will win the American League pennant, he would have to begin his analysis by considering standards against which to measure this prediction. He would probably arrive at such criteria as strong starting pitchers, sound relief pitching staff, high team batting average, power hitters capable of driving in runs, high fielding average, bench strength, and a coaching staff capable of motivating the players. The relevance of each of these standards to the overall judgment of "probable pennant winner" would constitute potential issues for debate.

In essence, then, the frame of definition suggests that we must know what it is we are looking for before we can find it. Critical terms in the statement of judgment must be defined. These definitions provide standards by which to compare the judgment against the external situation.

The frame of existence of fact. The total circumstances surrounding any judgment must be carefully examined. The frame of existence of fact suggests that there are always certain critical bits of information upon which a proposition of judgment rests. A prosecutor, in attempting to decide whether to charge a suspect with a specific crime, must determine if the available evidence against that individual is sufficient to meet the criteria for that type of crime. A father, trying to decide if his son is mature enough to take the family car on a date, will examine the boy's attitudes and behavior in past situations to see if they reveal the characteristics of maturity. A doctor, in determining if a patient is dead or alive, will examine his patient's heartbeat, respiration, and brain waves to see if they conform to the medical criteria for determining the existence of life.

To establish that the Detroit Tigers are likely to win the American League pennant it would be necessary to offer data showing that this team does, in fact, conform to the established criteria. Evidence relating to the records and earned run averages of the starting pitchers and relief pitchers might be offered to help establish that a strong pitching staff exists. One would also present evidence of high team batting average, number of home runs, and number of runs batted in to establish the hitting criteria. Fielding averages at the key positions as well as overall team fielding average would be presented to satisfy that criteria. Statements by key players and members of the local news media might be offered to establish the motivational abilities of the manager and the coaching staff.

It is important to note that the issues relevant to the frame of existence of fact are not concerned simply with the existence of certain facts; rather, the issues center around the conformity of the facts to the established criteria. Thus, the frame of existence of fact directs the advocate to look for those conditions, circumstances, or facts which are relevant to the criteria or definition. When the available facts conform to the criteria, an affirmative case can usually be said to have been established.

The frame of quality. The frame of quality is intended to alert the advocate to the fact that there may be certain special criteria or unusual facts which need to be considered before a judgment can be made. Judgments must sometimes be tempered by an examination of the situation from a different perspective.

Courts of law recognize the frame of quality by permitting the plea of innocence because of insanity. When this plea is entered, the prosecution must be prepared to establish all of the usual issues in a case for that crime and, in addition, must address itself to the special quality of insanity. This special consideration may change the perspective of the jury and alter its ultimate judgment.

In evaluating the probability of the Detroit Tigers winning the American League pennant, the frame of quality would require that any special extenuating circumstances be considered. These special circumstances might provide justification for ignoring certain of the normal criteria, or they might provide reasons for reversing the judgment even though the standard criteria had been satisfied. Thus, if it could be established that several key players were near retirement from the sport or were injury prone, or if it could be established that one of the other teams in the league met the established criteria even better than the Tigers, then the predictive judgment might have to be modified.

In effect, what the frame of quality does is to direct the advocate to look beyond the normal frames of reference to consider unusual circumstances and concepts. Valid judgments must be based upon appropriate perspectives.

The status system, then, provides three frames of reference from which to view propositions of judgment. The frames of definition, existence of fact, and quality can help an advocate know where to begin the search for issues and may suggest the general substance of those issues. Since each argument in a policy controversy is a statement of judgment, the status approach should be used in the secondary stages of analysis of policy questions.

SUMMARY

Analysis is the process of breaking down a controversy into component parts in order to discover the issues. Three assumptions underlie this process: (1) analysis is essentially a search for appropriate methodologies; (2) no one methodology provides a complete system for analysis; and (3) analysis requires in-depth investigation into the subject matter of the controversy.

Two general methodologies for analyzing controversies exist. They are the analysis of the background of the controversy and the application of analytical formulas. These two basic approaches should be thought of as complementary.

The study of the background of a controversy is a four-step process which includes consideration of the immediate causes for discussion, examination of the nature and history of the present policy or belief, examination of the nature and history of the proposed policy or belief, and the discovery of common ground.

The three analytical formulas which can be applied to controversies are the stock issues, systems, and status formulas.

The stock issues formula provides a systematic approach to questions of policy which can be focused into a clear statement of the specific course of action being advocated. The four stock issues are ill, blame, cure, and cost. Each of these categories corresponds to a logical obligation of the advocate of policy change.

The systems formula is adapted to policy controversies which are not yet focused on a specific policy proposal. A system is a whole which functions as a whole by virtue of the interdependence of its parts. Systems analysis is, therefore, an attempt to study interacting components as a whole. A systems analysis formula would involve the following processes: (1) system selection, (2) component selection, (3) relationship assessment, (4) goal determination, and (5) effect assessment and input experimentation.

The status formula provides a systematic approach to the analysis of propositions of judgment. It provides three frames of reference from which statements of fact or value may be examined. These three reference points are the frames of definition, existence of fact, and quality.

STUDY QUESTIONS

1. What are the differences between the concept of "issues" and the concept of "stock issues"?
2. Under what conditions would one prefer the systems analysis methodology over the stock issues analysis methodology?
3. Critics of the stock issues analysis methodology claim that this methodology is inferior to systems analysis because it encourages a "static" view of reality as compared to the emphasis on "process" reality encouraged by the systems analysis methodology. Do you agree with this criticism?
4. Critics of the systems analysis methodology claim that this methodology is arbitrary because component selection is dependent upon the personal judgment of the analyst. Do you agree with this criticism?
5. Why is it important for individuals analyzing propositions of policy to be able to analyze propositions of judgment?

EXERCISES

1. Using the current national debate proposition or any proposition of policy of your choosing, discuss the four elements of background analysis:
   a. The immediate causes for discussion.
   b. The nature and history of the present policy.
   c. The nature and history of the proposed policy.
   d. The possible sources of common ground.

2. Using the current national debate proposition or any proposition of policy of your choosing, prepare an analysis of the existing system using the first four steps of the *systems formula*. In addition to writing this preliminary analysis you may also want to try to diagram the system (indicating its goals, components, and their relationships).

3. Using the same proposition, suggest an *input* into the existing system and discuss its impact on the components, relationships, and goals of that system.

4. Phrase a negative *cost* argument on the current national debate proposition or any proposition of policy of your choosing and analyze it using the three-step *status formula*.

5. Phrase a proposition of judgment for which the *status formula frame of quality* would be particularly relevant. Briefly discuss the ways in which the *quality* analysis modifies the *definition* and *existence of fact* analysis.

4 The Discovery of Data

In Chapter 3 several methodologies were discussed which the student of argumentation might use in beginning the process of analyzing controversies. These analytical systems, however, provide only a general framework for beginning the process of analysis. To discover the real issues in any controversy, one must immerse himself in the subject matter of that controversy. Since the subject matter is the ultimate determinant of the issues, a thorough study of the subject itself is an essential part of the process of analysis.

When one begins the process of research into the subject matter of any controversy, he is immediately confronted with two questions: (1) What am I looking for? and (2) How do I go about finding it? The purpose of this chapter is to provide answers to both of these questions. In an attempt to answer the first question, the chapter will describe the general nature and various types of data. In response to the second question, the chapter will attempt to assist the advocate in beginning research by discussing the sources and mechanics of data collection.

THE NATURE OF DATA

When the student begins the process of researching the subject matter of a controversy, he is searching for data upon which he will build arguments and upon which he will ultimately build a total analysis of the proposition. Simply defined, *data is the starting point of argument, the substance from which we reason.* Data is to argument what a foundation is to a building. To be structurally adequate, a building must be built upon a sound foundation. To be logically adequate, arguments must be built upon sound data.

There are two general classes of data which are used as starting points for investigation and argument; these are premises and evidence. *Premises* are the fundamental assumptions or beliefs of an advocate or of an audience which will be accepted without external support. *Evidence* consists of source materials external to the advocate or audience which may be used to lend support or proof to a conclusion.

Both premises and evidence must be discovered, not created. When engaging in inquiry, an advocate must begin with an analysis of his own beliefs in order to discover what perceptions of reality he is willing to accept as starting points for his further investigation. When engaging in advocacy, a speaker must begin by analyzing his audience in order to discover what beliefs and values it holds as fundamental. Thus, premises are discovered within the system of belief of the individual advocate or the specific audience. Evidence is discovered through examination of real situations or through the study of materials written by others about their examinations of real situations. Since most advocacy situations offer only limited opportunities for presentation of real objects (i. e., the murder weapon) or for the conducting of controlled experiments, evidence used in argumentation is usually symbolic in nature and must be discovered in the reports of other people.

TYPES OF PREMISES

Before the appropriate logical tests can be applied to premises we must identify the types of premises which may be used as data. The two types of premises are perceptual premises and value premises.

PERCEPTUAL PREMISES

Perceptual premises are assumptions about the nature of things. These assumptions are based upon one's personal view of the world. For many years in the past men assumed that the earth was flat. This assumption grew out of the informal experiences of the men of that age. To the extent that this belief influenced their thinking on related matters, it functioned as a perceptual premise. Even today, many of our personal conclusions about what we should do or think are based upon perceptual premises. Differences within the American public regarding policies toward communist nations, for example, are, to a certain extent, based upon different perceptions of the nature of communism.

Perceptual premises function as data not because they are the end product of objective research. Rather, they may serve as the starting point of argument because they will be accepted without question. Ultimately, of course, perceptual premises derive their authority from past experience and past knowledge. Perceptions, however, tend to assume a certain face validity of their own, and they become ingrained and unchallenged even after the original basis for them is forgotten.

VALUE PREMISES

Simply defined, values are judgments concerning the worth of something. Value premises put into statement form our concepts of good and evil, right and wrong, and importance and unimportance. If data is the substance from which we reason then values must be considered to be data when they serve as the starting point for argument. Many people are surprised to discover just how frequently arguments are based upon stated or implied value judgments. In the 1971 clash between the *New York Times* and the federal government over the publication of the secret Vietnam war documents, known as the Pentagon Papers, both sides argued from value premises. The *Times* argued from the premise that the public's right to know was the most important value in the situation. The government, on the other hand, argued from the primacy of the value of protecting national security. Since these values provided the substance from which both sides reasoned, they must be thought of as data in this situation.

It is possible for an advocate to anticipate what his audience's feelings are likely to be in a specific situation. If he anticipates the proper feelings (discovers the right value), he may begin his argumentation at that point. Not all the values of a speaker or writer will necessarily serve as data; only those values which he holds in common with his audience are capable of acting as the starting point for argument.

TYPES OF EVIDENCE

There are two general types of evidence: factual evidence and expert opinion evidence. The categorization of evidence into these broad classes will become useful in the next chapter when the tests of evidence are discussed.

FACTUAL EVIDENCE

Factual evidence consists of potentially verifiable statements which describe real objects and events. Factual evidence is potentially verifiable because it seeks only to describe events and objects. If factual evidence takes the form of the results of a scientific experiment, it has the potential for verification by another scientist performing the same experiment. If factual evidence takes the form of a description of the scene of a record snowfall in an urban area, it can be verified if other people who witnessed the same scene can be found. While an advocate may not be in a position to verify a given piece of factual evidence, that piece of data still has the potential for verification because it seeks only to *describe* what was observed rather than to *explain or evaluate* what occurred.

Descriptions of objects and events (factual evidence) can appear in a variety of forms. One form is that of *verbal examples,* which are detailed descriptions of specific cases, instances, or situations. The detailed description of the scene after a tornado, for instance, would be a verbal example. The *U.S. Riot Commission Report* used the following verbal example as partial proof of the conclusion that national guardsmen frequently placed buildings under siege on the sketchiest reports of sniping during the 1967 Detroit riot.

> In one instance a report was received on the jeep radio that an Army bus was pinned down by sniper fire at an intersection. National Guardsmen and police, arriving from various directions, jumped out and began asking each other: "Where's the sniper fire coming from?" As one Guardsman pointed to a building, everyone rushed about, taking cover. A soldier, alighting from a jeep, accidentally pulled the trigger on his rifle. As the shot reverberated through the darkness an officer yelled: "What's going on?" "I don't know," came the answer. "Sniper, I guess." Without any clear authorization or direction someone opened fire upon the suspected building. A tank rolled up and sprayed the building with 50 caliber tracer bullets.[1]

Another form that factual evidence can take is that of *statistics.* While there is a tendency to think of them as something more, statistics are merely numerical representations of examples. Statistics may appear in a variety of forms—raw numbers, percentages, ratios, averages, etc.—but they are essentially convenient ways of expressing large numbers of examples. If a TV rating survey concludes that a certain program commands only 19 percent of the viewing audience, the statistic is a projection based upon a limited number of examples. Statistics give the impression of being more representative than isolated examples, and they usually are. But one needs to examine the ways in which the statistics were arrived at before reaching such a conclusion.

A final form that factual evidence can take is that of *descriptive historic statements.* Such statements observe that something happened

---

[1]*Report of the National Advisory Commission on Civil Disorders* (New York: Bantam Books, 1968), p. 97.

at a certain time and place in history. Descriptive historic statements are closely related to verbal examples but generally appear in less detail. The observation that President John F. Kennedy was assassinated on Friday, November 22, 1963 in Dallas, Texas is a descriptive historic statement.

EXPERT OPINION EVIDENCE

Expert opinion evidence consists of authoritative statements which explain factual evidence. While the statements of factual evidence simply *describe* objects and events, expert opinion evidence attempts to *interpret the meaning* of those objects and events. Such interpretations must be authoritative or expert. We shall accept interpretations of factual evidence only if we believe that the source of the opinion is qualified to make the interpretation. When a ballistics expert examines a bullet and a gun and concludes that the bullet was fired from that gun, we are likely to accept his opinion because of his specialized knowledge. When an economist interprets certain signs in the economy and concludes that we are heading for a recession, he is offering expert opinion which is both a conclusion and data for further argument.

It is important to remember that since expert opinion evidence consists of statements about statements, it is further away from the actual perception of objects and events than is factual evidence. It is hard enough for a reporter to describe accurately the events and objects he perceives. It is even harder to provide accurate interpretations of the meaning of those objects or events.

SEARCHING FOR DATA

Knowing what to look for is essential to the discovery of data, but knowing how to find it is equally important. This section, therefore, is concerned with the means of identifying premises and with the methods of researching for evidence.

IDENTIFYING PREMISES

The processes involved in identifying premises are the same whether one is looking for perceptual premises or value premises. Since perceptual and value premises have their origins within the advocate himself and within the audience to be addressed, it is necessary to examine these two sources.

PERSONAL PREMISES

The process of inquiring into a problem should begin with an examination of one's own beliefs and assumptions. Such an examination will usually reveal some previously accepted values or perceptions which would be difficult to justify to others or even to oneself. Premises such as these should be rejected as starting points for argument or inquiry. These premises will need to be tested and supported with external evidence. Other values and perceptions, however, will seem so self-evident as to be almost undeniable. These premises may be accepted as initial starting points for argumentation.

To separate self-evident premises from less fundamental beliefs, three questions should be asked: What do I believe? Why do I believe it? and Can the basis of my belief be reasonably denied? The ancient belief that the world was flat was based on personal perceptions of the world and was consistent with the limited knowledge of the physical universe. Thus, for many generations the flatness of the earth could not reasonably be denied.

In America today, certain members of the political right are vigorously opposed to any further expansion of economic or political contacts between the United States and the nations of the communist world. This belief is based upon certain other beliefs. These beliefs include the assumptions that communism seeks to destroy the free world and that expanded contacts with communist nations aid their efforts at world domination. No matter how deeply a member of the political right might believe these last two assumptions, he could not fairly call them self-evident since so many other "reasonable" people reject them. The search for self-evident premises, therefore, requires a consideration of the assumptions underlying this second level of beliefs. A premise basic to both of these second-level beliefs is that the free world should not be taken over by communism. However, even this statement is not universally self-evident to reasonable men. Still more fundamental premises have to be identified. Contained within the third level of belief is the idea that personal and political freedom are desirable. Since this concept is universally consistent with Western experience, it may be said to be self-evident, and it can be accepted as a starting point for investigation and argumentation.

By forcing one's analysis of beliefs to increasingly more fundamental and self-evident levels, it is possible to identify those personal perceptions and personal values which can serve as data. The test of "universal self-evident" is, of course, an arbitrary one, but it does provide a useful guideline as to the depth of premise analysis required.

The demands of truth require that all conclusions be based upon universally self-evident premises or upon sound evidence, but the circumstances of public advocacy may permit the use of less than universally self-evident premises in certain situations. Whenever the premises of an advocate coincide with the values and perceptions of his *specific* audience, those premises may be used as starting points for argument before *that* audience, even though they lack universal self-evidence.

Experienced advocates are generally aware that knowledge of their audience's premises can be enormously helpful in determining the starting point for their arguments. Skilled lawyers select jurors based, in part, upon what the prospective jurors reveal about their perceptions and values during the impaneling process. Successful politicians rely upon information about specific audiences which they receive from staff aids and local sources. An ethical advocate will not adjust his overall conclusions to conform to the beliefs of his audience, but whenever possible he will attempt to build his arguments upon the values and perceptual premises which he shares with his audience.

In order for an advocate to utilize his audience's premises effectively he must have gathered considerable information about the attitudes of the specific audience. There are three primary sources of information about specific audiences which can usually be utilized: audience-published documents, informal statements from established group members, and reports of nongroup members.

Documents or statements of principles published by groups provide a first major source of audience information. Service clubs, political organizations, and community and religious groups all exist to promote certain principles, and these principles are generally set down in some code, creed, or constitution. In addition, some groups also publish organizational magazines or newsletters which may furnish additional insights into the common premises of the group.

Informal statements from established group members can provide a second important source of audience information. An advocate does not normally appear before a group unannounced and uninvited. He usually speaks before a group only after some member has invited him to participate. This fact means that he has an opportunity to discuss the attitudes of the audience with at least one group member in advance of his public presentation. If the speaker happens to be personally acquainted with other members of the group, he can verify and enrich his understanding of the audience's beliefs through these additional contacts.

A final source of audience information is the reports of nongroup members. This source of information is particularly helpful when the audience to be addressed is not part of a formal organization but is a temporary group gathered for the express purpose of discussing a specific topic or hearing particular speakers. These outside sources may include such things as public-opinion polls, newspaper reports, and demographic data.

In general, the goal of the advocate should be to gain as comprehensive a knowledge of his audience's premises as possible. He must know *why* his audience believes as it does—not simply *what* it believes. Only when he understands the basis of his audience's beliefs can he hope to identify and build upon *commonly shared* premises.

RESEARCHING EVIDENCE

Research skills stand at the very heart of the inquiry phase of argumentation. Researching for evidence is as important in argumentation as it is in solving perplexing medical problems. No new vaccine or treatment for presently incurable diseases will be found without months and even years of thorough research. Likewise, we will not find the answers to our important personal problems or to the problems facing society until we first engage in research in our area of concern. Skill in research, then, is vital to any student of argumentation.

It is important to think of the process of researching for evidence as one of adventure and challenge. If we begin research with the assumption that the probable *truth* of any question is *out there to be found,* we will begin to view research as an exciting process of discovery, and we will begin to experience the same joy of discovery as do pioneers in any field. Moreover, if we begin to view research as discovery of truth, we will be less likely to distort the evidence we find to fit preconceived notions.

When faced with the task of research, the most common question which arises is, "Where do I begin?" The purpose of this section will be to provide assistance in finding a systematic approach to research. Specifically, it will seek to answer three questions: (1) Where do I find evidence? (2) How do I read for evidence? (3) How do I record evidence for future use?

SOURCES OF EVIDENCE

The first problem confronting any researcher is the problem of finding the best sources of evidence on his subject. In compiling a bibliography on any subject, the researcher must keep in mind that the thoroughness of his research and the completeness of his analysis are dependent upon finding the best sources of information.

The first step in the search for sources of evidence is to learn how to use the available library facilities efficiently. Most libraries publish "guides" to assist the researcher in using their resources. Many students are amazed at the time that can be saved by just spending an hour or two studying such a guide and familiarizing themselves with the layout of the library.

The second step is to become familiar with some of the most basic reference guides. This section will attempt to describe some of the more frequently used guides which can be of assistance in finding the best sources of evidence. Our discussion will be divided into six categories of sources (books, periodicals, newspapers, almanacs and fact books, government documents, and essays). The treatment here will be, of necessity, somewhat brief. The student who is interested in more detailed and complete reference source listings should consult Constance M. Winchell's *A Guide to Reference Books* or *Reference Books: How to Select and Use Them* by Saul Galin and Peter Spielberg.

Books. The researcher usually begins his search for sources of evidence by looking for books on the topic under consideration. Books are useful because they generally provide the most thorough treatment of a topic and because they are more likely to place the specific controversy in its historical context. The typical starting point in the search for books on a given topic is the card catalog of the campus or public library. This starting point is a logical one because the card catalog lists books which are readily available to the researcher. The weakness of any card catalog, of course, is that it is limited to the books contained in a given library. If that library happens to be weak in the area of your research, the card catalog will be of limited usefulness in preparing a meaningful book bibliography.

If the researcher wants to move beyond the resources of his campus or public library, the single most useful source is the *Cumulative Book Index* (prior to 1928, the *United States Catalog*). This work can be found in the reference room of most libraries and contains the most comprehensive record of books printed in the United States since 1928 (since 1899 if the *United States Catalog* is used). The book is organized alphabetically by author, by title, and by subject (although the entry under the author is more detailed than that under the title or subject). These twin works are especially useful for compiling a complete list of books printed in the United States on any given topic or for finding a comprehensive list of the works of any U. S. author.

Periodical articles. The major limitation of books as sources of evidence is that books become dated so quickly. Because of the time it takes to write and publish a book, even the most recently published books may contain dated information. To find current information and perspective on a topic the researcher turns to periodical articles. The most frequently used guide in this category is the *Reader's Guide to Periodical Literature.* The *Reader's Guide* indexes the most widely read general magazines published in the United States. It is organized alphabetically under author, under subject, and occasionally under the title of the article. The weakness of the *Reader's Guide* is that it lists few of the more specialized periodicals which are of frequent use to researchers.

For the researcher who is interested in finding more specialized periodical articles in a given field, the task is somewhat more difficult. Almost every field publishes some index of its own periodical literature. Many of these specialized indexes are noted in Galin and Spielberg's *Reference Books.* Three particularly useful indexes of more specialized periodical literature are the *Social Sciences and Humanities Index,* the *Public Affairs Information Service, and the Guide to Legal Periodicals.* The *Social Sciences and Humanities Index* (and its 1920–1964 predecessor, the *International Index)* covers articles in the humanities and social sciences over the past fifty years. It is organized alphabetically by author and subject. The *Public Affairs Information Service* is an indispensible index for locating current works in political science, government, economics, and sociology. Published since 1915, the *P. A. I. S.* is organized alphabetically by subject. The *Guide to Legal Periodicals* catalogues the articles in the many legal journals published in the United States as well as the publications of legal associations. Organized by subject, this guide is invaluable to anyone doing legal research.

Newspapers. When the researcher wants more detailed contemporary commentary on an event or topic, he will want to investigate newspaper sources. While many local newspapers attempt to keep current indexes of their articles, the only comprehensive index of an American newspaper which is available in most libraries is the *New York Times Index.* Because of the thorough coverage of national and international news in the *Times* and because of the *Times'* policy of printing important documents, Supreme Court opinions, and speeches, the *Times Index* becomes an excellent research tool. The *Times Index* includes summaries of news articles and editorials arranged under alphabetical subject headings. Entries under each heading are arranged chronologically. If one wishes to find commentary from more than one newspaper, he can use the *Times Index* to locate the event or item under consideration and then check copies of other newspapers for that same date to find further articles on the topic.

Almanacs and fact books. Frequently the researcher needs to find a fact or a date or a specific statistic. While these may be found in books or periodical articles, the use of almanacs and fact books can save a considerable amount of time. Three such sources are particularly valuable: (1) *The Statistical Abstract of the United States,* (2) the *World Almanac,* and (3) *Facts on File.*

The *Statistical Abstract of the United States* is probably the best source of statistics about all aspects of the United States. Statistics are compiled on literally every important aspect of American life, and these statistics usually cover a period of fifteen to twenty years before the publication date to assist in putting current statistical information into perspective. An additional feature of the *Statistical Abstract* is that sources are given for most statistics; this makes cross references possible when more detailed information is needed. Each volume contains an extensive subject index. Of the sources of statistical data, it is one of the best organized.

The *World Almanac* is similar to the *Statistical Abstract* although not quite as well organized. The *Almanac* probably contains a larger amount of data about the United States than does the *Statistical Abstract* and also contains sections on the history and present conditions of every country in the world. The book is organized alphabetically by subject, profession, and occupation.

Facts on File is a weekly (made cumulative monthly, quarterly, and yearly) summary of the most important facts from news events gathered from the major metropolitan newspapers. It is an encyclopedia of current events and is the place to look for brief summaries of the most important events of the week. Its subject indexes are precise and easy to use. The major limitation of *Facts on File* is that sources of information are not provided.

Government documents. The U. S. Government is a prolific publisher of books, hearings, pamphlets, bulletins, and the proceedings of Congress. On any question of public policy, the researcher will find government documents, especially hearings, to be an excellent source of expert testimony on all sides of the controversy. Unfortunately, most government publications are not indexed in the reference works described in this section. The *only* index which provides a comprehensive listing of all publications of all federal government agencies and departments is the *Monthly Catalog of United States Government Pub-*

lications. Although other indexes of government publications exist for the years preceding 1940, the *Monthly Catalog* is the only bibliography of government publications since that date. The organizational system of the *Monthly Catalog* is a bit complex, and some practice is necessary to learn to use it efficiently. The best method is to ask a reference librarian to show you how to use it and then to spend some time practicing with it.

Essays. Much of the valuable material for the scholar in any field exists not in book or periodical article form, but rather as essays in edited collections. The typical reference sources are not much help in locating such essays. Book sources will tend to list only the title of the total collection rather than the titles of individual essays, and periodical sources tend not to include essays in their listings. The work which fills this void is the *Essay and General Literature Index.* Published annually since 1900, this work is a guide to essays and short articles contained in collections. The works indexed are from most major fields, and the organization is alphabetical by author, subject, and occasionally by title. The work is invaluable in finding material which may not be published in book form or in periodicals.

READING FOR EVIDENCE

The gathering of the necessary sources of evidence is only the first step in research. Finding the right sources of evidence does not automatically guarantee that one will discover the evidence needed for his purposes. The researcher must now read the sources that he has gathered and make decisions on what evidence to record.

The most important thing to remember when reading for evidence is that such reading is *purposeful.* In other words, the researcher is reading with a limited purpose in mind and cannot afford to waste time reading what is tangential to his purpose. The first question which must be asked before beginning reading for evidence, then, is, "What am I looking for?" The clearer the researcher's concept of the purpose of his reading, the more profitable the reading will be.

The purpose of reading for evidence will vary depending upon the stage of research. In the early stages, one is frequently reading merely to discover whether or not the sources of evidence are relevant to the proposition under consideration. Book and article titles are frequently misleading, and the researcher must discover and quickly eliminate those sources which are tangential to the research purpose.

At this point, the research technique of skimming is desirable. By quickly checking chapter titles, prefaces, subheadings, and summaries, one can make a relatively rapid determination as to the potential usefulness of a source. Instead of wasting valuable time in careful reading of an irrelevant source, skimming allows one to dispose of such sources quickly.

In the first stages of research and analysis of a controversy, one is frequently reading for *ideas* as well as for *evidence.* At this point, the reading should be most careful and thorough to make sure that one fully understands the context of the ideas and evidence discovered. Because analysis is just beginning, it is difficult for the reader to determine what evidence will be useful. Much of the evidence recorded at this point in research will end up being of little use in the ultimate analysis of the proposition. This does not mean, however, that evidence should not be recorded during this stage. On the contrary, since it is much easier to discard unneeded evidence than it is to find relevant evidence which has been read earlier but not recorded, one should record any potentially useful evidence during the early stages of research. The purpose of reading at this stage is to gather as many relevant ideas and as much evidence to support those ideas as possible.

In the later stages of research and analysis, the purpose of reading for evidence changes. With the analysis nearly complete and a considerable amount of evidence already recorded, the purpose of such reading becomes much more specific. At this point, the *quantity* of evidence becomes less important and the *quality* of the evidence becomes the controlling factor. At this stage of research one is usually looking for relatively few items of evidence to support specific arguments. One is no longer engaged in general research on the topic. Rather than consulting general books or articles on the proposition, one is more likely to be working with much more specialized sources. Since the research purpose is specific, the technique of skimming becomes useful again. Sources are now skimmed, not for their general relevance to the proposition, but rather for their likelihood of containing a specific item of evidence. While the early stages of reading for evidence may produce much recorded material, in the later stages it is not uncommon to spend hours searching for one specific item.

Reading for evidence, then, is purposeful. If the researcher has a clear concept of the purpose of his reading at any point in time, he is much less likely to waste time on sources which are irrelevant to his specific needs. Since the reason for reading for evidence varies with the stage of research one must adapt his reading methods to the purpose of the reading.

Since few of us have photographic memories, it will be necessary for us to record the evidence which we discover. Whether we are preparing a term paper or gathering material for a debate, evidence must be recorded for future reference. This section will address itself to the problems involved in recording evidence. These problems center around two questions: (1) What should be recorded? (the evidence itself) and (2) How should it be recorded? (documentation form).

Recording the evidence itself. There is no method available which will guarantee that the researcher will record all of the right evidence needed on a specific research project. The choice of what evidence to record is ultimately a subjective judgment of the individual researcher dependent upon the nature of the specific research project, the nature of the subject matter, and the type of evidence that the researcher is looking for at any point in time. While specific content rules cannot be generalized here, four formal guidelines for the recording of evidence may be helpful: (1) record single ideas, (2) record reasons rather than conclusions, (3) record evidence consistent with its context, and (4) record evidence in a length appropriate to its anticipated use.

The suggestion that single ideas be recorded is made to make the process of information retrieval possible. Evidence is recorded in order to be used in the future. As we will suggest later, evidence should be recorded on index cards and filed under subject headings. If a particular piece of evidence contains more than a single idea, it becomes impossible to file it accurately without duplicating it. When a quotation contains multiple ideas which are of use to the researcher, they should be separated and recorded individually.

Second, the evidence recorded should consist of reasons rather than just conclusions. It is important to remember that data is the starting point of argument. If we record only conclusions, we have recorded only authoritative restatements of the arguments which we seek to support. Evidence which gives the reasons for these conclusions provides a more specific and acceptable basis for our own arguments.

Third, the evidence recorded should be consistent with the context within which it exists. The researcher is faced with an ethical decision here. Frequently, by taking evidence out of its context one can change substantially the meaning and impact intended by the source. On rare occasions, a researcher can justify the usefulness of a piece of evidence which is inconsistent with its context, but in such cases he should at least note on the index card that the context differs with the specific piece of evidence. One should be especially careful if editing or paraphrasing of evidence is necessary, since chances for misrepresentation are multiplied in these cases. As a general rule, the researcher should record evidence in the *exact form* in which it is found, noting any inconsistencies in context. If editing or paraphrasing is necessary, this should be done only after the accurate, complete recording of the evidence is accomplished.

Finally, the evidence should be recorded in a length appropriate to its anticipated use. If the research is in preparation for a term paper or other forms of scholarly writing, then it may be appropriate to record rather lengthy quotations on occasion to insure completeness of context. If the evidence is to be used orally in support of an argument, on the other hand, the demands of the oral communication situation require that shorter quotations be used. In recording evidence for possible oral presentation, it may be wise to break up a longer quotation into several shorter, more specific ones.

Documenting the source of evidence. Accurate and complete documentation of all evidence recorded is vital no matter what the purpose of the research. In any research project, there are always occasions when the researcher will wish to go back to a previously read and recorded source for one reason or another. Adequate documentation the first time around makes this process faster and more efficient. Thorough documentation is also helpful in evaluating the comparative worth of evidence when making decisions on which items of evidence to use in a paper or speech. In addition, careful documentation is essential in order that others may be able to examine the accuracy of your research. There are, unfortunately, too many verified instances of the falsification and misrepresentation of evidence to ignore the importance of this safeguard.

A suggested form for documentation is contained in the accompanying illustration of a sample evidence card. First of all, evidence should be recorded on index cards to facilitate organized filing. The suggested inclusion of an index topic further assists the process of filing the evidence for systematic retrieval. The name of the author and the inclusion of his qualifications assist in evaluating the comparative credibility of the evidence. The details on the source of the evidence make checking and further reference possible. The footnote form used for most term papers and theses and the *Debate Program and Tournament Standards* of the American Forensic Association both require the researcher to be able to supply the following source information: the

name of the book, magazine, or other publication, the date of publication, and the specific page quoted from.

Index Topic

Author
Position (why he is an authority)
Source details (title, book or magazine, date, page)

"Exact quotation of only the information which is pertinent. Make the quotation
as short as possible without distorting the author's meaning or removing his words
from their proper context. Deletions should be indicated by three dots (...)."

ETHICAL USE OF EVIDENCE

Throughout this chapter numerous references have been made to
the importance of fairness and accuracy in the recording and use of
evidence. Inaccuracy and unfairness in the use of evidence may result
from many circumstances—from deliberate deception, from hurried
and careless recording of evidence, or from the use of evidence inaccurately recorded by someone else. The misuse and distortion of evidence
has been repeatedly documented in many areas of inquiry and advocacy. Championship college debaters, lawyers, government researchers, and even college presidents have been discovered misusing
and fabricating evidence.

Fortunately, the very nature of our processes of inquiry and advocacy makes it unlikely that distorted evidence will go undetected for
very long. Because other investigators often conduct parallel or related
research and because opposing advocates usually check each other's
sources, fabricated or inaccurately used evidence is likely to be revealed soonor or later.

Even short-term distortions can, however, have serious consequences. Since data is the basis of all argument and analysis, errors in
evidence can lead to faulty conclusions and to inappropriate solutions.
Years of an individual's life may be wasted in prison or millions of
dollars may be wasted on unwise programs before false evidence is
discovered.

Not only may the specific consequences of the misuse of evidence
be undesirable, but the possible impact of numerous distortions is
equally serious. The result of the repeated unethical use of evidence
may be to undermine overall confidence in the reliability of the meth-

ods of argumentation. Once loss of faith in reasoned inquiry and advocacy occurs, then only intuition and propaganda will be left as our guides.

Adherence to a few simple guidelines can help the advocate to avoid even unintentional distortions of evidence: (1) do as much of your own research as possible; (2) record all evidence carefully and accurately; (3) use evidence in ways consistent with its context; (4) never use evidence collected by inexperienced or unreliable persons or groups.

SUMMARY

Data is the starting point of argument, the substance from which we reason. Premises and evidence constitute the two major classes of data. Premises are the fundamental assumptions or beliefs which will be accepted without external support. Evidence consists of external source materials which may be used to lend support. Both premises and evidence must be discovered and not created.

There are two types of premises: perceptual and value. Perceptual premises are assumptions made about the nature of things; they are based on our personal view of the world. Value premises are statements which express the worth of something. Both perceptual premises and value premises have their origins within the advocate and within the audience to be addressed.

There are two types of evidence: facts and expert opinions. Factual evidence consists of potentially verifiable statements which describe real objects or events. Factual evidence can appear in the form of verbal examples, statistics, or descriptive historic statements. Expert opinion evidence consists of authoritative statements which explain or interpret factual data.

The process of inquiring into a problem should begin with an examination of one's own beliefs. To arrive at those personal premises which can be used as data three questions should be asked: What do I believe? Why do I believe it? and Can the basis of my belief be reasonably denied? The desire to discover probable truth requires that only those personal values and personal perceptual premises which meet the test of universal self-evidence be accepted as data.

The circumstances of public advocacy permit the use of less than universally self-evident premises as data when the premises of an advocate coincide with the values and perceptions of his *specific* audience. Information about audience premises may be gained from group publications and documents, informal statements from group members, and the reports of nongroup members.

There are a number of excellent guides available to assist researchers in the discovery of both factual and expert opinion evidence. The card catalog of any library will list all of the books available in that specific library. The most comprehensive list of books printed in the United States may be found in the *Cumulative Book Index.* The most widely read general periodicals are listed in the *Reader's Guide to Periodical Literature.* The *Social Science and Humanities Index,* the *Public Affairs Information Service,* and the *Guide to Legal Periodicals* are among the more important specialized periodical indexes. The most readily available newspaper index is the *New York Times Index.* Specific dates, statistics, and other factual evidence can be most easily found in such sources as the *Statistical Abstract of the United States,* the *World Almanac,* and *Facts on File.* The *Essay and General Literature Index* provides a systematic guide to essays and short articles contained in collections.

Reading for evidence should be purposeful. In the early stages of research one may skim articles to determine if they are related to the proposition. Later, a researcher must read carefully since he will want to understand ideas as well as collect evidence. Still later in his study, the researcher will seek more specific evidence, and he will rely on more specialized sources and more selective reading.

Four guidelines should be followed in recording evidence: (1) record single ideas; (2) record reasons rather than just conclusions; (3) record evidence consistent with its context; and (4) record evidence in a length appropriate to its anticipated use.

Accurate and complete documentation of all evidence recorded is essential. Complete documentation requires that the author's name, his special qualifications, the title of the book or periodical, the date, and the specific page be listed.

The ethical use of evidence requires that you (1) do as much of your own research as possible, (2) record all evidence carefully and accurately, (3) use evidence in ways consistent with its context, and (4) never use evidence collected by inexperienced or unreliable persons or groups.

STUDY QUESTIONS

1. What is the essential difference between *premises* and *evidence?*
2. To what extent is the usefulness of perceptual and value premises as data dependent upon the nature of the audience in a communication situation?
3. What is the essential characteristic which distinguishes a *fact* from an *opinion?*

4. Why is it dangerous to record evidence in paraphrased form?
5. What ethical responsibilities does the researcher have in recording and using evidence?

EXERCISES

1. Using the transcript of a contemporary public speech, identify all of the arguments used by the speaker and the data for each of these arguments. For each of the items of data indicate whether it is a perceptual premise, a value premise, factual evidence, or expert opinion evidence.
2. Build a preliminary bibliography on an argumentative proposition which you are currently working on by finding and recording three sources from each of the following bibliographic guides:
   a. The card catalog of your campus or public library.
   b. The *Reader's Guide to Periodical Literature.*
   c. The *Public Affairs Information Service.*
   d. The *New York Times Index.*
   e. The *Monthly Catalog of United States Government Publications.*
   f. The *Essay and General Literature Index.*
   g. The *Cumulative Book Index.*
3. Build four arguments for oral presentation as follows:
   a. One argument based on a perceptual premise.
   b. One argument based on a value premise.
   c. One argument based on one of the forms of factual evidence.
   d. One argument based on expert opinion evidence.
4. Prepare fifteen evidence cards to be turned in to your instructor. In recording this evidence you should attempt to follow the four guidelines for recording evidence and the documentation form suggested in this chapter.

5 The Testing of Data

Each day we are bombarded with a multitude of facts and opinions concerning the important questions of our society. Whether we are listening to a newscast, chatting with friends, or reading a magazine or newspaper, we are confronted with various types of data which are frequently in conflict with each other. Unfortunately, many people become the mental slaves of what they read or listen to because they do not have criteria by which to measure the accuracy or acceptability of the premises and evidence offered. How does one determine whether or not a given piece of data is logically sufficient to serve as the starting point for argument? The attempt to answer this question constitutes the purpose of this chapter.

The importance of this task should be obvious. If an argument is insufficient at the outset—if the data upon which it is based is inadequate—then the most careful reasoning process and the most clearly phrased conclusions will not salvage it. The tests of data outlined in this chapter serve not only as criteria for selecting data for use when inquiring into a problem, but also as tests for examining and refuting data offered by opponents who advocate a specific position.

The chapter will be divided into three sections. The first section outlines tests which can be applied to all data; the second considers tests unique to factual and opinion evidence; the third presents tests appropriate to premises.

GENERAL TESTS OF DATA

While tests which are unique to specific types of data will be outlined later in this chapter, there are three general tests which can be applied to all data. These are the test of internal consistency, the test of external consistency, and the test of relevancy.

THE TEST OF INTERNAL CONSISTENCY

The test of internal consistency asks the question, "Is the data consistent with other data from the *same source?*" This test suggests that we must look carefully at the premises, facts, and opinions expressed by a source to determine whether or not they are consistent with each other. Inconsistencies between or among premises, facts, and opinions expressed in a single source raise serious questions concerning the credibility of the source of the data. Unexplained inconsistencies at any level of data suggest that the source of the data is guilty of careless thinking and superficial analysis. Such data are always an inadequate basis for argument and are easily and persuasively refuted by anyone familiar with the consistency problems of the source.

An example of inconsistent opinion data is found in the analysis by the *Tampa Times* of the role of marijuana in a multiple ax-slaying:

> ... it may or may not be wholly true that the pernicious marijuana cigarette is responsible for the murderous mania of a Tampa young man in exterminating all of the members of his family within his reach—but whether or not the poisonous mind-wrecking weed is mainly account- able for the tragedy, its sale should not be and should never have been permitted here or elsewhere. ... It required five murders to impress the Tampa public and Tampa officials with the serious effects of the habit.[1]

This editorial first admits uncertainty as to the causal connection be- tween marijuana and the killing but then goes on to assume that causal- ity has been established. Such a blatant inconsistency in opinion undermines any assumption of expertness in this matter on the part of the source of the data, the *Tampa Times.*

THE TEST OF EXTERNAL CONSISTENCY

The test of external consistency asks the question, "Is the data consistent with other data from *unrelated sources?*" This test suggests that each piece of data must be examined in the light of other known data from other sources. A *New York Times* feature writer once ap- plied the test of external consistency to refute the claim that pollution control costs are causing business failures:

> Headlines such as "Pollution Laws Closing Plants by the Hundreds" and "A Drive to Find Jobs for Victims of the Pollution War" have ap- peared in both business and lay periodicals. A Department of Commerce publication said recently, "More plant closings are being reported daily from countless small communities throughout the nation."
>
> However, a nationwide check by *The New York Times,* corroborated by Government reports, provides little substantiation for such assertions and apprehensions.
>
> To the contrary, the survey yielded indications—supported by a num- ber of officials, economists and other observers—that the costs of pollu- tion control, while they may be causing dislocations in a few specialized situations, could also be a constructive element in terms of plant modern- ization and increased efficiency.[2]

The discovery of inconsistencies between unrelated sources does not automatically invalidate the credibility of the data, but it does require that further examination be conducted to determine which of

---

[1] *Tampa Times,* October 20, 1973, p. 11.
[2] Gladwin Hill, "The Cost of Cleanup," *New York Times,* June 4, 1972, quoted from the *Congressional Record,* July 18, 1972, p. S11111.

the sources is more credible in the matter under consideration. Such further examination leads to the tests specific to the individual types of data. These tests will be outlined in the final two sections of this chapter. Problems with external consistency, then, are a tip-off that further testing of the data must be conducted.

The test of external consistency can be used positively to validate data as well as negatively to question the validity of data. When used in the positive sense it becomes the test of "independent corroboration." Historian Louis Gottschalk defines the concept of independent corroboration when he says, "The general rule of historians is to accept as historical only those particulars which rest upon the independent testimony of two or more reliable witnesses."[3] If two unrelated (independent) sources provide us with the same premises, facts, or opinions, the credibility of our data is more firmly established.

THE TEST OF RELEVANCY

The test of relevancy asks the question, "Does the data support the conclusion it is asserted to support?" This test suggests that data can be credible in every other respect but may still be an insufficient basis for argument because it is tangent to the conclusion being forwarded. It is not infrequent for a conclusion to assert one thing and for the data to establish something slightly different. If, for example, an advocate set forth the conclusion that no one in America suffers from hunger or malnutrition and proceeded to cite expert opinion evidence which stated, "No one in America *need* go without adequate food," the evidence would be irrelevant to the claim. In examining the relevancy of data to any given conclusion, then, one must always ask the question, "Does this data really support this conclusion?" If the data is tangential to the conclusion, it provides no probative force and may be dismissed as irrelevant.

TESTS OF FACTUAL AND EXPERT OPINION EVIDENCE

While the three tests outlined above can be applied to all types of data, there are other tests which are unique to factual and expert opinion evidence. These include the test of recency, the test of source identification, the test of source ability, the test of source willingness, the test of context, and the tests of statistical evidence.

[3]Louis Gottschalk, *Understanding History* (New York: Alfred A. Knopf, Inc., 1963), p. 166.

THE TEST OF RECENCY

The test of recency asks the question, "Is the statement of the evidence based upon recent observations of the real situation?" Since the world is constantly changing, most facts and opinions have maximum validity for only a limited period of time. The test of recency simply asks if the evidence is recent enough so that important facts have not changed in the elapsed time. Factual evidence concerning wage levels in a given profession, for example, can be badly dated in even a year or two. The same is true of data on unemployment, prices, economic growth, etc. Expert opinions which interpret such dated facts must also be carefully examined.

An article in the *Christopher News Notes* used the test of recency in rejecting often-cited statistical estimates of the number of deaths from illegal abortions:

> Estimates widely quoted as recently as 1967, based for the most part on a study by Taussig in 1932, put the number of such deaths each year between 5,000 and 10,000. This study was done before the advent of antibiotics, therapeutic medicine and frequent transfusions—all of which have sharply reduced the medical risks.[4]

Note that in applying the test of recency the author referred both to the fact that the statistics were forty years old and to the fact that conditions had changed during that period.

In applying the test of recency, the advocate should be especially aware of recent statements of old facts. It is not uncommon for current books or articles to base conclusions on evidence from older sources. Books are especially suspect on this count since there is frequently a time lapse of several years between the writing of certain sections of a book and its actual publication.

THE TEST OF SOURCE IDENTIFICATION

The test of source identification asks the question, "Is the source of the evidence identifiable?" This test suggests that each piece of evidence should be traceable to a specific source. Without adequate source identification, complete testing of evidence is impossible. The credibility of factual and expert opinion evidence is, in large part, dependent upon the ability and willingness of a source to perceive and interpret the situation accurately and fairly. Without source identification we cannot make these vital credibility judgments.

[4]*Christopher News Notes,* Pamphlet #195.

Frequently we are confronted with general documentation such as "sources close to the President," or "according to *Newsweek,*" or "economists believe." Such general documentation may make arguments easier to read or listen to, but it also renders adequate source evaluation impossible. Every time such general documentation is encountered, one must ask why the documentation was not more specific and must examine whether or not those using the evidence may have reasons for not disclosing the full identification of their sources.

THE TEST OF SOURCE ABILITY

The test of source ability asks the question, "Is the source of the evidence *able* to report or interpret the situation accurately?" Since the factual and expert opinion evidence used in argumentation must be reported, it is necessary to examine the source of the evidence as well as the fact or expert opinion itself. In questioning a source's ability to report or interpret the situation accurately it is vital to consider both the source's accessibility to the situation and his expertness.

It is first important to determine a source's geographical and chronological nearness to the elements of the situation which he is reporting or interpreting. Lack of direct accessibility results in a source who is dependent upon other sources for his information. When the source is separated from the situation, the facts and opinions must be sifted through a variety of individual perceptions and interpretations and, therefore, are more subject to distortion and misrepresentation. As a general rule, then, the more a source is separated from direct access to the important elements of a situation, the less accurate his report or interpretation is likely to be. In our courts of law, as well as in society in general, eyewitness accounts are considered more credible than hearsay evidence.

In addition to examining source *accessibility* one must also consider source *expertness.* More specifically, one must question whether or not the source is qualified by experience, training, or position to interpret the situation. These factors of expertness are crucial in determining whether or not the source of the evidence is able to tell the truth. Even superior access to the situation may not be helpful if specialized knowledge or background is necessary to understand the event.

The *experience* test suggests that a source should have worked with the situation sufficiently to enable him to report or interpret the elements of that situation accurately. An experienced diplomat is much better able to interpret the public statements of a foreign power than is a novice news reporter. To the novice reporter, a foreign policy statement may seem to be the same as previous statements. The experienced diplomat, on the other hand, may be able to read between the lines of the statement to see subtle shifts of policy.

In many situations, *specific training* may be necessary to interpret events or even merely to report them. News reporters receive intensive training before being sent to cover combat situations. Military combat situations are so complex that specialized training is necessary in order simply to report events intelligently. In deciding the complex constitutional questions in our society, years of legal training are a vital prerequisite. The layman simply lacks the specialized training necessary to permit an authoritative interpretation of complex legal issues.

Another measure of source expertness is that of *position.* The concept of position is closely related to the test of accessibility. A source's position may give him access to information denied to most people thereby providing him with a degree of expertise. The perfect example, of course, is the position of President of the United States. No matter which individual occupies this office, the position permits access to otherwise classified information. That access enables the President to view and interpret events in a perspective denied to most other people. In much the same way, a Senator who is a member of the Senate Judiciary Committee has access to important information on judicial issues. He becomes an expert on these issues, not because of any personal qualities which he possesses, but rather because of the position he holds.

In examining a source's ability to report or interpret situations accurately, then, we must consider a source's accessibility to the situation and his experience, training, and position with reference to that situation. If a source has problems in any of these areas, it should lead to a search for independent corroboration by sources with superior accessibility, experience, training, or position.

THE TEST OF SOURCE WILLINGNESS

The test of source willingness asks the question, "Is the source of the evidence *willing* to report or interpret the situation fairly?" While a source may be in an excellent position to perceive the truth accurately, conditions may exist which may cause him to distort the reporting or interpretation of situations. In examining source willingness to report or interpret accurately, one must consider both the self-interest and writing style of the source.

The first question to ask is, "Does the *self-interest* of the source or his sponsor prejudice the evidence?" If the source of the evidence could profit from a given reporting or interpretation of the situation, we have grounds for questioning the fairness of the source. This was the basis for Senator Frank Moss's rejection of an American Medical Association report on cigarette smoking. "The American Medical Association," he charged, "accepted $10 million for research from the tobacco industry and announced soon afterward that the evidence against smoking was inconclusive."[5] While bias does not automatically negate the validity of the reporting or interpretation, it causes us to doubt objectivity and to look to the other tests of the credibility of the evidence.

We must question not only the self-interest of the source but also the interests of the organization for whom he works. A source may be consciously restrained from telling the whole truth by the organization with which he is associated if the whole truth is deemed in conflict with the interests of that organization. Such restraint is even more likely if the report of a source must be filtered by the organization.

In assessing source willingness to report or interpret events fairly we must also question whether or not the *writing style* of the source has sacrificed accuracy. Frequently the necessity of writing in a style which is acceptable to given readers results in compromises with accurate reporting and interpreting of the situation. This test is especially important when we evaluate the reporting of sources who write for popular periodicals. The need to make the report simple and interesting to the general reading public frequently leads to over-generalization of evidence.

THE TEST OF CONTEXT

The test of context asks the question, "Is the evidence used in a manner consistent with the *meaning and intent* of the source?" Inevitably, facts and expert opinions exist in a context broader than that used by the advocate. Since evidence gathering and use are selective processes, it is vital to examine the context of any piece of evidence to insure that the meaning or intent of the source is not misrepresented. We frequently hear public figures decry the fact that their words have been taken out of context.

The test of contextual accuracy is one of the more difficult tests of evidence to apply because of its inherent subjectivity. The evidence selected for use by an advocate is almost always an incomplete representation of the total argument of the source. The test of context is used to determine whether or not the advocate has violated the intent of the source in his selection of evidence from that source.

[5]Senator Frank Moss, *Congressional Record,* January 25, 1972, p. S467.

An example of the application of the test of context occurred in the final round of the 1966 National Debate Tournament. The affirmative was arguing that the gambling element of organized crime was careful to avoid engaging in interstate commerce in order to avoid falling within the jurisdiction of federal law-enforcement agencies. The negative, as part of its attempt to refute this argument, challenged the affirmative evidence as being out of context.

> ... Now Mike came back with a *Wall Street Journal* article that said, "The more knowledgeable gamblers have tailored their operations so they don't become a part of interstate commerce." Mr. Denger, in his eagerness, forgot to read two words in that quotation. "The more knowledgeable gamblers have *attempted* to tailor their operations so they stay out of interstate commerce." I want proof that they have. I want proof that they don't use the telephone, that they don't use the mails, and that they don't use the interstate commerce in any way whatsoever.[6]

TESTS OF STATISTICAL EVIDENCE

When evidence takes the form of statistics, a variety of special tests of the measurement procedures must be applied. These special tests are necessitated by the symbolic nature of statistics. Since items are collected and given a numerical symbol, the resultant statistic exists on a higher level of abstraction than the examples it represents. Because of this symbolic abstraction, statistics are subject to manipulation, and the underlying truth can be lost or distorted. Therefore, in addition to applying the general tests of evidence, four special tests should be considered when evaluating statistical evidence.

Are the statistics based upon adequate sampling techniques? Many people assume that the figures which they read regarding such matters as the level of unemployment or the number of new housing starts represent real numerical counts of those situations. Such statistics are not, of course, true counts but are rather projections based upon limited samples. The validity of such statistics, therefore, rests heavily upon the reasonableness of the sampling techniques used in the projections.

Unfortunately information concerning the size or representativeness of the sample used to arrive at a statistical statement is not always provided. Yet, such information must be sought if intelligent judgments concerning the credibility of statistical evidence are to be made.

[6]*Twentieth National Debate Tournament* (West Point, New York: United States Military Academy, 1966), p. 61.

If a sample does not adequately represent all of the elements within a class, the resultant statistic will be quite misleading. When college debaters discussed the question of compulsory health insurance, many of them came upon a survey of medical financing in the city of Baltimore. The findings of this study seemed to support the negative claim that failure to receive adequate medical care was not related to ability to pay. Because these findings contradicted most affirmative studies, the better debaters sought to find out more about the survey. When they examined the survey techniques underlying the study, they discovered that all people earning less than the national median income had been excluded from the survey sample. An unrepresentative sample made the survey invalid.

Even if the sample is representative, it must be large enough to guarantee that chance deviation is not operating. The size required will depend upon the homogeneity of the items being measured and the representativeness of the items within the sample. It is important, therefore, to seek explanation and justification of the sampling techniques when examining statistical evidence. The best sources of statistical evidence are sources which provide such explanations and justifications.

Is the statistical unit an appropriate one? All statistics view phenomena from a particular perspective, and the statistical unit selected determines what that perspective is. The answer to so simple a question as "What is the average income of an American factory worker" depends, in large part, upon the statistical unit used to measure "average income." Three statistical measures of average are commonly used: the median, the mean, and the mode. The *median* is the exact middle point; in the number series one through seven it would be the number four. The *mean* is the true numerical average; it is arrived at by adding all the numbers of a series together and dividing by the number of items in the series. The *mode* is the point around which the largest number of items cluster; it is the item which occurs most often. There are no firm rules for determining which of these measures is most appropriate. In general, if there are a few extreme numbers in a series which will distort the mean, the median or mode should be used.

The problem of selecting an appropriate statistical unit is by no means limited to the measurement of averages. There are a variety of potentially appropriate units which can be used to describe most situations. If, for example, we wished to discuss poverty or unemployment or crime, we could express the extent of these problems in absolute terms (1.2 million unemployed), or as percentages of the total population (6 percent unemployment), or as ratios (one out of every seventeen adult workers is unemployed), or as a percentage increase or decrease from a previous period (a 25 percent decrease from last year), or in a number of other ways.

The selection of the most appropriate statistical unit became the basis of a critical issue in the 1960 presidential election campaign. John F. Kennedy, the Democratic nominee, charged that under the Republican Eisenhower Administration the United States' rate of economic growth had not kept pace with the Russians' rate of growth. Richard Nixon, the Republican candidate, responded that percentage figures were not a fair measure of growth. He claimed that the Soviet economy was a much poorer one so that even minor economic expansions sharply increased its rate of growth while the United States' economic base was so large that even large expansions affected the rate of growth only slightly. Thus, the two candidates' perspectives and conclusions were affected by their choice of particular statistical measuring units.

In general, the more one knows about what it is he wants to measure and the more one knows about what it is a particular statistical unit measures, the more likely he is to select an appropriate unit.

Do the statistics cover an appropriate time period? Many times statistics are used to describe a situation over a given period of time. It then becomes critical to know whether the time period selected is appropriate for the purposes at hand. In measuring concepts like economic growth, inflation, and employment, the selection of base years and the length of time measured can have a significant effect upon the impression created by the statistic. By selecting an exceptionally high or an exceptionally low base year, an advocate can sometimes suggest the existence of a trend favorable to his side. The cause of truth, however, dictates that base years be selected not on the basis of personal advantage but on the basis of representativeness and reasonableness.

Are comparisons between comparable units? The old adage that you cannot compare apples and oranges has a significant application to statistical evidence. One of the most common uses of statistical evidence is the attempt to compare conditions. When statistical evidence is used in this comparative sense it is vital to determine whether or not the statistical units are comparable. Before attempting to compare the rates of juvenile crime in two cities, an advocate must determine if the two jurisdictions include the same group of people in the category of juvenile. Some cities define anyone under twenty-one years of age as a juvenile, while others include only those sixteen and under in the class of juveniles. Similarly, when one is comparing the economic growth of two countries it is important to determine whether or not these countries measure economic growth in the same way. If one country measures economic growth using only gross national product statistics while the other country adjusts gross national product statistics to allow for inflation, a comparison between such statistical units is meaningless.

TESTS OF VALUE PREMISES

Chapter 4 identified two types of premises which may be used as data: perceptual premises and value premises. There are no logical tests which are unique to perceptual premises, although the general tests of data should, of course, be applied to them. Value premises, on the other hand, do have certain specialized tests which are peculiar to them.

The claim is frequently made that when we reduce an argument to its underlying value premises we have arrived at a point where we can no longer apply tests of logical adequacy. To be sure, values are emotional in nature and are more difficult to test than any of the other types of data. Nevertheless, it is possible to test the adequacy of values as data by asking the following three questions: (1) Does the value really represent a good? (2) Is there a more important value? (3) Is the meaning of the value properly interpreted?

DOES THE VALUE
REALLY REPRESENT A GOOD?

Values, when used as data, must always be related to factual situations. Few values are universally applicable. There frequently exist situations in which the value cannot be applied without qualification. The value judgment that it is wrong to take another human life, for instance, is modified under conditions of war and self-defense. To deny the universal application of a value, one must show that the value does not constitute an ultimate good in a specific situation. Values, then, must be relevant to the factual situation under consideration.

A debater in the final round of the 1969 Heart of America Debate Tournament refuted an alleged disadvantage to the affirmative proposal for United States withdrawal from Vietnam by denying the worth of an underlying negative value.

... Consider finally the proliferation [of nuclear weapons] disadvantages. He says it's harmful in Asia. I deny this: so does Fred Green in 1968 of Williams College. "Over the long run, the United States would find that proliferation among its Asian allies and friends would make more harmonious relations with them easier to attain." I suggest no disadvantage.[7]

IS THERE A MORE IMPORTANT VALUE?

It is frequently possible to test a value or principle by asking whether or not a more important value should be applied to a given situation. A value premise, to begin with, is a concept of the "most important." To suggest that there is another consideration which is even more important is to deny the primacy of the original value as the basis for argument.

The identification of value conflicts is a realistic approach to human controversies since the acceptance of the primacy of a specific value usually precludes the realization or at least the maximization of other values. Students must frequently establish priorities among their desires to get good grades, to participate in extracurricular activities, and to earn money for small luxuries. Similarly, politicians ask us to choose between our wish for lower taxes and the need for improved public services. In the following editorial, the writer rejects the idea of government-supervised television programming because he considers freedom from censorship to be a more important value than improved programming.

> Rep. John Murphy, New York Democrat, wants to jab TV and radio networks with the pitchfork of $10,000 a day fines if they fail to provide "balanced programming" in prime time. The whole idea should be consigned to limbo. ...
> In effect, his plan would censor the networks after-the-fact by imposing fines for failure to conform to a government-decreed pattern of programming. ...
> Aside from the question of censorship, however, we wonder how any congressman or regulatory agency would define Murphy's brand of programming. What, exactly, is better, balanced programming in the public interest? ...
> TV is not perfect. Far from it. But we prefer the imperfection of freedom to some arbitrary concept of perfection imposed by politicians and federal bureaucrats.[8]

[7] Final Debate, Heart of America Debate Tournament, University of Kansas, Lawrence, Kansas, March 8, 1969.
[8] *The Detroit News,* June 9, 1972, Sec. A, p. 14.

It is important to remember that value premises are highly abstract linguistic constructs. It may be possible to agree with the primacy of a value while at the same time questioning the interpretation of that value used by an advocate. This abstract nature of value premises makes it possible for people who hold different positions to claim support for the same value.

In the debates over United States policy in Southeast Asia both sides claimed that withdrawal was their primary goal. To those opposed to the war in Vietnam, withdrawal meant an immediate absence of all United States men and materials from the conflict. To the supporter of United States involvement, however, withdrawal meant a gradual and conditional disengagement from active participation in the conflict. Outwardly, both sides had the same goal, but what they actually meant by that value term was quite different.

Some years ago when compulsory arbitration of labor disputes was debated, a negative team effectively applied the test of properly interpreting the meaning of the value. The affirmative team established as its initial premise that reason is a better means of solving disputes than is force. The negative accepted this value judgment but reinterpreted the meaning of reason and force in labor-management disputes. The affirmative case had suggested that strikes were a form of force and that compulsory arbitration represented reason. The negative, however, claimed that strikes do not force either side to capitulate; rather, they establish a pressure situation which encourages free and reasonable compromise at the bargaining table. The negative further asserted that the only situation in which labor and management could be forced to accept a contract was when government imposed one through compulsory arbitration. Thus, by reinterpreting the meaning of the value, the negative was able to accept the affirmative's premise without accepting its conclusion.

SUMMARY

This chapter has addressed the problem of determining the logical adequacy of the various types of data. The tests of data outlined in the chapter serve as criteria for selecting data as well as criteria to test the data offered by public advocates.

There are three general tests which can be applied to all types of data. The test of internal consistency asks the question, "Is the data consistent with other data from the same source?" The test of external consistency asks the question, "Is the data consistent with other data from unrelated sources?" The test of relevancy asks the question, "Do the data support the conclusion it is asserted to support?"

Six tests are unique to factual and expert opinion evidence. The test of recency asks the question, "Is the statement of the evidence based upon recent observations of the real situation?" The test of identification asks the question, "Is the source of the evidence identifiable?" The test of source ability asks the question, "Is the source of the evidence able to report or interpret the situation accurately?" This test considers a source's accessibility to the situation and his experience, training, and position with reference to that situation. The test of source willingness asks the question, "Is the source of the evidence willing to report or interpret the situation fairly?" This test takes into consideration the self-interest of the source and his sponsor and the writing style of the source. The test of context asks the question, "Is the evidence used in a manner consistent with the meaning and intent of the source?" The tests unique to statistical data require the answering of four specific questions: (1) Are the statistics based upon adequate sampling techniques? (2) Is the statistical unit an appropriate one? (3) Do the statistics cover an appropriate time period? (4) Are comparisons between comparable units?

Tests specific to value premises are threefold: (1) Does the value really represent a good? (2) Is there a more important value? (3) Is the meaning of the value properly interpreted?

STUDY QUESTIONS

1. How do the tests of internal and external consistency apply to perceptual premises and value premises?
2. What criteria can be used to determine whether or not an item of evidence is consistent with the meaning and intent of the source?
3. To what extent do the tests of value premises outlined in this chapter depend upon the beliefs of the audience for which the ultimate communication is intended?

EXERCISES

1. Examine the editorial and feature pages of your local newspaper and try to find examples of writers applying the tests of data to opposing arguments.

2. Try to discover through library research the statistical bases for:
   a. The Bureau of Labor Statistics' unemployment figures.
   b. The Bureau of the Census population figures.
   c. The Gallup Poll's opinion research studies.
3. Practice refuting value premises by having one student present an argument based on a value judgment and having a second student attack the judgment through application of one of the appropriate tests.
4. Apply the tests of factual and expert opinion evidence to any evidence which you have collected. Be prepared to discuss any problems you had in applying the tests.

6 The Nature of Argument

Even before a baby begins to talk there are signs that he has begun to make simple associations between the satisfaction of certain of his physical wants and his external environment. As the baby grows into childhood and then adulthood this process of making associations continues. To become aware of associations among things, events, or concepts is to think. For a baby or young child most thinking occurs at a fairly concrete level. His associations tend to be among things he can see and touch. However, once the child develops the ability to use language he can begin to deal with the world indirectly through symbols. He thereby enormously increases his range of potential associations and his ability to think.

Unfortunately, not all of the associations which men make during their lifetimes are valid ones. If a young man interprets the friendly smile of an attractive girl as a sign that she wants affection, he may be reasoning incorrectly and get his face slapped. In this instance, no serious harm will have occurred. On the other hand, if a baby reasons that one orange-flavored aspirin tastes good and that several more aspirin would be even better, the health and life of that baby could be seriously endangered. Or if, during an economic recession, national policy makers wrongly interpret certain economic indicators as signs of an upturn and fail to enact appropriate measures to deal with the recession, months of additional lost production and personal hardship may result.

Certainly, not all errors in reasoning can be avoided, but the more one understands how relationships are drawn, the better equipped he is to guard against mistakes. In an attempt to achieve such an understanding, this chapter will focus on the nature of argument. More specifically, the chapter has a threefold purpose: (1) to identify the elements of an argument, (2) to examine the assumption of uniformity which underlies the reasoning process, and (3) to describe the two fundamental processes of reasoning.

ELEMENTS OF ARGUMENT

An argument may be thought of as a complete unit of logical proof. As such, an argument consists of three basic elements. These elements are the data, the reasoning process, and the conclusion. Each of these elements is essential to the establishment of logical sufficiency. In the presentation of arguments certain of these elements may sometimes be omitted on the assumption that the audience will supply the missing element from its own experiences. Because of the brevity and clarity necessary for the communication act, such omissions are often justified.

Nevertheless, it is important to know what constitutes a complete unit of logical proof so that missing elements can be identified and subjected to the same kind of scrutiny as the stated elements.

DATA

In Chapter 4 data was defined as the starting point of argument, the substance from which we reason. Data consist of those things which we are willing to accept as true without further support. It is the basic raw material which calls for interpretation or association. Data may exist as premises (perceptual or value) or as evidence (facts or expert opinions). Arguments may be built upon any of these forms of data. If the data upon which an argument is based are not true (does not conform to reality), the conclusion of that argument will not be true.

REASONING PROCESS

The reasoning process is the procedure which associates data in order to give it meaning. It involves the discovery of a pattern or relationship among the data. Even if an argument is based upon accurate data, its conclusion may still be false if improper associations have been drawn. The nature of these associations will be discussed in the last major section of this chapter and in all of Chapter 7.

CONCLUSION

The conclusion describes the specific condition or relationship identified by the reasoning process's interpretation of the data. All conclusions are aimed at providing answers to one of three fundamental questions: Is it? (question of existence), What is it? (question of essence), or Why is it? (question of explanation).

Conclusions of existence. Conclusions of existence assert that something is real or manifest or in a state of being. When economists refer to reduced unemployment, declining investment, and lowered production and conclude that we are in a recession, they are attempting to prove the existence of a specific economic condition. Conclusions which prove existence are specific to a particular case or a limited group.

Conclusions of essence. Conclusions of essence identify an essential feature or basic attribute or characteristic property of something. When economists cite lost production during the recessions of 1957,

1961, and 1970 and conclude that during recessions production is lost, they are concerned with establishing the essence or nature (lost production) of recessions. Conclusions which prove essence are universal in that they include all members of a class.

Conclusions of explanation. Conclusions of explanation relate phenomena so as to account for their existence or to make their existence intelligible. When economists observe that a restricted money supply preceded each of our recessions and conclude that the recessions were caused by a restricted money supply, they are attempting to provide an explanation of why the recessions occurred. Conclusions of explanation may be specific or universal depending upon the data and reasoning process utilized.

MODEL OF ARGUMENT

The following model illustrates the process involved in creating an argument.

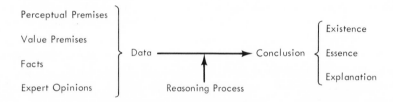

ASSUMPTION OF UNIFORMITY

The reasoning process which allows us to relate data and reach conclusions rests upon an important fundamental assumption. That assumption is called the *assumption of uniformity.* This concept simply describes the belief that there is order and regularity in the universe.

That the assumption of uniformity is justified there can be little doubt. It is the orderliness of nature that allows the biologist to classify plants and animals into species and genus. It is the universe's unvarying characteristics which make it possible for the physicist's laws of energy and motion to predict physical behavior. And it is the consistency of the world which makes the mathematician's tools of statistical analysis useful.

Because uniformity does exist, we can expect to find similarities among phenomena and to discover that experiences reoccur. It is these similarities and this repetition which are the bases for the associations we make when we reason. Without uniformity there would be no basis for predicting future relationships or interpreting past ones. Thus, an awareness of the principle of uniformity is essential to an understanding of how conclusions may be drawn and how knowledge can be projected beyond the immediate situation.

FUNDAMENTAL PROCESSES OF REASONING

Knowing that nature is orderly and regular helps to explain why it is possible to relate experiences, but it does not identify the specific ways in which relationships may be drawn. Basically, the reasoning process associates phenomena in one of two manners, either inductively or deductively.

INDUCTIVE REASONING

Inductive reasoning is sometimes defined as reasoning from the specific to the general. This definition is inadequate on two counts. First, it fails to identify the nature of the process which is involved in moving from the data to the conclusion. This movement from data to conclusion involves a process essentially different from that of deductive reasoning.

Second, defining inductive reasoning as reasoning from the specific to the general does not accurately describe the nature of all inductive conclusions. While it is true that inductive reasoning may involve the examination of numerous particular instances in order to arrive at a general (or class inclusion) statement, it is also true that it may involve a comparison among particulars to arrive at a conclusion specific to only one instance. For example, if we examined fifty cows and discovered that all of them gave milk, we might arrive at the generalization that all cows give milk. But if we examined road and weather conditions in two neighboring states and determined that they were similar and if we discovered that studded snow tires had reduced accidents in one of the states, we might arrive at the specific conclusion that studded snow tires would reduce accidents in the second state. In both cases the reasoning process began with specific data, but in the latter instance the reasoning led to a specific conclusion rather than to a class conclusion. Thus, while it is proper to say that inductive reasoning proceeds from specifics, it is misleading to indicate that induction always results in generalized conclusions.

Properly conceived, inductive reasoning may be thought of as the synthetic process used in moving from particulars to probable conclusions.

Synthetic process. The process of synthesis involves the bringing together of elements into a whole. Inductive reasoning is synthetic in nature because it is concerned with bringing data together into a meaningful pattern or whole. Raw data does not interpret itself. Therefore, any effort to establish relationships requires some extension beyond the data. This extension beyond the data is known as the *inferential leap.* In the illustration with the cows, the conclusion that all cows give milk was possible only because we were willing to move beyond fifty cows to state a general conclusion about all cows. In the studded snow tire example, the similarities between the two neighboring states with regard to road and weather conditions encouraged the extension of the comparison to the third condition, the success of studded snow tires. Inductive reasoning, then, is synthetic in that it reaches beyond the data through an inferential leap to identify a uniform pattern.

Begins with particulars. Induction begins with particulars which may be specific cases, instances, or situations. Sometimes the particulars are drawn from our own experiences, but more often they are based upon other people's descriptions of real experiences. When a number of examples are required, statistical summaries are helpful. Our illustration with the cows was presumably based on direct personal experience, but note how that experience was expressed in a statistical summary (50 cows). Statistical measurements may also be useful in making specific detailed comparisons. The comparison of road and weather conditions in our other example would require detailed statistical descriptions of the two states with regard to the number of miles of paved road, the amount of snowfall, the variations in temperature, etc. While statistics are helpful in capsulizing and presenting particulars, it should be remembered that it is the real instances or situations, and not the numbers, which are the ultimate basis of the reasoning process.

Probable conclusions. The conclusions arrived at through induction are only probably true. Since induction requires a movement beyond the raw data, inductive conclusions are always less certain than the original data. If we had actually observed fifty cows giving milk, we could be reasonably certain of our initial data, but because we have not had direct experience with all cows we cannot be as certain of our conclusion. Thus, even if the absolute validity of the initial data could be established, the *form* of inductive reasoning does not allow for structural certainty.

DEDUCTIVE REASONING

Deductive reasoning is often defined as reasoning from the general to the specific. This definition, like its counterpart definition of induction, is inadequate on two counts. First, it too fails to describe the nature of the process which is involved in moving from the data to the conclusion. We must distinguish between the *synthetic process* of induction and the *analytic process* of deduction.

Second, defining deductive reasoning as reasoning from the general to the specific does not accurately describe the nature of all deductive conclusions. While it is true that all deductive reasoning moves from the more general to the less general, deductive conclusions are not necessarily specific. For example, if we begin with the general statement that all medical doctors have college degrees and then identify Mr. Smith as a medical doctor, we would arrive at the specific conclusion that Mr. Smith has a college degree. On the other hand, if we begin with the general statement that all buildings should be built on solid foundations and then place houses in the category of buildings, we arrive at the less general—but not specific—conclusion that all houses should be built on solid foundations. Thus, deductive reasoning proceeds from general statements and arrives at specific applications or less general class conclusions.

Properly conceived, deductive reasoning may be thought of as the analytic process used in moving from generalities to structurally certain conclusions.

Analytic process. The process of deduction is analytical in nature because it is concerned with the breaking down of a whole into its parts. The synthesis of induction seeks to arrive at new insights by bringing concepts together through an inferential leap, whereas the analysis of deduction attempts to apply established insights to new or different situations by including or excluding the parts of a whole. In the medical doctor illustration, the assertion that all medical doctors have college degrees was the established insight. By including Mr. Smith in the category of medical doctors we were able to apply our established insight to a part (Mr. Smith) of the whole class (all medical doctors). In the other illustration, the need of all buildings for solid foundations was the established insight. By including houses in the category of buildings we were able to apply our established insight to a part (houses) of the whole class (buildings). Deductive reasoning, then, is analytical in that it relates parts to the whole through inclusion in or exclusion from a class.

Begins with generalities. Deductive reasoning begins with general statements which may be descriptive or evaluative in nature. But whether descriptive or evaluative, these initial generalizations must be universal—they must apply to all members of a class. A statement which is less than universal does not provide any clear guidelines for inclusion or exclusion of the parts of the whole. If the initial generalization in the medical doctors illustration declared that some medical doctors have college degrees, we would not know whether Mr. Smith fell within the category of those medical doctors who possess college degrees or not. Thus, in order to provide for definite categories, the beginning generalization must indicate a universal inclusion or exclusion.

Structurally certain conclusions. The form of deductive reasoning provides for a conclusion which is *structurally* certain. The conclusion of a deductive argument does not extend beyond the original data but rather is contained within the initial generalization. So long as none of the rules of deduction are violated, the *form* of inclusion in, or exclusion from, the terms of the original statement provides for a conclusion which follows certainly. In our examples, once we included Mr. Smith in the category of medical doctors and once we included houses in the category of buildings, the conclusions followed inevitably. In deductive reasoning, then, it is possible to be as certain of the truth of our conclusions as we are of the truth of the first statements. If the content of the initial generalization is incorrect, the content of the conclusion will probably be incorrect, but the *structure* of the deductive process assures that conclusions will follow consistently.

A COMPARISON

In studying the basic processes of reasoning there is a temptation to compare the two approaches in order to try to decide which method is better. The answer is that neither one is any better than the other. The determination of which process to use is not based upon any qualitative measure but rather upon the kind of data with which one has to work. Inductive reasoning is sometimes referred to as the scientific method and deductive reasoning as the philosophical method, not because scientists and philosophers have any special preference for those methods, but because the kinds of data with which they work lend themselves to the one more than the other. However, since most of us—scientists and philosophers included—will on some occasions be called upon to reason from both particulars and generalities, it is important that we understand and are able to apply both the inductive and the deductive processes.

A second comparison of the two processes is often made in terms of which process is the more basic. In an ultimate sense, it may be true that the initial generalizations of deductive reasoning are derived from the inductive synthesis of raw data. However, as individuals, we frequently acquire generalizations about phenomena before we have had any extensive first-hand experience with them. Most of us, for example, have not had any extensive first-hand acquaintance with the Communist Chinese people or with millionaires, yet we have certain preconceptions regarding these groups. Moreover, in many situations, the processes of induction and deduction so interact that it is difficult to call one more basic than the other. In investigating problems, conclusions are drawn from the examination of raw data; these conclusions are used to deduce other conclusions, which in turn are tested by returning to more raw data.

SUMMARY

An argument is a complete unit of logical proof. It consists of three elements: data, reasoning process, and conclusion. The conclusions of all arguments are ultimately intended to answer one of three questions: Is it? (question of existence), What is it? (question of essence), and Why is it? (question of explanation).

The reasoning process is based upon the assumption of uniformity. This assumption describes the alleged order and regularity of the universe. Without such an assumption it would not be possible to relate data to arrive at conclusions.

There are two basic processes of reasoning by which data may be related. Inductive reasoning is a synthetic process which begins with particulars and arrives at probable conclusions. Deductive reasoning is an analytic process which begins with generalities and arrives at structurally certain conclusions. The nature of the data will determine which of these two processes is used in a particular situation.

STUDY QUESTIONS

1. What is the difference between the term "argument," as defined in this chapter, and the term "issue," as defined in Chapter 2?
2. Why is inductive reasoning commonly linked to "scientific method" and deductive reasoning linked to "philosophical" method?
3. What is the difference between a "structurally valid" conclusion and a "materially valid" conclusion?

1. Select ten sample arguments from speeches, editorials, or articles:
    a. In each sample try to identify the three elements of the argument (data, reasoning process, and conclusion). Where an element is missing, try to supply it.
    b. Do the conclusions in the sample arguments assert existence, essence, or explanation?

2. Examine textbooks in mathematics and science, and see what evidence you can discover to support the assumption of uniformity. To what extent do the principles of these fields describe uniform conditions?

3. Prepare a brief report in which you explain the differences between the processes of synthesis and analysis. Examine unabridged dictionaries, encyclopedias, and science textbooks in preparing your report.

7 The Forms of Argument

The explanation of the nature of argument presented in the preceding chapter was intended to provide a basic understanding of the process of argumentation. Before the validity of individual arguments can be examined, however, it is necessary to know how these processes are used to create different classes or forms of argument since the tests of validity differ according to which form is used. Five basic forms of argument may be identified. Three of the forms are based upon the inductive process and two upon the deductive process.

INDUCTIVE FORMS

The three forms of argument which rely upon inductive reasoning are the argument by example, the argument by analogy, and the argument by causal correlation. Because they are inductive, each of these three utilizes the process of synthesis to move from particulars to arrive at probable conclusions. The three forms of inductive argument differ from each other in terms of the *kind of uniformity* (regularity, similarity, or functional correlation) assumed in the inferential leap and in terms of the *basic question* (existence, essence, or explanation) which is answered by the conclusion.

ARGUMENT BY EXAMPLE

Regularity of a characteristic within a class. The first inductive form of argument is the argument by example—or the argument by generalization, as it is sometimes called. *This form of argument examines several specific cases in a given class and assumes that if the known cases are alike with regard to a specific characteristic then other unknown cases in the same class will exhibit the same characteristic.* The conclusion of an argument by example rests upon the assumption of the *regularity* of the specific characteristic within the class.

When an automobile manufacturer discovers a defect in the brake mechanism of twenty cars of the same year and model and decides to recall the entire run of that model to inspect and repair the brake mechanism, he is reasoning by example. He has examined only a limited sample from a given class (twenty cars of the same year and model) and has discovered that a specific characteristic (brake defect) exists in this sample. His decision to recall all of the cars of that year and model for brake inspection and repair was based on the assumption of the regularity of the characteristic of a brake defect in the unknown cases of cars in this class.

The use of an argument by example in an actual communication is provided by a student speaker from the University of Minnesota:

> Meet Sam Running. Sam is one of a large family which was unable to meet the financial strain brought about by the depression. As a result, his education was interrupted and he was forced to seek employment. Resentment and loneliness started him drinking. He worked in garages and became an accomplished body and fender man. Any employer would be glad to hire Sam—but Sam is a "deehorn." That is, he drinks anything with alcohol in it—anything from vanilla extract to bay rum. . . .
>
> Next, shake the hand of William Nelson. I met Bill when he washed dishes for me. Bill is a man who has had three years of college. . . . It seems that Bill had been a successful merchant in a small Minnesota town. However, because of general economic conditions his business failed. Shortly thereafter his wife became ill and required expensive medical treatment which Bill couldn't provide. Possibly because of the lack of medical treatment—she died. This dual misfortune caused Bill to withdraw to the irresponsible life of the bowery. . . .
>
> Now I would like you to meet Alfred "Buck" Jones. Buck is forty-three years old, married, has two children, and ran away from his faithless wife. I've known Buck, who is a machinist, for several years, and Buck is a person who attempts to give the impression he's enjoying the life of a derelict on Washington Avenue. But he's not. . . .
>
> Yes—I could go on giving you many more examples of men like Sam, Bill, and Buck. I merely wanted to suggest that many men on skid row have the ability and capacity to become productive human beings.[1]

In this speech the speaker offers a limited number of instances from a given class (three men from the class of skid row residents) and identifies a specific characteristic (ability to be productive) which exists in each of the instances. The conclusion that many men on skid row have the ability to be productive rests on the assumption of the regularity of the characteristic in unknown cases of the class.

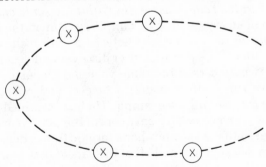

[1]Peter A Karos, "The Haven of the Defeated," *Winning Orations of the Northern Oratorical League,* 1945–1950 (Minneapolis: The Northwestern Press, 1951).

The argument by example can be further illustrated in diagram form. In the diagram on page 96 the small circles represent individual cases or examples, and the X's represent the specific characteristic under examination. The dotted line represents the conclusion which includes, and generalizes beyond, the individual cases.

Generalized conclusion of essence or existence. The conclusion of an argument by example extends beyond the cases considered to include yet unexamined cases. It is in this sense that the conclusion is a generalization. That generalization, however, does not necessarily have to be a universal statement. The generalization of the conclusion may be limited by any one of a number of qualifiers—many, most, some, and so on. When the generalization is universal, it answers the question, What is it? (question of essence). The conclusion that all cows give milk, drawn from an examination of fifty cows, is a universal conclusion concerning the essence of cows. When the generalization is qualified, it answers the question, Is it? (question of existence). The conclusion that many men on skid row have the ability to be productive, drawn from an examination of three skid row residents, is a qualified conclusion which established the existence of a characteristic.

ARGUMENT BY ANALOGY

Similarity of characteristics between cases. The second form of argument which is purely inductive in nature is the argument by analogy. *This form of argument examines a limited number of specific cases, usually only two, and compares their essential characteristics. If the cases are alike in all known essential characteristics, it is assumed that they will be alike with regard to a characteristic known in the one case but not known in the other.* The conclusion of an argument by analogy rests upon the assumption of the essential *sameness* of characteristics within the compared cases.

The student who reasons that he will receive an "A" in a course because his test scores, term-paper grade, and class participation are the same as the test scores, term-paper grade, and class participation of a student in the previous semester who had received an "A," is reasoning by analogy. The two cases are alike in all known essential characteristics (test scores, term-paper grade, and class participation), and it is assumed that they will be alike with regard to a characteristic (final grade of "A") known in one case but not known in the other.

Senator Edward Kennedy used an analogy to argue that people will not find the licensing of guns a burdensome requirement:

Opponents of firearms laws insist that gun licenses and record-keeping requirements are burdensome and inconvenient. Yet they don't object to licensing automobile drivers, hunters, or those who enjoy fishing. If the only price of gun licensing or record-keeping requirements is the inconvenience to gun users, then the public will have received a special bargain. Certainly sportsmen will gladly tolerate minor inconvenience in order to protect the lives of their families, friends, and neighbors.[2]

In his argument, Senator Kennedy asserts that gun licensing is like automobile, hunting, and fishing licensing in an essential characteristic (inconvenience), and he suggests that it will be like the other forms of licensing with regard to the characteristic (tolerance) known in the other forms but not known in the instance of guns.

In the diagram below, the large circles represent the two cases being compared, and the letters indicate similar characteristics. The X indicates the characteristic known in the one case but not in the other. The dotted line suggests the inferential leap to the conclusion of similarity in regard to characteristic X.

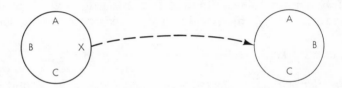

Specific conclusion of existence or of essence. The form of the argument by analogy calls for specific conclusions. These conclusions do not extend to new cases or classes but, rather, are limited to one of the compared instances. The analogy may be used either to establish existence (Is it?) or essence (What is it?). In the first example above, the conclusion, "I will receive an 'A' in this course," was limited to one of the compared instances and did not extend to include new cases. This conclusion was used to establish existence, answering the question, "Is it or is it not going to be an 'A'?"

Sometimes analogies are drawn between *related classes* rather than between *specific cases within a class.* In an analogy between classes, each characteristic of the classes is, itself, a generalization derived from an argument by example. If the class characteristics are

[2]Edward Kennedy, quoted in "Tighter Gun Controls—Both Sides of the Dispute," *U.S. News and World Report,* July 10, 1972, p. 69.

all in the form of universally true generalizations, the conclusion will be one of essence. If the class characteristics are in the form of qualified generalizations, the conclusion will establish existence.

In the analogy used by Senator Kennedy the comparison is between different classes (gun users compared to automobile drivers, hunters, and fishermen). The class characteristic (inconvenience) is presented as a universally true generalization so that the conclusion is an unqualified one of essence (hunters will tolerate). The conclusion is specific to one of the compared classes but applies universally within the class.

Literal and figurative analogies. Two kinds of analogies are often presented. The *literal analogy* is the type which we have been describing and the only one which has the force of logical support. The literal analogy involves a comparison between cases, classes, or objects of the same kind. The *figurative analogy,* on the other hand, is concerned with comparisons between unlike categories. Although the figurative analogy is often useful in illustrating an idea, it is generally not considered to constitute logical proof. The fact that the comparison of the figurative analogy is between unlike categories suggests initially that the objects or cases being compared are fundamentally dissimilar, and this therefore undermines the logical assumption of uniformity.

The analogy below is a figurative analogy because the comparison is between a physical characteristic of a mythical character and an intellectual characteristic of modern man. In this example, as in most figurative analogies, the comparison rests more on imaginative and literary similarities than upon fundamental likenesses.

> The Cyclops was a being of gigantic size and immeasurable strength. He was gifted with acute senses. And his only defect was that he had but one eye placed squarely in the midst of his forehead. This weakness was fatal. For he was brought to his knees by one far smaller in stature than he who was clever enough to deprive him of his eyesight. Thus being blinded, his great strength was useless.
>
> In a way, modern man is an image of Cyclops. For though he possesses two eyes and two ears, he has only one intellect. It is this mind of his that gives man the power to look deep into things and understand them. And yet today millions of men have suffered a cyclopean wound. Their mind's eye is blinded. They are deprived of the vision that their intellect should give them.[3]

[3]Daniel McDonald, *The Language of Argument* (Scranton: Chandler Publishing Company, 1971), p. 154.

While the figurative analogy is not exact enough to serve as *proof* of a conclusion, it may, of course, be helpful in *clarifying* an idea.

ARGUMENT BY CAUSAL CORRELATION

Functional correlation between elements of cases. The third form of argument which is inductive in nature is the argument by causal correlation. *This form of argument examines particular cases and attempts to discover a functional correlation between certain elements of the cases.* Since a correlation is involved, the patterned appearance of at least *two* elements within the cases must be identified. To say that the correlation should be functional means only that the *elements should act upon one another.* It is not necessary to establish that a single element is solely responsible for the other. If it can be shown that, under a given set of circumstances, a particular element is either necessary or sufficient to bring forth the other element, a causal correlation has been established. Usually the correlated elements appear in a regular time sequence. When this occurs, the element which appears first is referred to as a cause, and the one which follows is called an effect.

Mill's canons. The English philosopher John Stuart Mill identified certain procedures which can be used to discover causal relationships. These procedures are often referred to as Mill's Experimental Method.[4]

The first of Mill's procedures is the *method of concomitant variation.*

> Whatever phenomenon varies in any manner whenever another phenomenon varies in some particular manner, is either a cause or an effect of that phenomenon, or is connected with it through some fact of causation.

This method rests not simply upon the establishment of the coexistence of two elements, but also requires some patterned behavior of the elements. Thus, if the cause varies from time to time by a large amount, the effect might be expected to vary significantly from time to time. This type of relationship is illustrated at the top of page 101. In this diagram *C* stands for varying quantities of the alleged cause and *E* stands for the equally varying quantities of the alleged effect.

[4]John Stuart Mill, *System of Logic* (London: Longmans, Green and Company, 1900), pp. 255–66.

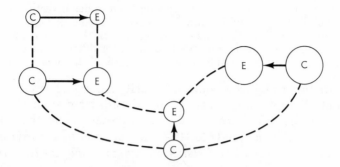

The method of concomitant variation could be used, for instance, to show the effect of a police force on the crime rate. If it could be shown that as the size of the police force was increased or decreased by a certain percentage, the crime rate increased or decreased by a similar percentage, a cause and effect relationship would be suggested.

The second of Mill's procedures is the *method of agreement:*

> If two or more instances of the phenomenon under investigation have only one circumstance in common, the circumstance in which alone all the instances agree is the cause (or effect) of the given phenomenon.

This procedure attempts to find something in common among essentially dissimilar cases. It may be represented by the diagram below in which *E* stands for *the phenomenon under investigation* and *C* stands for the *one circumstance in common.*

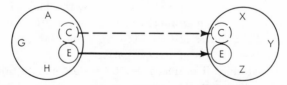

The method of agreement could be used, for instance, by a group of people attempting to discover the cause of their shared food poisoning. By the process of elimination, it could be determined that the group had shared only one meal together, and by comparing what they had eaten at this meal, a single common food might be identified as the cause of their poisoning. In this example the shared food poisoning is the *phenomenon under investigation* and the single common food is the *one circumstance in common.*

The third of Mill's procedures is the *method of differences:*

>   If an instance in which the phenomenon under investigation occurs,
> and an instance in which it does not occur, have every circumstance in
> common save one, that one occurring only in the former, then the cir-
> cumstance in which alone the two instances differ, is the effect, or the
> cause, or an indispensable part of the cause, of the phenomenon.

This procedure recognizes one dissimilarity among otherwise identical
cases and attempts to discover in the dissimilar case an element to
account for the difference. It may be represented by the following
diagram in which *E* stands for the *phenomenon under investigation*
and *C* stands for *the circumstance in which alone the two instances
differ.*

The method of disagreement was used, for instance, by a town
attempting to discover why a new downtown shopping mall had failed
to bring the marked increase in retail sales which similar malls had
brought elsewhere. Comparisons with other towns with successful
malls revealed similar populations, comparable variety and quality of
stores, and equal access to parking. The one difference was that all of
the other malls had direct bus service from all parts of town while the
unsuccessful mall had no such service. Thus, the lack of bus service
(the circumstance in which alone the two instances differ) was assumed
to be the cause of the mall's failure to bring a marked increase in retail
sales (the phenomenon under investigation).

In many instances it is necessary to use a combination of procedures in order to demonstrate a credible cause and effect relationship.
The United States Surgeon General's Advisory Committee on Smoking
and Health used all three of Mill's methods at various stages of its
report on smoking and lung cancer. The report identified the presence
of a *concomitant variation* when it reported:

>   The systematic evidence for the association between smoking and lung
> cancer comes primarily from 29 retrospective studies of groups of persons
> with lung cancer and appropriate "controls" without lung cancer. . . . The
> 29 retrospective studies . . . varied considerably in design and method.
> Despite these variations, every one of the retrospective studies showed
> an association between smoking and lung cancer. . . .

The differences are statistically significant in all the studies. Thirteen of the studies, combining all forms of tobacco consumption, found a significant association between smoking of any type and lung cancer; 16 studies yielded an even stronger association with cigarettes alone. The degree of association between smoking and lung cancer increased as the amounts of smoking increased.[5]

The Surgeon General's committee used the *method of agreement* to isolate smoking as a sufficient causative factor.

In lung cancer, we are dealing with relative risk ratios averaging 9.0 to 10.0 for cigarette smokers compared to non-smokers. This is an excess of 900 to 1,000 percent among smokers of cigarettes. Similarly, this means that of the total load of lung cancer in males about 90 percent is associated with cigarette smoking. In order to account for risk ratios of this magnitude as due to an association of smoking history with still another causative factor X (hormonal, constitutional, or other), a necessary condition would be that factor X be present at least nine times more frequently among smokers than non-smokers. No such factors with such high relative prevalence among smokers have yet been demonstrated.[6]

A number of specific research studies cited in the report attempted to factor out, and thereby control, certain specific variables. To the extent that such controls created more homogeneous groups, they allowed for the application of the *method of difference.*

In a well-conceived analytic study, Sadowsky *et al.,* recognizing that duration of smoking is a function of age, controlled the age variable, and found an increasing prevalence rate of lung cancer with an increase in duration of smoking among all age groups.[7]

General or specific conclusions of explanation. The conclusion of an argument by causal correlation will be general or specific depending upon which of Mill's three methods is utilized. The method of concomitant variation will provide a class conclusion if a series of instances is observed, or it can render a specific conclusion if a single situation is observed over a period of time. The method of agreement and the method of difference lead to conclusions which are specific to the compared instances. Repeated comparisons of agreement or of difference can, of course, result in generalized conclusions. The food poisoning and shopping mall illustrations provide examples of specific conclu-

[5]Report of the Advisory Committee to the Surgeon General, "Smoking and Health" (Washington, D.C.: U.S. Department of Health, Education and Welfare, 1964), p. 230.
[6]Advisory Committee on Smoking and Health, p. 184.
[7]Advisory Committee on Smoking and Health, p. 158.

sions. The report "Smoking and Health" offers examples of generalized causal conclusions.

Causal correlations render conclusions which answer the question, Why is it? They attempt to explain the existence of one element of a situation in terms of its relationship to another element of the situation. While the conclusion of an argument by analogy identifies the existence of a single element and the conclusion of an argument by example either describes an essential characteristic of an entire class or indicates the existence of a specific element among many members of a class, the conclusion of an argument by causal correlation establishes an interdependent relationship between two or more elements.

DEDUCTIVE FORMS

The two forms of argument which rely upon deductive reasoning are the argument from sign and the argument from causal generalization. Because they are deductive, each of these forms utilizes the process of analysis to move from generalities to arrive at structurally certain conclusions. The two forms of deductive argument differ from each other in terms of the kinds of relationship (substance-attribute or explanation) asserted by the initial generalization and in terms of the basic question (existence, essence, or explanation) which is answered by the conclusion.

ARGUMENT FROM SIGN

Substance-attribute relationship.   The first deductive form of argument is the argument from sign (or argument from circumstantial evidence, as it is sometimes known). *This form of argument is based upon the assumption of a substance-attribute relationship.* This assumption suggests that every substance (object, event, person, etc.) has certain distinguishing characteristics or attributes (size, shape, sound, color, etc.) and that the presence or absence of either the substance or the attribute may be taken as a sign of the presence or absence of the other.

The individual who experiences periodic attacks characterized by wheezing respiration, shortness of breath, and an annoying cough and reasons that he should have his doctor check him for bronchial asthma is reasoning from sign. He assumes the existence of a substance (bronchial asthma) because of the existence of certain attributes (wheezing, shortness of breath, and coughing) which his medical guide describes as symptoms of this disease.

In the following diagram, the attributes are indicated by small circles (*A, B,* and *C*). The substance is represented by the large circle. Since the attributes are parts of the substance, the existence of either the large circle or the small circles may be assumed to indicate the existence of the other.

In most sign arguments, the relationship between the substance and the attribute is never explicitly stated. Typically, the presence of the attribute (or substance) is noted and the existence of the substance (or attribute) is stated as a conclusion. In the example below, taken from a newspaper account, the underlying substance-attribute relationship is assumed, but not expressed.

> Until this [anticrime] campaign begins to make headway, life in the District of Columbia will reflect fear, especially after dark.
>
> Cruise through downtown Washington in a police car on a Saturday night and the mood can be felt. On F Street, the main downtown shopping street, merchants lock their doors at 6 p.m. Many put up iron grillwork nightly to protect their windows. Shoppers and employees hurry to the bus stops. Many employees who fear the lonely walk at the end of the bus ride, wait in the stores until their spouses drive by to take them home. . . .
>
> "Watch the people," advises a seasoned policeman. "See how they walk quickly and with a purpose. There's no casual strolling. People don't come into this town at night unless they have a specific destination in mind. They go straight to it and then go home as fast as possible."[8]

The unstated initial generalization of this argument is that doors locked early, grill-work, and hurrying people are attributes of the substance, fear. Since these attributes or characteristics are shown to exist, it is concluded that the substance (fear) also exists.

The assumed substance-attribute relationship of a sign argument may have either a natural or a conceptual basis. Natural signs are correlations which may be observed in nature and which exist as an inherent part of one of nature's processes. The farmer who observes hard crusted soil and concludes that there will be a poor potato crop is

[8]Karmin W. Monroe, *Wall Street Journal,* February 11, 1970, p. 16.

reasoning from natural sign. The relationship between the symptoms and the existence of bronchial asthma is also one of natural sign.[9]

Conceptual signs are correlations which exist as a result of custom or of definition. The substance of conceptual signs may or may not have a real physical basis. When one refers to a Cadillac as an indication of wealth, he is reasoning from a conceptual sign based upon custom. When one reasons that a whale is a mammal because it nourishes its young with milk, he is reasoning from a conceptual sign based upon a definition. The conclusion that life in the District of Columbia reflects fear also illustrates the use of conceptual signs based upon definition (fear is defined in terms of locking doors early, putting up grill-work, hurrying, etc.). Signs based upon definition are particularly important since all moral and legal questions are ultimately dependent upon them.

Conclusion of existence or essence. The conclusions of sign arguments establish either existence or essence. When the substance-attribute relationship is applied to a specific member or to a specific part of a class, the conclusion demonstrates existence. In the case of the individual concerned with the symptoms of wheezing, shortness of breath, and coughing, the conclusion was applied to a specific member of a class and, therefore, demonstrated the possible existence of bronchial asthma. When the substance-attribute relationship is applied to an entire subgroup within a class, the conclusion asserts essence. If we reason that all whales are mammals because all whales nourish their young with milk, the conclusion is applied to an entire subgroup and, therefore, asserts essence.

ARGUMENT FROM CAUSAL GENERALIZATION

Inclusion in or exclusion from functional correlation. The second deductive form of argument is the argument from causal generalization. *This form of argument applies an assumed or inductively established causal correlation to specific cases or classes.* By including (or excluding) a specific instance in the category of the general cause (or the general effect), the functioning of the effect (or the cause) can be established in that instance. If we start with the causal correlation that

[9]Arguments from natural signs may ultimately involve unidentified causal relationships. However, the possible existence of a cause and effect relationship is really irrelevant to natural signs since sign arguments begin with generalizations which assert coexistence rather than functional correlations and end with conclusions of existence (or essence) rather than conclusions of explanation.

heavy smokers are more likely than nonsmokers to develop lung cancer, observe that John is a heavy smoker, and conclude that John is more likely than nonsmokers to develop lung cancer, we have reasoned from causal generalization.

An argument from causal generalization was used in a final round of the National Debate Tournament to establish that the affirmative proposal would achieve its goal.

> Reduction of our commitments in Northeast Asia will encourage improved U.S.-Chinese relations. It will encourage improved U.S.-Chinese relations, first, because the affirmative proposal will remove major barriers to improved U.S.-Chinese relations. What are those barriers? We turn to *Current History* of September 1966. They tell us that "China's Vice Premier Chen Yi reiterated the primary importance of the Taiwan issue as a key to improving relations between China and the United States . . . violation of China's air space and territorial waters and the establishment of a chain of military bases surrounding China took second and third place. . . ."
>
> Now how does this affirmative proposal affect those barriers? Number one, by ceasing to recognize Taiwan's claim to all of China, and by removing all of our troops from Taiwan, we remove Taiwan as the major source of controversy between China and the United States. Second, by removing the Seventh Fleet from the Straits of Taiwan, we stop the violation of territorial waters. Third, by removing our troops from Korea, Japan, and Taiwan, we break the chain of American military bases surrounding China. That is why we conclude that the affirmative proposal does remove major barriers to improved U.S.-Chinese relations.[10]

In this example, the initial causal generalization was that the removal of major barriers will improve relations with Communist China. By including specific examples (Taiwan's claim to all of China, U.S. troops in Taiwan, Korea, and Japan, and the presence of the Seventh Fleet in the Straits of Taiwan) in the general category of causes (major barriers), it was possible to forecast the functioning of the effect (improved relations).

In the diagram at the top of page 108, the two large circles represent the categories of cause and effect and the arrows represent the functional relationship between the cause and the effect. If P is included within the cause and the cause is functionally related to the effect, then P must have a functional counterpart within the effect category. In our smoking example, the cause is smoking and the effect is likelihood of lung cancer. Our P (John) is placed within the cause circle and is assumed also to exist within the effect circle.

---

[10]"1967 National Debate Tournament Final Debate," *Journal of the American Forensic Association* 4, no. 3 (Fall 1967): 120–21.

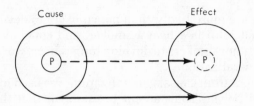

The relationship of exclusion is indicated by the diagram below. The two large circles represent the categories of alleged causes and alleged effects. Since, in this situation, it is known that there is no functional relationship between the alleged causes and the alleged effects, the arrows connecting the two circles are broken. If P is included within the alleged causes, but the alleged causes are not related to the alleged effects, then P is excluded from causing any part of the alleged effects.

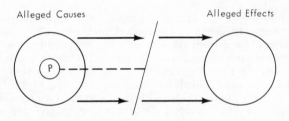

If, for instance, we begin with the generalization that there is no significant correlation between low high-school grades and failure in college and observe that Mary has low high-school grades, we have no basis for predicting college failure for Mary.

General or specific conclusion of explanation. The conclusions of arguments from causal generalization may be either specific to an individual case or general for an entire class. When a general conclusion results, the class identified within the conclusion will always be a more specific subgroup of the initial generalization.

Arguments from causal generalization provide conclusions of explanation. While sign arguments show existence or identify essence, they do not *account for* the existence or the essence. The conclusions of arguments from causal generalizations provide explanations by asserting functional relationships between phenomena.

SUMMARY

There are five basic forms of argument. Three of them utilize the inductive process and two use the deductive process. Within each of these two general categories of reasoning the forms differ from one another in terms of the ways in which they relate data and in terms of the kinds of questions answered by the conclusions.

The three forms of inductive argument are argument by example, argument by analogy, and argument by causal correlation. The argument by example seeks to identify a regular characteristic within a given class in order to arrive at a generalized conclusion of essence or existence. The argument by analogy attempts to discover similarities of characteristics between cases to establish a specific conclusion of existence. The argument by causal correlation tries to establish a functional relationship between certain elements of the cases in order to achieve a general or specific conclusion of explanation.

The two forms of deductive argument are argument from sign and argument from causal generalization. The argument from sign utilizes a substance-attribute relationship to show existence or essence. The argument from causal generalization includes or excludes specific cases or classes from the initial generalization to arrive at a less general conclusion of explanation.

STUDY QUESTIONS

1. After reviewing the three types of conclusions outlined in Chapter 6 (existence, essence, and explanation), discuss the following:
   a. Why does an argument by example not reach conclusions of explanation?
   b. Why does an argument by analogy not reach conclusions of explanation?
   c. Why does an argument by causal correlation not reach conclusions of essence or existence?
   d. Why does an argument from sign not reach conclusions of explanation?
   e. Why does an argument from causal generalization not reach conclusions of existence?
2. Arguments by example and arguments from sign are frequently confused with each other. Why does this confusion occur? Differentiate between these two forms of argument.
3. This chapter outlines two forms of causal argument: an inductive form (argument by causal correlation) and a deductive form (argument from causal generalization). In what ways are these two forms of causal argument similar and different?

EXERCISES

1. Prepare a notebook in which you collect examples of each of the forms of argument.
   a. Label each argument.
   b. Indicate whether it utilizes the inductive or deductive process.

  c. Is the conclusion of the argument one of essence, existence, or explanation?

  d. Are all three elements of a complete argument (data, reasoning process, and conclusion) presented? If not, try to supply the missing element.

2. Examine government reports such as those on marijuana, crime and violence, birth control pills, etc. Try to determine how each of these reports approached the problem of establishing causation. Note especially any attempt to use the method of concomitant variation, the method of agreement, or the method of difference to demonstrate a cause and effect relationship.

3. Bring several examples of figurative analogies to class, and be prepared to explain why they lack the force of logical proof.

8 The Testing of Argument

I. Tests Specific to the Forms of Argument
  A. Argument by Example
    1. Are the examples typical?
    2. Have a sufficient number of examples been examined?
    3. Are negative instances adequately accounted for?
  B. Argument by Analogy
    1. Are the compared cases alike in all essential regards?
    2. Are the compared characteristics accurately described?
  C. Argument by Causal Correlation
    1. Is the association between the alleged cause and the alleged effect a consistent one?
    2. Is the association between the alleged cause and the alleged effect a strong one?
    3. Do the alleged cause and the alleged effect appear in a regular time sequence?
    4. Is the association between the alleged cause and the alleged effect coherent?
  D. Argument from Sign
    1. Are the substance and the attribute invariable indicators of the presence of each other?

      2. Are sufficient signs presented?

      3. Are contradictory signs adequately considered?

   E. Argument from Causal Generalization

      1. Will intervening factors preclude an expected cause and effect relationship?

      2. Is the cause sufficient to bring about the effect?

      3. Will the cause result in other unspecified effects?

II. Tests Specific to the Structure of Deduction

   A. Tests of Categorical Syllogisms

      1. Is the middle term used in a universal or unqualified sense in at least one of the premises?

      2. If a term is universal in the conclusion, was it universal in the premises?

      3. Is at least one of the premises an affirmative statement?

      4. If one premise is negative, is the conclusion negative?

      5. Are the terms of the syllogism used in the same sense throughout?

   B. Tests of Hypothetical Syllogisms

      1. If the minor premise affirms the antecedent, does the conclusion affirm the consequent?

      2. If the minor premise denies the consequent, does the conclusion deny the antecedent?

   C. Tests of Disjunctive Syllogisms

      1. If the minor premise affirms (or denies) one of the alternatives, does the conclusion deny (or affirm) the other alternative?

      2. Are the alternatives presented in the first premise mutually exclusive?

      3. Does the major premise include all of the possible alternatives?

III. Summary

We live in a verbal society. Through radio, television, newspapers, magazines, books, direct conversations, public speeches, and a variety of forms of mass advertising we are constantly subjected to the ideas and claims of thousands of different individuals and groups. Most of these ideas will not be of great importance to us and will be largely ignored. Other ideas, however, will demand our immediate attention and will require thoughtful consideration. If we are to evaluate the claims of others and to determine what is the probable truth of a situation, we must have some criteria for measuring the validity of arguments. Chapter 5 presented tests to aid in determining the substantive accuracy and source credibility of data. This chapter will provide criteria for evaluating how the data is used by the reasoning process in arriving at conclusions.

The ability to evaluate arguments is important in both the inquiry and advocacy phases of argumentation. In the inquiry phase, the testing of arguments helps us to judge the validity of the claims of others and to evaluate our own conclusions. In the advocacy phase, the testing of arguments is essential to the refutation of opposing ideas.

In this chapter, the testing of arguments will be discussed from two perspectives. First, tests specific to the five forms of argument will be presented, and second, tests specific to the structure of the deductive process will be described. The tests of the three inductive forms of argument—example, analogy, and causal correlation—are intended to help assure that the conclusions of these arguments are consistent with known data. The tests of the two deductive forms—sign and causal generalization—are concerned with the examination of reservations to or qualifications of the initial generalization. The tests of the deductive process, presented in the second half of this chapter, may be used to examine the structural consistency of arguments from sign and causal generalization.

TESTS SPECIFIC TO THE FORMS OF ARGUMENT

The previous chapter described five forms of argument: example, analogy, causal correlation, sign, and causal generalization. Once one of these specific forms of argument is identified in a particular situation, the appropriate tests for that form may be applied.

ARGUMENT BY EXAMPLE

The argument by example utilizes the inductive process to identify a regular characteristic within a class. The conclusions of arguments by example may be either universal generalizations of essence or qualified generalizations of existence. Three tests may be applied in evaluating this type of argument.

Are the examples typical? For a generalization to be true it must be based upon an examination of representative instances. If the instances are not typical of the entire class of things, then any conclusion based upon them will be invalid when extended to include all cases within the class. For instance, a survey of the housing needs of the nation based upon examples drawn just from the upper economic classes of our society would not provide a fair indication of the housing needs of the total population.

Most of us are inclined to accept our own personal experiences as the ultimate test of what is true. One of the dangers of excessive reliance upon personal experience, however, is that our experiences may not be typical, and thus, generalizations based upon them may not be valid. Examples taken from a variety of situations, or over a period of time, or by a number of different people are more likely to be typical than examples drawn from one situation, at one time, by one person.

Have a sufficient number of examples been examined? A number of cases must be considered in order to establish the regularity of the characteristic. In presenting an argument, a single case may be sufficient to *illustrate* the generalization, but a single example cannot *support the claim of regularity.*

The question of how many examples are sufficient is one to which there is no absolute answer. In general, it may be said that the less homogeneous the class, the greater the number of examples that will be needed. If one wished, for example, to draw a reliable generalization about all smokers of tobacco, he would require more supporting cases than if he wished to generalize about all male pipe smokers. It may also be said that the more sweeping the conclusion, the greater the number of examples required. A generalization which asserts that *some* dogs are black would require fewer examples than one which claims that *most* dogs are black.

Are negative instances adequately accounted for? It is a common experience when studying a number of specific cases to discover one or more instances which do not seem to conform to the general pattern of the class. These atypical instances must not be ignored when drawing conclusions. Sometimes the negative instances will be taken into consideration through the use of appropriate qualifying phrases such as "many," "most," or "some." Notice that the use of such qualifiers precludes universal conclusions of essence while permitting qualified conclusions of existence.

When the negative instances can be explained away in terms of special circumstances, appropriately phrased conclusions of essence may still be warranted. For example, if we discovered that 93 percent of the elementary school teachers in a specific state had college degrees and that the 7 percent who did not have degrees were in nonpublic schools, we might legitimately conclude that all *public* school elementary teachers have college degrees. By limiting the conclusion to *public* school elementary teachers it was possible to arrive at a universal generalization of essence. The omission of the qualifying term *public* would have resulted in a conclusion which did not account for the negative instances.

ARGUMENT BY ANALOGY

The argument by analogy uses the inductive process to establish uniform characteristics among specific members of a class. The conclusions of arguments by analogy establish existence in specific instances. There are two essential tests of analogies.

Are the compared cases alike in all essential regards? The compared cases must be fundamentally alike in order to justify the assumption of the uniformity of the unknown characteristic. It is not necessary to demonstrate absolute similarity. Minor or noncritical dissimilarities may exist even among basically similar instances. If, for example, it could be demonstrated that the batting averages, pitching staffs, and fielding records of two baseball teams were similar, sufficient basis for an analogy would exist even though the specific personnel of the teams were different. The requirement, then, is for fundamental similarity, rather than for complete sameness.

The question of what constitutes a critical or essential characteristic requires judgment in the specific situation. If we were to compare two cities in an effort to predict the probable success or failure of a mass transit system, we would need to consider such factors as the size of the metropolitan populations, the degree of concentration of the populations, the extent of express highways, and the geographical location of the downtown area in relation to suburban areas. On the other hand, if we were to compare the same two cities in order to predict the success or failure of specific programs of job training, then different factors—the educational level of the unemployed and the nature of available jobs—would become more critical. In general, the determination of what is essential depends upon the nature of the things being compared and upon the substance of the conclusion being drawn.

Are the compared characteristics accurately described? It is particularly important that the data used as a basis for comparison be examined and its accuracy assured. This is true because the question of what constitutes sameness is as much a matter of judgment as is the question of what constitutes essentiality. To say that two cities have the same needs for public housing because 20 percent of the housing facilities in both cities are more than fifty years old may misrepresent the real situation. If in one of the cities the fifty-year-old housing units were cheaply constructed frame structures, while in the other city the older units were well-constructed brick and stone buildings, the comparison would be invalid.

Even where quantitative comparisons are used, as in the preceding example, questions may be raised regarding the comparability of the units measured or the point at which two measured quantities are similar. When qualitative, rather than quantitative, comparisons are made, the possibilities for misinterpretation of the data are even greater. Moreover, many analogies are developed at fairly abstract levels so that the sameness of the characteristics is only asserted and not demonstrated in detail. The accuracy of the initial comparison, then, should be carefully scrutinized.

ARGUMENT BY CAUSAL CORRELATION

The argument by causal correlation utilizes the inductive process to determine a functional correlation between elements of a case or cases. The conclusions of arguments by causal correlation provide explanations. There are four tests which should be applied to this form of argument.

Is the association between the alleged cause and the alleged effect a consistent one? This criterion suggests that repeated examinations of the association under a variety of circumstances should reveal similar relationships. This test does not demand that the cause and effect appear together in *every* instance. Rather, it requires that a significant and relatively predictable rate of association must be established. When studies made at different times or with different subjects or under different conditions fail to indicate similar correlations, the alleged cause and effect relationship is undermined. If a study of juvenile delinquency made in Atlanta during a recession period revealed a high correlation between poverty and juvenile delinquency but another study made in Chicago five years later during a period of prosperity indicated no such correlation, then the relationship between poverty and juvenile delinquency would not be a consistent one. Such inconsistency undermines the validity of the causal correlation. Only by accounting for the inconsistent study through claims of bias or poor design or other special conditioning factors could the association be resubstantiated.

Is the association between the alleged cause and the alleged effect a strong one? Because a number of causal factors may be operating within a situation, it is important to be able to indicate the relative strength of any specific cause. A measure of the strength of a specific causal correlation can be provided by comparing the extent of the effect in situations where a specific causal factor is not present with the extent of the effect in situations where that causal factor is present. To study the possible effectiveness of a new medicine, for example, we would need to compare the rate of recovery of patients who were given the new medicine with the recovery rate of those who had not been treated with it. The higher the incident of the effect (recovery) in those situations where the specific cause (new medicine) operated, as compared to those situations where it did not, the greater the strength of the association. If the incidence of the effect was not significantly higher in those situations in which the specific cause operated, then the causal link should be a relatively weak one.

Do the alleged cause and the alleged effect appear in a regular time sequence? The functional nature of a cause and effect relationship suggests that the two elements should appear in a regular time sequence. As a general rule, the cause occurs before the effect, although in nature the cause and effect sometimes appear to occur simultaneously. In no instance may an effect occur before the cause. A bullet could not be said to have caused a man's death if it could be established that the man had died before the bullet was fired. The period of time between the appearance of the cause and the appearance of the effect may vary from case to case, but the same order of appearance must remain.

If it can be shown that an alleged cause and effect relationship is based upon an irregular time sequence, the causal correlation is denied. It should be noted, however, that while the irregularity of a time sequence is sufficient to negate a causal association, the mere existence of a regular sequence of events is not sufficient *by itself* to establish causation. During the period of atmospheric atomic tests, many people attempted to attribute the peculiar weather patterns which followed certain tests to the atomic bombs. The attempt to assert a causal correlation based simply on a temporal relationship results in what is known as the *post hoc* fallacy (*post hoc ergo propter hoc*—after this therefore because of this).

Is the association between the alleged cause and the alleged effect coherent? This test suggests that any alleged cause and effect relationship should be consistent with other related data. In every causal situation there is likely to be a body of data which is not directly useful in establishing a causal correlation but which is indirectly related to the causal experience. Such data may be capable of explaining, or of being explained by, the causal correlation. The Surgeon General's report

"Smoking and Health" found indirect evidence which was consistent with a causal correlation and which illuminated a number of other facts. Data from a number of pathologic studies helped to explain the physiological basis of the correlation, and the correlation in turn helped to explain a number of other phenomena such as the disparities between male and female lung cancer rates. When such indirect evidence contradicts the causal correlation rather than adding to our understanding of it, the evidence undermines confidence in the causal relationship. The test of coherence simply asks, "Is the causal relationship reasonable in light of other known data?"

ARGUMENT FROM SIGN

The argument from sign uses the deductive process to apply a general substance-attribute relationship to a more specific situation. The conclusions of sign arguments establish existence when applied to a specific member or specific part of a class, and they demonstrate essence when applied to an entire subgroup. There are three tests of the argument from sign.

Are the substance and the attribute invariable indicators of the presence of each other? This test seeks to determine if the substance only appears when the attribute is present and if the attribute exists only when the substance is present. It is possible for the attribute to be an invariable indicator of the substance, and it is also possible for the substance to exist apart from the attribute. A bullet-ridden body may be an invariable indication of the existence of a spent firearm, but a spent firearm can exist without indicating the presence of a bullet-ridden body. Similarly, it is possible for the substance always to reveal the presence of the attribute while it is also possible for the attribute to exist without the substance. A traffic jam may always suggest the presence of cars, but a car can exist without a traffic jam occurring. It is not necessary that both the substance and the attribute be invariable indicators of the other. When an invariable relationship of any kind is assumed, however, the identification of one contrary instance is sufficient to undermine confidence in the conclusion.

Are sufficient signs presented? If the relationship between a single attribute is not an invariable one, then it is necessary to offer a number of supporting signs. A series of signs may be considered sufficient when it establishes either invariability or probability. While no one sign may be capable of providing an invariable indicator, a group of signs may often accomplish the same purpose. Most illnesses, for example, require the identification of several symptoms before an accurate diagnosis can be made. Although the presence of chest pains does not necessarily indicate heart disease, chest pains when combined with other symptoms can provide an invariable indication of heart trouble. In other situations, however, it is difficult to establish an invariable relationship between even a group of attributes and a substance or between a group of substances and an attribute. In such instances, the probability of the conclusion rests both upon the degree of reliability of the individual substance-attribute relationships and upon the number of such relationships presented. If we know that in most periods of history the buildup of weapons and the expression of hostility toward neighboring nations have preceded the outbreak of wars, then we may be willing to predict the future existence of a war based upon only these two signs. On the other hand, if only occasionally have the buildup of weapons and the expression of hostility preceded wars, then we would probably require several more supporting signs before accepting the conclusion that war is inevitable in this situation.

Are contradictory signs adequately considered? The existence of contradicting signs undermines confidence in the conclusion of a sign argument. An asserted sign relationship may be weakened by demonstrating the existence of even one contrary sign. A sign relationship may be completely denied by showing that the preponderance of signs are contrary ones or that the single contrary sign has an inevitable relationship to the substance.

If the existence of an elected government, competing political parties, and universal suffrage were offered as indications that a particular country has a democratic government, the claimed sign relationship could be undermined by pointing to the lack of a free press as a contrary sign. By demonstrating that the existence of a free press was an invariable indicator of democracy or that such other signs of democracy as freedom of speech, freedom of assembly, and fair election procedures were also lacking, the original claim of democracy could be not only weakened but denied.

ARGUMENT FROM CAUSAL GENERALIZATION

The argument from causal generalization utilizes the deductive process to include (or exclude) specific cases or classes within its initial generalization. The conclusions of arguments from causal generalization provide less general statements of explanation. There are three tests for arguments based on causal generalizations.

Will intervening factors preclude an expected cause and effect relationship? This test recognizes that cause and effect relationships do not normally function in environments free from other influences. Since other influences may be operating, there is the possibility that a normal cause and effect relationship may be blocked or at least altered. Placing a finger on a hot iron to see if it is ready for use would normally be expected to result in burnt flesh. If, however, a bit of saliva is placed on the finger and then the iron is touched, no burn will result.

In order to undermine the conclusion of a causal generalization, it is not enough simply to show the possibility of some intervening factor. Both the likelihood that intervening factors exist and that they will negate or significantly change the predicted cause and effect relationship must be demonstrated. It should be noted that this test does not wholly deny the original causal generalization; it only identifies a reservation to its application in a specific situation.

Is the cause sufficient to bring about the effect? This test accepts the idea that a specific cause and effect may be functionally related to each other, but it suggests that the specific cause, acting alone, will not be adequate to bring about the effect. According to this test, other causal forces must be present before the effect will occur. By demonstrating that the effect will not occur in the absence of the other factors, a one-to-one cause and effect relationship is denied, and the significance of the causal force is weakened. Money, for example, may be functionally related to the solution of such domestic problems as poverty and inadequate housing, but if it can be shown that money alone, without effective programs and wise administration, is not sufficient to solve these problems, the causal generalization is undermined. Causal generalizations which fail to meet this test are said to be guilty of the *fallacy of part cause* or *insufficient cause.*

Will the cause result in other unspecified effects? Not only may there be other causes than those suggested by the initial causal generalization, but there may also be other effects. Many causal forces set off a series of reactions rather than resulting in a single effect. The benefits of certain modern medicines, for example, are sometimes offset by their side effects. While the identification of such other effects does not directly negate the conclusion of an argument from causal generalization, it does allow for a fairer evaluation of the impact of the cause.

TESTS SPECIFIC TO THE STRUCTURE OF DEDUCTION

Two of the five forms of argument—argument from sign and argument from causal generalization—involve the deductive process. The deductive process relates parts to wholes or members of a class to the whole class. The mechanism through which this is accomplished is the syllogism. The initial generalizations upon which arguments from sign and arguments from causal generalization rest are often not expressed when these arguments are used in actual discourse. It is, nevertheless, important to be aware of these missing statements and to be able to cast these arguments in complete syllogistic form.

Only by casting deductive arguments in syllogistic form is it possible to examine their structural accuracy or formal validity. The tests specific to the argument from sign and the argument from causal generalization, given in the previous section, are tests of the substantive accuracy or material validity of their initial generalizations. However, since deductive arguments apply these initial statements to new situations, it is necessary to test not only the accuracy of the original statements but also the ways in which they are utilized. The syllogism, thus, tests the *form* of the argument or the validity of the *relationship* between the statements.

A syllogism consists of three statements and three terms (words, phrases, concepts). Each statement contains only two of the terms, and each of the statements relates a different set of the terms. The statements of a syllogism are known as the major premise, the minor premise, and the conclusion. The *major premise* states a generalization (All apples are fruit). The *minor premise* relates a specific case or class to the generalization (Jonathans are apples). The *conclusion* follows from the premises (Therefore, Jonathans are fruit).

The terms of a syllogism are known as the major term, the middle term, and the minor term. The *major term* (fruit) appears in the major premise and in the conclusion. It is the term which includes or excludes the middle term. The *middle term* (apples) appears in the major and the minor premises but not in the conclusion. It is included in or excluded from the major term, and it includes or excludes the minor term. The *minor term* (Jonathans) appears in the minor premise and in the conclusion. It is the term which is included in or excluded from the middle term.

The statements of a syllogism relate the terms to one another based upon three logical principles which are known as Aristotle's laws of thought. These laws are the *law of identity* ($A = A$), the *law of contradiction* (every A has its non-A), and the *law of the excluded middle* (B is either A or non-A). These laws assume that it is possible to separate out phenomena and to define terms categorically. By establishing precise categories, classes are set up which include or exclude other terms.

There are three types of syllogisms based upon the structure of the major premise. They are the categorical syllogism, the hypothetical syllogism, and the disjunctive syllogism. All three types are based upon the laws of thought, and all involve three premises and three terms. The structure of an argument from sign or an argument from causal generalization may involve any one of these three types.

TESTS OF CATEGORICAL SYLLOGISMS

A categorical syllogism is a syllogism whose major premise classifies without qualifications. Such major premises are characterized by words such as "all," "every," "each," "none," or "no." An example of a categorical syllogism would be:

> All Christians believe in the divinity of Christ.
> John is a Christian.
> John believes in the divinity of Christ.

There are five basic tests of the logical validity of the categorical syllogism.

Is the middle term used in a universal or unqualified sense in at least one of the premises? The middle term must apply universally to every member of the class in order to provide a clear basis for inclusion or exclusion. If the middle term were not universal and applied only to some members of the class, there would be no basis for predicting whether or not a specific member of the class was included within the generalization of the first premise. The following is an example of an invalid syllogism based upon a nonuniversal (or undistributed) middle term:

> Some history professors are poor lecturers.
> Dr. Robinson is a history professor.
> Dr. Robinson is a poor lecturer. (Invalid)

The middle term, "history professors," is not universal, so there is no way of knowing whether or not Dr. Robinson is part of the group of history professors who are poor lecturers.

If a term is universal in the conclusion, was it universal in the premises? A term which is qualified in one of the premises cannot assume universality in the conclusion. Deductive arguments provide structural certainty because the conclusions do not extend beyond the initial data. To assert universality in the conclusion when the terms of the premises were limited would be an unwarranted extension of the argument and would violate the certainty of the conclusion. Consider the following example:

All people with poor vision should wear glasses.
Many college graduates have poor vision.
All college graduates should wear glasses. (Invalid)

The minor term, "Many college graduates," was not universal in the minor premise but became so in the conclusion. The inclusion of "many college graduates" in the category of "people with poor vision" does not justify the inclusion of all college graduates in that category.

Is at least one of the premises an affirmative statement? Affirmative statements are necessary in order to establish class-inclusive relationships. Negative statements indicate relationships of exclusion. If both premises are negative statements, both the major and the minor terms are excluded from the middle term. With the major and minor terms excluded from the middle term, there is no way of relating the major and minor terms to each other. A syllogism with two negative premises is illustrated here:

No Arabs are Zionists.
Harry is not an Arab.
Harry is a Zionist. (Invalid)

The first premise excludes Zionists (major term) from the class of Arabs (middle term). The second premise excludes Harry (minor term) from the class of Arabs. The fact that Arabs are not Zionists does not assure us that non-Arab Harry is a Zionist. Lacking a positive statement of inclusion in at least one premise, there is no way of linking the major and minor terms through the middle term.

If one premise is negative, is the conclusion negative? A negative premise excludes the term of that premise from the middle term. Therefore, the only relationship which can be identified between the major and minor terms is a negative one of exclusion. This rule is violated in the following example:

No Russian believes in capitalism.
Ivan is a Russian.
Ivan believes in capitalism. (Invalid)

In this sample syllogism the first premise is a negative one which excludes all Russians from believing in capitalism. Since Ivan is included in the category of Russians, he must be excluded (along with all other Russians) from the category of those who believe in capitalism.

Are the terms of the syllogism used in the same sense throughout? As was explained earlier, syllogisms are based upon precise definitions of terms. If the meaning of a term is not precise and shifts during the development of an argument, a fourth category may inadvertently be introduced. Since the form of the syllogism only permits three terms to be related at a time, the introduction of a fourth term (in the form of a shift in meaning) precludes any valid conclusion. Observe how the shift in the concept of communism creates a fourth term in the following syllogism:

> All communists were opposed to United States involvement in Vietnam.
> All those who believe in the collective ownership of property are communists.
> All those who believe in the collective ownership of property were opposed to United States involvement in Vietnam. (Invalid)

In this example, the term communist is used to refer to a political viewpoint in the first premise, but in the second premise it refers to an economic concept. Since the political viewpoint and the economic concept do not necessarily coincide, a fourth term was introduced into the syllogism. When an advocate changes the meaning of a critical term during the course of an argument, he is said to be guilty of the *fallacy of equivocation.*

TESTS OF HYPOTHETICAL SYLLOGISMS

A hypothetical syllogism is a syllogism whose major premise is concerned with uncertain or conditional happenings which may or may not exist or occur. The uncertain condition is usually indicated by such terms as "if," "when," "assuming," or "in the event of." An example of a hypothetical syllogism would be:

> If a system of compulsory health insurance is financed through the income tax, it will win approval.
> The proposed system of compulsory health insurance is financed through the income tax.
> The proposed system of compulsory health insurance will win approval.

There are two basic tests of the hypothetical syllogism.

If the minor premise affirms the antecedent, does the conclusion affirm the consequent? The antecedent is the conditional clause, and the consequent is the independent clause. If the minor premise denies the antecedent, no valid conclusion can be drawn. When the antecedent is denied, the condition of the first premise has not been met, and we have no basis for predicting what will happen. The second premise of the following syllogism denies the antecedent:

If you have outstanding grades, you will be admitted to law school.
You do not have outstanding grades.
You will not be admitted to law school. (Invalid)

The first premise indicates only the positive results of outstanding grades. It does not suggest the possible consequences of less than outstanding grades. The conclusion predicting nonadmission to law school is, therefore, unjustified.

If the minor premise denies the consequent, does the conclusion deny the antecedent? By knowing that the consequent does not exist, we must also know that the condition which would have resulted in its existence does not exist. However, if the minor premise affirms the consequent, we do not necessarily know that the antecedent has occurred. It may be that the condition of the antecedent is only one of many conditions which could cause the consequent to exist. Thus, when the minor premise affirms the consequent, no valid conclusion can be drawn. Observe the following example:

Whenever I eat too much, I get sick.
I got sick.
I ate too much. (Invalid)

Since conditions other than eating too much might cause us to get sick, the conclusion does not necessarily follow.

TESTS OF DISJUNCTIVE SYLLOGISMS

A disjunctive syllogism is one whose major premise presents alternatives. The alternatives are usually indicated by such terms as "either . . . or," "neither . . . nor," or "but." An example of a disjunctive syllogism would be:

Either the state must keep its spending more in line with its revenue or it will go bankrupt.
The state will keep its spending more in line with its revenue.
It will not go bankrupt.

There are three tests of disjunctive syllogisms.

If the minor premise affirms (or denies) one of the alternatives, does the conclusion deny (or affirm) the other alternative? Since the major premise establishes alternatives, one of the alternatives must be accepted and the other denied. It does not matter whether the minor premise affirms or denies one of the alternatives so long as the conclusion does the opposite. Note the following violation of this test:

> Either I must get a part-time job or else I will have to quit school.
> I did not get a part-time job.
> I will not have to quit school. (Invalid)

In this example, the conclusion is inconsistent with the other two premises. If the choice is truly between working part-time or quitting school, then the rejection of part-time work requires the acceptance of the other alternative (quitting school).

Are the alternatives presented in the first premise mutually exclusive? The alternatives presented in the first premise must automatically exclude each other. If the acceptance of one alternative does not necessarily force the rejection of the other, the alternatives are not mutually exclusive. A syllogism in which the terms are not mutually exclusive is illustrated below:

> Either we must take plenty of time or we must be unfair.
> We will take plenty of time.
> We will not be unfair.

The conclusion follows consistently, but the first premise is inadequate. It is possible both to take plenty of time and to be unfair; therefore the alternatives are not mutually exclusive.

Does the major premise include all of the possible alternatives? The major premise of a disjunctive syllogism must not ignore possible alternatives. If other alternatives than those indicated in the first premise exist, the conclusion can be denied by pointing to the incompleteness of the original premise. Notice the incompleteness of the disjunction in the following syllogism:

> Judging from his poor work, he must be either stupid or lazy.
> He is not stupid.
> He is lazy.

Although the conclusion follows consistently from the major premise, the major premise is faulty. There are many other possible explanations for the poor work—he may have been too busy to do it well, emotional problems may have precluded a good job, etc.

SUMMARY

Specific tests may be applied to each of the five forms of argument. The tests of the three inductive forms—example, analogy, and causal correlation—provide means of examining the conclusion's consistency with known data. The tests of the two deductive forms—sign and causal generalization—are concerned with the examination of reservations to or qualifications of the initial generalization.

There are three tests for the argument by example: (1) Are the examples typical? (2) Have a sufficient number of examples been examined? (3) Are negative instances adequately accounted for?

The argument by analogy has two tests: (1) Are the compared cases alike in all essential regards? (2) Are the compared characteristics accurately described?

Four tests may be applied to the argument by causal correlation: (1) Is the association between the alleged cause and the alleged effect a consistent one? (2) Is the association between the alleged cause and the alleged effect a strong one? (3) Do the alleged cause and the alleged effect appear in a regular time sequence? (4) Is the association between the alleged cause and the alleged effect coherent?

The argument from sign may be examined through the application of three tests: (1) Are the substance and the attribute invariable indicators of the presence of each other? (2) Are sufficient signs presented? (3) Are contradictory signs adequately considered?

There are three tests for arguments from causal generalization: (1) Will intervening factors preclude an expected cause and effect relationship? (2) Is the cause sufficient to bring about the effect? (3) Will the cause result in other unspecified effects?

The structural consistency of arguments from sign and arguments from causal generalization may be examined by applying the tests of the deductive process. In order to test the structure of deductive arguments they must be cast in full syllogistic form. A syllogism consists of three statements and three terms which are related to one another through inclusion in or exclusion from classes.

A categorical syllogism is one whose major premise classifies without qualification. Five basic tests of a categorical syllogism exist: (1) Is the middle term used in a universal or unqualified sense in at least one premise? (2) If a term is universal in the conclusion, was it universal in the premises? (3) Is at least one of the premises an affirmative statement? (4) If one premise is negative, is the conclusion negative? (5) Are the terms of the syllogism used in the same sense throughout?

A hypothetical syllogism is one whose major premise is concerned with uncertain or conditional happenings which may or may not exist or occur. There are two basic tests of the hypothetical form: (1) If the minor premise affirms the antecedent, does the conclusion affirm the consequent? (2) If the minor premise denies the consequent, does the conclusion deny the antecedent?

A disjunctive syllogism is one whose major premise presents alternatives. Three basic tests of the disjunctive syllogism may be identified: (1) If the minor premise affirms (denies) one of the alternatives, does the conclusion deny (affirm) the other alternative? (2) Are the alternatives presented in the first premise mutually exclusive? (3) Does the major premise include all of the possible alternatives?

STUDY QUESTIONS

1. The tests specific to the five forms of argument are tests of "material validity" whereas the tests specific to the structure of deduction are tests of "formal or structural validity." Explain this distinction.

2. Why is it necessary to cast deductive arguments in full syllogistic form in order to apply the tests of the logical structure of deduction?

3. Provide the rationale for the following statements about deductive arguments:
   a. "A deductive argument may be structurally valid yet materially invalid."
   b. "A deductive argument may move from materially valid premises to a materially invalid conclusion."

EXERCISES

1. If you started a notebook of arguments (as suggested in the exercises for Chapter 7) add a section to your notebook on the testing of arguments. Collect examples of people actually applying the tests of argument to other people's statements. In each instance, indicate the specific test which was used. Newspaper editorials, letters to the editor, legislative hearings, and transcripts of debates provide particularly useful sources for this exercise.

2. Have various members of the class present sample arguments. After each argument is presented the other class members should attempt to apply the appropriate tests to it.

3. Create or find in printed sources two examples of arguments from sign and two examples of arguments from causal generalization. Cast each of these examples into full syllogistic form. Bring both the original argument and its syllogistic statement to class.

9 The Organization of Argument

In order to form a reasonable argumentative case or position, one must be able to organize individual arguments in a meaningful and consistent manner. The logical outline provides a sound and useful means of accomplishing this objective. It is a sound system of organization because it utilizes logical, grammatical, and visual concepts for structuring and testing relationships. It is particularly useful because it allows for the structuring of both inductive and deductive relationships and because it permits different forms of argument to be related to one another.

In considering the organization of argument, this chapter will describe the nature of the logical outline, identify the principles of logical outlining, and suggest some specific benefits to be derived from skill in outlining.

THE NATURE OF THE LOGICAL OUTLINE

An outline consists of a number of statements which are arranged in a series. There are essentially two kinds of idea relationships which can exist between main points and subordinate points. An idea relationship of "parts-to-the-whole" is the essential characteristic of a *topical outline*, while the idea relationship of "support" constitutes the essential characteristic of the *logical outline.*

A topical outline breaks a whole down into its parts for purposes of clarity. In this type of outlining, the subpoints do not *support* the main point, but rather constitute *parts* of the main point. This type of outlining is generally used for informative discourse. In Chapter 2 our development of the concept of propositions was in the form of a topical outline. We took the whole topic of propositions and broke it down into two parts: propositions of judgment and propositions of policy. Our further division of propositions of judgment into descriptive, predictive, and evaluative judgments continued the parts-to-the-whole division. In outline form, this topical outline segment would appear as follows:

I. Types of propositions
   A. Propositions of judgment
      1. Descriptive judgments
      2. Predictive judgments
      3. Evaluative judgments
   B. Propositions of policy

In this chapter our primary concern is with logical outlining rather than with topical outlining. *In a logical outline the relationship between the different levels of statements is one of support.* In other words, each statement in a logical outline provides either data in support of the validity of the statement to which it is subordinate or a reason for the acceptance of that statement. Logical outlines are used for argumentative discourse while topical outlines are used for informative discourse.

The following sample outline illustrates both the form and the relationships involved in logical outlining.

Sample Logical Outline

I. Money bail is unnecessary to assure the appearance of a criminal suspect at trial.
   A. In jurisdictions with money bail 96 percent of the criminal suspects released returned for trial.
   B. In jurisdictions without any system of monetary guarantee 98 percent of the criminal suspects released returned for trial.
II. Money bail is ineffective in protecting society against the recommission of crimes.
   A. Citizens have a right to money bail.
      1. The U.S. Constitution guarantees such a right in all federal courts.
      2. Nearly all state constitutions assure such a right except for capital offenses.
   B. Professional criminals have little difficulty in raising the necessary money for bail.
III. Money bail is undesirable.
   A. The system of money bail discriminates against the poor.
      1. Many poor cannot afford to put up even twenty-five or fifty dollars in bail money.
      2. More affluent citizens can meet bonds of $10,000 or more.
         a. Some citizens have enough cash and collateral to pay the bail directly out of their own resources.
         b. Other citizens have at least enough resources to meet the fee of a professional bail bondsman.
   B. The system of money bail is costly to the state.
      1. It typically costs the state $500 or more to hold a suspect in custody pending trial.
      2. Prolonged pretrial detention of a family's breadwinner forces it onto welfare.
   C. The system of money bail is damaging to the person who is detained.
      1. He is subject to assault and homosexual rape.
      2. He is more likely to be convicted.
         a. He is less able to help in the preparation of his own defense.
         b. Studies have shown that those detained in jail during the pretrial period are twice as likely to be convicted as those released during that period.

THE PRINCIPLES OF LOGICAL OUTLINING

The basic principles of logical outlining provide both guidelines for constructing outlines and tests of their logical adequacy. Failure to adhere to any one of these principles when organizing arguments is an indication of an inconsistent, incomplete, or unclear relationship.

COORDINATION

At any given level of the outline form, statements should have some common relationship to one another. The common element or elements connecting such statements are determined by the statement to which they are subordinate. When unrelated or unequal statements appear at the same level of the outline form, an inconsistent relationship is revealed.

In the example below, note that items A, B, and D are all related to one another in that they identify specific manifestations of inflation's harm. Item C, on the other hand, indicates the magnitude of inflation, rather than its effect or harm. Statements A, B, and D are coordinate; statement C breaks the pattern of coordination.

I. Inflation is harmful to the nation. (because)
   A. Inflation erodes the purchasing power of those on fixed incomes.
   B. Inflation encourages unsound business speculation.
   C. Inflation has been increasing at the rate of 5 percent per year.
   D. Inflation makes the financing of state and local services more difficult.

SUBORDINATION

Those statements which are placed in a lower order in the outline form should justify, support, or prove the statement to which they are subordinate. Since the support for the higher-order statement may be based upon either inductive or deductive reasoning, the subordinate statements may be either more or less specific than the higher-order statements. In the first example below, the higher-order statement is the conclusion of a deductive argument. Since the lower-order statements are the premises upon which the conclusion is based, they are more general than the higher-order statement.

I. High unemployment will be necessary to halt our present inflation. (because)

A. In the past, inflation has never been halted until after unemployment became severe.
B. The present inflation is not different from earlier inflations.

In the second example, the higher-order statement is the conclusion of an inductive argument, and the supporting lower-order statements are less general.

I. Inflation has never been halted until after unemployment became severe. (because)
   A. The inflation of the late 1920s was not stopped until the depression and high unemployment of the early 1930s.
   B. The inflation of 1952 ended with the high unemployment of 1954.
   C. The inflation of 1956 ended with the high unemployment of 1957.

Whether more general or less general, subordinate points must lend support to the claim of the higher-order statement. When they do not, they are out of place in the outline form and logically irrelevant. In the following specimen, both points B and C are irrelevant to the statement of point I because they fail to justify a belief in that statement.

I. To be poor is to subsist on an inadequate diet. (because)
   A. Many poor families have meat to eat less than twice a week.
   B. There are millions of poor people living in America today.
   C. The heads of most poor households are either women or aged men.

DIVISION

At least two subordinate points must be presented for each subdivided statement within the outline. The fact that every argument involves two elements other than the conclusion—the data and the reasoning process—suggests that there must be at least two elements of subordination. All deductive arguments derive their conclusions from two premises and, therefore, demand two elements of subordination. The nature of each of the forms of induction requires at least two elements of data. The argument by example requires a minimum of two examples in order to establish the assumption of regularity. The argument by analogy requires the identification of one or more points of similarity and the discounting of all dissimilarities. The argument by causal correlation requires the examination of at least two cases in order to establish concomitant variation, similarities, or differences. Thus, the use of less than two subordinate points in a logical outline is contrary to the principles of argumentation.

The appearance of a single subordinate point in an outline indicates an incomplete deductive argument or insufficient support for the conclusion of an inductive argument. When only one subordinate point is presented, it may mean that a premise of a deductive argument has been overlooked. This is the error in the following example.

I. The economy is heading out of its recessionary downturn. (because)
   A. Car sales have been increasing.

The support for this argument could be made complete by adding a second subordinate point expressing the major premise of the argument.

   B. An increase in car sales is a reliable indicator of an economic upturn.

Single subpoints may also indicate insufficient support for the conclusion of an inductive argument rather than incomplete deductive reasoning. In the following outline segment, one example is not sufficient to support the general claim of the major premise.

I. Nationalism is capable of stopping communism. (because)
   A. Nationalism has thwarted communism in Thailand.

Either other supporting examples should be found or else the claims of the argument should be limited to the one example.

COMPLETENESS

Subordinate points should provide support for all of the concepts included within the statement of the superior point. This principle recognizes that the proof requirements of all propositions and arguments flow from their statement and that even sentences which are simple in structure and focus may contain several different concepts. The inclusion or exclusion of a single modifying term may change the proof requirements of any statement and, hence, the number and kind of subordinate points required. The failure of the subordinate points to support the claim of any concept of a statement results in a logically incomplete outline.

In the outline segment below the two subpoints do not provide complete support for the major idea since the concept of "harmful" is not established.

    I. Continued reliance on the property tax harmfully limits the expansion and upgrading of education. (because)
        A. The property tax continues to be the major source of revenue for education.
        B. The expansion and upgrading of education have been limited by the lack of funds.

The inclusion of an additional subpoint would make the outline segment logically complete.

        C. Failure to expand and upgrade educational opportunities has resulted in the waste of human resources.

SIMPLICITY

Each point in a logical outline should be stated in the form of a simple declarative sentence. A simple sentence is, by definition, a single unit of thought. Any collection of words which is less than a simple sentence does not express a complete idea. Phrases do not focus or limit thoughts, and for this reason it is not possible to determine their relationship to other ideas or concepts. Examine the two outline segments below. Notice how much clearer the relationships are in the second segment because the use of complete sentences has focused and limited the ideas.

    I. Pollution
        A. Getting worse
        B. People die
        C. Property damage

    I. Increasing levels of air pollution have resulted in serious costs to the nation. (because)
        A. Air pollution is increasing.
        B. Air pollution results in serious costs.
            1. Air inversions have resulted in many deaths.
            2. Chemical particles in polluted air dirty and decompose physical structures.

Compound and complex sentences are expressions of the relationships between two or more complete units of thought. Compound sentences indicate two independent ideas, while complex sentences indicate a dependent or conditional relationship between clauses. Because compound and complex sentences constitute larger units of thought and more varied relationships than do simple sentences, they do not permit the diagramming of clear and consistent relationships. Multiple units of thought should be expressed in two or more simple sentences, and the outline form, rather than the sentence structure, should be used to indicate appropriate relationships between thought units. In the illustration below, the statement of the first outline is a complex sentence. Notice how the second outline segment visually illustrates the subordinate nature of the concept of the dependent clause, while more clearly emphasizing the overall importance of the independent clause.

I. Although a system of mass transit will be expensive to build and operate, Metropolis should begin construction immediately.

I. The cost of a mass transit system should not prevent Metropolis from beginning immediate construction.   (because)
   A. The cost of building the system can be paid off over a period of years.
   B. The cost of operating the system will be offset by the economic benefits to the city.

In the next set of examples, the statement in the first outline is a compound sentence, while the two statements of the second outline are simple sentences. Since the two clauses of the statement in segment one are of equal importance, they should be structured as coordinate points.

I. The city is capable of bearing the cost of constructing a mass transit system, and the benefits would be great.

I. The city is capable of bearing the costs of constructing a mass transit system.
II. The benefits of a mass transit system would be great.

DISCRETENESS

The ideas presented in an outline must be expressed so that each statement is a separate and discrete unit of thought. Overlapping statements indicate indistinct and unclear relationships between ideas.

In the first outline segment below, the statement of point A is simply a different way of expressing the idea of I. In the second segment, point C is contained within the ideas of point B. Both outlines are logically unsatisfactory because they violate the principle of discreteness.

I. A communist monolith no longer exists. (because)
   A. Unity within the communist world does not exist.
   B. Russia and China have conflicting economic and political objectives.
   C. Yugoslavia and Albania are not members of the Warsaw Pact.

I. Racial discrimination is socially unacceptable. (because)
   A. Racial discrimination creates antagonism between the races.
   B. Racial discrimination prevents the maximum development of our human resources.
   C. Racial discrimination denies equal educational opportunity.

SYMBOLIZATION

Each statement in an outline requires a letter or number which will indicate its relative rank with reference to the other ideas in the outline. Points having similar symbols are expected to be of comparable importance. Common practice recommends the use of roman numerals for main points, capital letters for the first level of subordination, arabic numbers for the second level of subordination, and lower-case letters for the third level of subordination.

When symbols are not used in a consistent manner the logical relationship between points becomes confused. The use of more than one symbol for a single statement reveals an incomplete subordination. Notice how, in the following outline segment, the shift from arabic numbers to lower-case letters confuses the relationship between the three subpoints of B. Notice, also, that the use of two symbols at the A level of the outline reveals an omitted conclusion. The arabic numbers (1 and 2) should be subpoints of a statement (A) such as: "Corruption of state and local officials is widespread."

I. The widespread corruption of state and local officials protects the activities of organized crime. (because)
   A. 1. The criminal syndicate is alleged to control the state of Louisiana.
      2. The criminal syndicate controls major public officials in all of our larger cities.

B. Corruption protects the activities of organized crime. (because)
   a. Corrupted officials fail to report illegal activities.
   b. Corrupted officials warn of planned raids.
   c. Corrupted officials thwart the prosecution process.

BENEFITS OF LOGICAL OUTLINING

The development of skill in logical outlining requires considerable effort and experience, but once acquired, this skill is of great assistance in the preparation of entire argumentative cases and in the consideration of particular series of arguments. There are three reasons why logical outlining is so helpful.

First, the logical outline offers the only structure available for testing the relationships *among* individual arguments. The principles of logical outlining make it possible to organize all the forms of argument together within a single framework and to examine the relationships in terms of basic logical concepts. The principles of coordination and subordination provide guidelines for consistency of relationships. The principles of division and completeness test the comprehensiveness of the development, and the principles of simplicity, discreteness, and symbolization are directed at the clarity of the relationships. Thus, by working out an outline of arguments, an advocate can help to assure that he is prepared to support a given proposition in a consistent, comprehensive, and clear manner.

Second, the logical outline is helpful because it encourages careful attention to the wording of arguments. Within the framework of the logical outline, only as many separate ideas can be related as can be expressed within the structure of a single simple sentence, and every idea expressed within that sentence must be supported by subpoints. Thus, an advocate must develop skill at phrasing conclusions in order to focus relationships while at the same time limiting his claim.

Finally, the logical outline organizes ideas in a manner which can be easily communicated to others. When supporting arguments are presented before more general conclusions, listeners (or readers) may be confused about the purpose of the communication, but when conclusions are set forth before supporting arguments, receivers of the communication can more easily follow the presentation. Since this latter ordering of ideas is required by the logical outline, it helps to develop a pattern of thinking which is conducive to clear communication.

SUMMARY

An outline consists of a number of statements which are arranged in a series. The idea relationship of a topical outline is one of parts-to-the-whole. The idea relationship of a logical outline is based on the principle of support. In other words, each statement in a logical outline provides either evidence of the validity of the statement to which it is subordinate or a reason for the acceptance of that statement.

There are seven basic principles which should be observed when preparing logical outlines: (1) The principle of coordination requires that statements at any given level of the outline form have some common relationship to one another. (2) The principle of subordination declares that those statements which are placed in a lower order should support or prove the statement to which they are subordinate. (3) The principle of division states that at least two subordinate points must be presented for each supported statement. (4) The concept of completeness requires that subordinate points must provide support for all of the ideas included within the statement of the superior point. (5) The simplicity principle indicates that each point in a logical outline should be stated in the form of a simple declarative sentence. (6) Discreteness refers to the principle that ideas presented in the outline must be expressed so that each statement is a separate and distinct unit of thought. (7) The principle of symbolization declares that each statement in the outline must have a letter or number which will indicate its relative rank with reference to the other ideas in the outline.

Skill in logical outlining is helpful in preparing for argumentation. The logical outline offers the only structure available for testing the relationships *among* individual arguments. It encourages careful attention to the wording of arguments. It organizes the ideas in a manner which can be easily communicated to others.

STUDY QUESTIONS

1. What is the advantage of defining the types of outlines in terms of "idea relationships" instead of in terms of "sentence structure" as is usually done?

2. Why does the appearance of a single subordinate point in an outline indicate an incomplete deductive argument or insufficient support for the conclusion of an inductive argument?

3. Why is it important to take special care in "wording" the statements of arguments in a logical outline?

EXERCISES

1. Select a proposition for debate and prepare a logical outline of the issues and supporting arguments on one side of that controversy. Be sure your outline conforms to the principles of logical outlining.
2. Prepare a one- or two-page logical outline on any controversial topic. While making most of the outline conform to the principles of logical outlining, deliberately violate two or three of the principles at certain points in the outline. Exchange outlines with other class members and see if you can detect each others' errors.
3. Turn to the sample debate in Appendix A, and try to prepare a logical outline of the first affirmative speech. What does your outline tell you about the completeness, consistency, and clarity of the arguments presented?

III Argumentation as Advocacy

10 Situations for Advocacy

The consideration of advocacy situations can be thought of as the bridge between inquiry and advocacy. In a sense, analysis of advocacy situations is still very much within the framework of inquiry since the process continues to be investigative. That investigation, however, no longer focuses on the discovery of truth within a given controversy, but rather becomes an analysis of the specific situation in which that truth will be presented. In dealing with advocacy situations this chapter seeks to classify them in a way which permits description and illustration of their essential components. In attempting to accomplish this goal, the chapter will do three things: (1) discuss the importance of the analysis of advocacy situations, (2) outline a continuum which will serve as the base for classifying advocacy situations, and (3) provide a more detailed discussion of the specialized advocacy formats used in educational debate.

IMPORTANCE OF ADVOCACY SITUATIONS

To this point our discussion has centered on the attitudes and skills necessary for the student of argumentation to discover the truth within any given controversy. Generally, however, this search for truth is not an isolated endeavor, but is instead part of a total process which culminates in the student of argumentation becoming an advocate of that truth in a specific advocacy situation. As the individual turns from inquiry to advocacy, however, he must begin to realize that advocacy situations differ considerably from each other and that argumentative strategies which are appropriate in one situation may not be transferable to another. In a very real sense, the nature and demands of advocacy situations exert a controlling influence over the advocate.

One way in which advocacy situations exert this influence is that the situational goal may not be consistent with the goal of the advocate. The goal of a lawyer, for instance, is to win his case in court, but the goal of the courtroom situation in which his advocacy takes place is to determine the truth of the question under consideration. The rules and procedures which characterize legal advocacy situations respond to the situational goal, not the goal of the individual advocate. In much the same way, the goal of a politician on a press interview program will be to build his own political support. He may find himself, however, in an advocacy situation which is structured to force him to answer many questions which may be damaging to his political objectives. In approaching advocacy, therefore, the advocate must consider not only his personal goal but must also analyze the goal of the advocacy situation to determine its influence upon his advocacy.

Advocacy situations also exert a controlling influence in that they determine the location and extent of presumption and burden of proof. The concepts of presumption and burden of proof are logical concepts which are central to inquiry processes. Their application in advocacy situations, however, is by no means consistent. In situations which are designed to keep advocacy within a logical framework, such as legal situations and academic debate formats, the logical concepts of presumption and burden of proof will be directly relevant. In many advocacy situations, however, these concepts cannot be strictly applied. When advocacy takes place before general public audiences, for instance, consideration of audience attitudes and values becomes more important than the application of presumption and burden of proof. An advocate who would defend an existing system cannot begin with the assumption that a general public audience will understand his logical presumption and impose a burden of proof upon the advocate of change. Advocacy situations, therefore, must be analyzed to determine the extent to which the concepts of presumption and burden of proof are functionally relevant.

A final influence of the advocacy situation is the determination of the amount and kinds of proof which must be presented. Some advocacy situations impose strict logical proof requirements upon the advocate. Legal situations, for instance, severely limit the types of evidence which may be presented as proof. In less structured situations before less specialized audiences, on the other hand, proof requirements are significantly altered. More time may have to be spent in illustrating concepts than in proving them. Such situations may also demand that the advocate's proof be derived from the premises of his audience rather than from external evidence.

Advocacy situations, therefore, exert a controlling influence upon the advocate. An advocate must understand the components of the situation in which his advocacy takes place in order to understand the demands which these components make upon his advocacy. Failure to understand the nature of the specific advocacy situation and failure to adapt appropriately to the demands of that situation significantly reduce the likelihood of successful advocacy.

CONTINUUM OF ADVOCACY SITUATIONS

Advocacy situations may be thought of as existing on a continuum according to their goals, the nature of their procedures, and the nature of their audiences. On one end of this continuum are advocacy situations which are characterized by highly formalized procedures and specialized audiences. On the other end of the continuum exist advocacy situations with no formal procedures and nonspecialized audiences. In the model below, the advocacy situations have been placed on this continuum and have been grouped according to three situational goals: (1) immediate truth determination, (2) information seeking, and (3) audience activation.

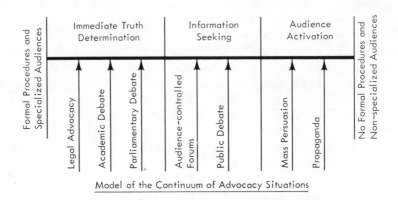

Model of the Continuum of Advocacy Situations

TRUTH DETERMINATION SITUATIONS

The goal of those advocacy situations with the most specialized audiences and rules of procedure is generally to determine truth in the immediate situation. Included within this goal grouping are legal advocacy, academic debate, and parliamentary debate. In these situations specific rules of procedure are drawn up and decision making is left to specialized audiences in order to insure that the goal of truth determination is not subverted by the individual advocates who participate within the situation. Since such situations are designed to encourage logical rigor, the standards of argumentative inquiry can be expected to be most relevant here. A more thorough understanding of these situations can come through a deeper analysis of the rules of procedure and the type of audience which characterizes each of these situations.

Legal advocacy. More than any other single advocacy situation, courtroom advocacy is structured to attempt to determine the truth in the immediate situation. All of the rules of procedure in legal advocacy are designed to insure that the situational goal of truth determination prevails over the individual goals of the participants in the situation. The rules of procedure call for a precise statement of the proposition for debate (indictment) and rigidly apply the concepts of presumption and burden of proof. The advocacy format guarantees direct and thorough refutation of ideas presented by participating advocates. Strict rules of evidence severely limit the types of supporting materials which are appropriate in this advocacy situation.

Consistent with the situational goal of truth determination, audiences in legal advocacy situations receive specific training in how to evaluate the advocacy of the participants in the dispute. Frequently the audience is a single judge or a panel of judges who have received extensive training in the law and in legal procedures. Even when the decision-making audience is a lay jury, the members of the jury receive specific instructions concerning the criteria by which they must evaluate the advocacy. Juries are further assisted by the judge who is able to instruct them even during the advocacy and who exercises a controlling influence within the situation.

The concepts and standards of argumentative inquiry apply most directly to legal advocacy situations because such situations are characterized by rules of procedure and specialized audiences which insure that logical standards will be applied in the evaluation of advocacy. To be sure, motivational elements are present even within the restrictive framework of legal advocacy. Despite the existence of rigid procedures and trained audiences, judges and juries are human and subject to motive appeals. Yet, within the framework of free human decision making, legal advocacy situations come the closest to the ideal of guaranteeing immediate truth determination.

Academic debate. When one examines the advocacy formats for academic debate one sees striking similarities to legal advocacy. Like legal advocacy, academic debate requires a statement of proposition which provides the framework within which advocacy must take place. The concepts of presumption and burden of proof are applied in a manner similar to their usage in legal advocacy. Like the format of legal advocacy, the formats of academic debate are designed to encourage direct and thorough clash of ideas. Evidence rules are also applied, although not as rigidly as in legal advocacy.

The nature of the decision-making audience in academic debate situations is also quite similar to that of legal advocacy. In most academic debate situations the audience is composed of a single judge or a panel of judges who is trained to apply the rules and procedures of academic debate. The judges in academic debate, however, do not exert quite as much influence as the judges in legal situations because they are not generally free to interrupt the proceedings, to correct procedural errors, or to declare elements of the advocacy to be irrelevant to the proceedings. These judges are also not as directly concerned with immediate truth determination as are the judges in legal advocacy situations. Since academic debate situations function as training grounds for reasoned advocacy, judges are frequently as concerned with skill development as they are with truth determination.

The similarities between legal advocacy and academic debate, however, seem to justify the frequent claim that academic debate provides excellent training for legal advocacy. While legal advocacy is more directly committed to truth determination in the real world and while the judges in legal advocacy situations exert a stronger influence than the judges in academic debate, the similarities between the two advocacy situations certainly outnumber the differences. The next section of this chapter will direct itself to a more detailed examination of specific academic debate formats.

Parliamentary debate. While parliamentary debate can be characterized as a truth determination situation, its rules of procedure and its audiences do not insure the same level of logical rigor as do legal advocacy situations and academic debate situations. Generally, parliamentary debate may occur only after a specific motion or resolution has been made and seconded. Attempts are made to keep debate relevant to the specific motion or resolution at hand by empowering the chairman to declare irrelevant debate out of order. Parliamentary debate guarantees the opportunity for the presentation of opposing views, but the rules of procedure do not guarantee direct clash of ideas. Unlike legal advocacy and academic debate situations, the concepts of presumption and burden of proof are not rigidly applied and evidence rules are notably absent.

The level of audience specialization can vary significantly among parliamentary situations. In general, the potential advocates and the decision-making audience are composed of the same individuals. Parliamentary debate situations rely heavily on the training of the chairman and parliamentarian. The chairman and parliamentarian have reasonably broad powers to insure that debate stays within the limits of the prescribed rules and procedures. To the extent that these two individuals understand the procedures of parliamentary debate and are willing and able to use their powers appropriately, parliamentary debate can be kept within the goal of truth determination. Chaos can result, however, if these individuals are either untrained or are unwilling to use their powers at the right time.

Parliamentary debate, then, while committed to the goal of truth determination, lacks many of the rules and procedures which insure the accomplishment of this goal. Its rules and procedures are designed to keep order and to provide an opportunity for all views to be heard rather than to insure logical rigor. Audience specialization is also more likely to vary in parliamentary situations than it is in legal advocacy or in academic debate situations. Parliamentary debate, then, creates a higher degree of freedom for the individual advocate. His choices of arguments and of supporting materials are not nearly as limited as in the other two situations described in this section.

INFORMATION-SEEKING SITUATIONS

In the middle of the continuum are advocacy situations which have been classified as essentially information-seeking in nature. Such situations have elements of truth determination and audience activation in them but are designed to achieve the primary objective of gathering information. Within this classification are included audience-controlled forums and public debates. They are placed in the middle of the continuum because they have either less rigorous rules and procedures or less specialized audiences than do truth determination situations.

Audience-controlled forums. Audience-controlled forums are public advocacy situations in which the direction of the advocacy is strongly controlled by the immediate audience in order for it to obtain desired information. Such situations include committee hearings, press conferences, and the full range of broadcast programs in which an advocate is questioned by a professional interviewer or a panel of newsmen. When compared with truth determination situations, audience-controlled forums lack rigid rules of procedure. Such forums, for instance, frequently operate from open-ended questions rather than from precise statements of proposition. The formats do not guarantee an in-depth discussion of a single question but rather frequently permit the discussion to wander from question to question with a minimal degree of purposefulness. The concepts of burden of proof and presumption are not consistently applied and rules of evidence are also not characteristic of such forums. The degree to which rules of procedure are applied and the degree to which the audience really controls the forum will vary significantly within this classification of advocacy situations.

With wide variations in rules of procedure among audience-controlled forums, such advocacy situations depend heavily upon the specialized training of the primary audience members. When audience-controlled forums are composed of highly trained and perceptive audience members, the search for information becomes more systematic and logically rigorous. The members of congressional committees, for example, frequently become experts at cross-examination. Trained newsmen also develop the skill of asking the right questions at the right time. Such expertise can help to bring a degree of logical rigor to audience-controlled forums. Yet, that logical rigor is not guaranteed by formalized rules and procedures as it is in most truth determination situations. It is the dependence upon the nonguaranteed variable of audience training which motivates the placement of audience-controlled forums in the middle of the continuum.

As a general rule, the advocate has greater latitude in the presentation of his ideas within audience-controlled forums than he does in truth determination situations. He is much freer, for instance, to rely on his own opinions as opposed to the rigorous supporting material demanded in legal advocacy and academic debate situations. The logical rigor demanded of the advocate will be entirely dependent upon the cross-examination skill of the controlling audience members. While the relaxed rules and procedures of audience-controlled forums give the advocate greater freedom, they also create an additional responsibility. In preparing for such situations, the advocate must begin to take into account the opinions and values of the members of the audience. He cannot be assured that his advocacy will be evaluated on logical criteria. This is especially true in those audience-controlled forums, such as televised press conferences and interviews, where there is a secondary audience. This audience does not participate directly in the questioning of the advocate, but frequently this is the audience which the advocate wishes to influence. The reaction of this nonparticipating audience may be of vital concern, then, when one is engaged in audience-controlled forums.

Public debate. Public debate refers to all advocacy situations which guarantee presentation of both sides of a controversy before general public audiences. Such advocacy situations are classified as essentially information-seeking rather than as truth determination situations because of relatively lax rules of procedure and because they generally occur before nonspecialized audiences. They differ from audience-controlled forums in that they guarantee pro and con advocacy. The audiences in such situations, however, tend to be more passive than those of audience-controlled forums. In a sense, public debates could be termed format-controlled forums.

There are great variations in rules of procedure among public debate situations. Frequently, for instance, the essence of the controversy is not clearly stated beyond the identification of a topic. The more precise the statement of the debate proposition, the more such situations begin to demand a degree of logical rigor. Such precise statements, however, are not guaranteed in public debate situations. As in audience-controlled forums, the concepts of presumption and burden of proof are rarely applied and specific rules of evidence seldom exist. The advocacy situation is totally dependent upon the specific debate format to be used and upon the refutation skill of the individual advocates. The audience becomes a variable in the rules of procedure only to the extent that the format permits direct questioning from the audience. The factor which keeps public debate from being classified as an audience activation situation is the guarantee that both sides of the controversy will be heard.

In public debate situations, audience expertise and training cannot generally be assumed. The audience cannot be depended upon to apply the standards of reasoned inquiry. Truth determination, then, is entirely dependent upon the format for the debate and upon the skill of the opposing advocates. However, the opinions and values of the audience begin to become more vital to the advocate. Since audience members will tend to evaluate the advocacy in terms of their own opinions and values, the advocate must seriously consider these factors as well as the arguments of the opposition. The fact that audience attitudes and values become pivotal factors in public debates moves such situations well down the continuum from pure truth determination. As one moves closer to audience activation and away from truth determination as the controlling goal of the advocacy situation, the standards of reasoned inquiry outlined in the first half of this book begin to be applied less consistently.

AUDIENCE ACTIVATION SITUATIONS

Audience activation is the goal of those advocacy situations at the extreme end of the continuum. In these situations few, if any, rules of procedure exist, and the goal becomes the motivation of a nonspecialized, nonparticipating audience. Hopefully, advocates in these situations will have utilized the standards of reasoned inquiry in arriving at their positions, but in seeking to activate audiences they will tend to place greater emphasis on motivational factors as opposed to purely logical forms of proof and development.

Mass persuasion, propaganda, and advertising are terms which can be used as synonyms for audience activation. In such situations none of the rules of procedure which encourage logical rigor can be guaranteed. In fact, a distinguishing feature of audience activation situations is the complete lack of predictable rules of procedure. Nothing exists within the advocacy situation to guarantee that advocacy will remain focused on a specific proposition. Logical presumption, burden of proof, and specific evidence rules are totally absent. Whereas other advocacy situations permit and even encourage the presentation of opposition views, audience activation situations are characterized by one-sided presentations.

The only possible controls in audience activation situations are the ethical and logical standards of the advocate and the information level and logical capacities of the audience. These factors, however, are not guaranteed by the advocacy situation. Audience activation situations, more than any other type of advocacy situation, permit the motives of the advocate to dominate the situation. It is in such situations that the standards of reasoned inquiry have the least relevance, for such situations are controlled by the objectives of the advocate and the attitudes and values of the audience rather than by any logical guidelines or rules of procedure. Nothing, outside of the advocate's own standards, exists in audience activation situations to guarantee logical adequacy.

Advocacy situations, therefore, have been explained in terms of a continuum moving from those situations which are designed to determine the truth in the immediate situation to those situations where the desire to activate a specific audience is the dominant objective. At the former end of the continuum the standards of reasoned inquiry are applied most directly because specific rules of procedure and specialized audiences guarantee their importance in the advocacy situation. At the latter end of the continuum, advocacy situations demand consideration of audience attitudes and values over purely logical factors, thus guaranteeing no consistent application of the standards of reasoned inquiry.

SPECIALIZED FORMATS
FOR EDUCATIONAL DEBATE

This final section of the chapter will be devoted to a more detailed examination of the formats which students most frequently encounter in educational debate training. Such formats constitute the advocacy situations designed to teach the skills of reasoned inquiry and reasoned advocacy. Specifically, this section will consider the standard interscholastic debate formats and formats for use in audience debate experiences.

STANDARD INTERSCHOLASTIC
DEBATE FORMATS

Any student who anticipates participating in interscholastic debate will soon have to become familiar with the standard debate formats which constitute the framework of the advocacy situation for academic debate. While a variety of debate formats are in use in high school and college debating, the two formats outlined below are encountered most frequently. They are known as the traditional "10-5" format and the cross-examination format.

Traditional 10–5 Format

1st Affirmative Constructive	10 minutes
1st Negative Constructive	10 minutes
2nd Affirmative Constructive	10 minutes
2nd Negative Constructive	10 minutes
1st Negative Rebuttal	5 minutes
1st Affirmative Rebuttal	5 minutes
2nd Negative Rebuttal	5 minutes
2nd Affirmative Rebuttal	5 minutes

Cross-examination Format

1st Affirmative Constructive	8 minutes
Negative Cross-examination of 1st Affirmative	3 minutes
1st Negative Constructive	8 minutes
Affirmative Cross-examination of 1st Negative	3 minutes
2nd Affirmative Constructive	8 minutes
Negative Cross-examination of 2nd Affirmative	3 minutes
2nd Negative Constructive	8 minutes
Affirmative Cross-examination of 2nd Negative	3 minutes
1st Negative Rebuttal	4 minutes
1st Affirmative Rebuttal	4 minutes
2nd Negative Rebuttal	4 minutes
2nd Affirmative Rebuttal	4 minutes

A quick glance at these two formats reveals an obvious but extremely important characteristic of academic debate: academic debate activities are structured as team activities. This means that the student who anticipates participating in academic debate must not only prepare himself for advocacy, but must also prepare to work closely with a partner in advocacy. An important first step in understanding academic debate advocacy situations, then, is to understand the basic responsibilities of each speaker within the standard debate formats. While there are variations in the approaches to using these formats, certain practices have become standard. In analyzing these formats it is helpful to discuss three aspects separately: (1) the constructive speeches, (2) the rebuttal speeches, and (3) the handling of cross-examination time.

Constructive speeches. In both formats there are four constructive speeches; one is presented by each of the participating advocates. In both formats, the constructive speeches receive the largest time allocation, indicating that the most thorough development of the arguments occurs in these speeches. In recognition of the logical presumption of the negative and the burden of proof of the affirmative, the advocate of change (affirmative) always speaks first.

In the *first affirmative constructive speech* it has become standard practice for the speaker to develop the basic outline of the entire affirmative case. This outline generally includes not only the affirmative's rationale for change but also a sketch of the specific proposal forwarded by the affirmative team. This development is frequently preceded by a statement of the affirmative philosophy with reference to the specific debate proposition and by definitions of important terms which are not made clear by the affirmative proposal. The first affirmative constructive speech sets the organizational framework within which the next two constructive speeches operate.

The *first negative constructive speech* is generally devoted to refutation of the affirmative rationale for change. It has become standard procedure to leave the analysis of the specific affirmative plan for the second negative constructive speech. If the affirmative plan is not clear or if it appears incomplete, the first negative will frequently ask questions to force the second affirmative to provide the necessary clarifications or additions. The first negative constructive speech frequently begins with a brief development of the negative philosophy on the resolution. The rest of the speech, however, generally follows the organizational structure of the rationale for change outlined in the first affirmative constructive speech. The basic duty of the first negative constructive speech is to refute, in some way, the affirmative's rationale for change.

The *second affirmative constructive speech* generally focuses on the rebuilding of the affirmative analysis in light of the refutation of the first negative constructive. While this speech usually follows the organizational structure set up in the first affirmative speech, its initial few minutes may have to be spent dealing with the negative philosophy, answering questions concerning the affirmative proposal, and clarifying any definitional questions. The speech deals with negative refutation within the affirmative organizational framework and attempts to forward the basic affirmative analysis by providing more details and more supporting materials.

The *second negative constructive speech* generally breaks with the organizational pattern of the first three speeches. In academic debate practice this speech is usually devoted exclusively to an analysis of the specific affirmative proposal. The second negative speaker sets up his own organizational structure built around the stock issues of cure and cost. His analysis generally focuses on the inability of the affirmative proposal to solve the problems outlined by the affirmative, on the workability problems of the proposal, and on the potential new problems which the proposal could create if adopted.

Rebuttal speeches. Both formats permit each advocate one rebuttal speech during the debate. The time allocated for rebuttal speeches is exactly half of that devoted to constructive speeches, indicating that the rebuttal speeches are used more for focusing of the debate rather than for the thorough development of initial arguments. With the exception of the first negative rebuttal, the rebuttal speeches must also cover twice as much argumentative ground as the constructive speeches.

The *first negative rebuttal* can really be viewed as an extension of the second negative constructive speech. Since no affirmative speech comes between these two speeches, the two are usually treated as one complete speech delivered by two advocates. Whereas the second negative constructive speech generally focuses exclusively upon the affirmative proposal, the first negative rebuttal returns to the negative arguments raised against the affirmative rationale for change in order to complete the negative attack. Using the structure of the first affirmative constructive speech, the first negative rebuttal attempts to reestablish the focus of the attack which was outlined in the first negative constructive speech. The speech must be responsive to the arguments developed in the second affirmative constructive speech.

The *first affirmative rebuttal* is the most difficult speech in the debate because it must deal with a block of negative speaking three times its own length. It must respond to the negative analysis of the affirmative plan as well as attempt to rebuild the affirmative rationale for change. Because of the short amount of time allotted to this speech, organization must be tight and argument development precise. The general practice is to begin the speech by dealing with the plan attacks outlined in the second negative constructive and then to move to the rebuilding of the affirmative case structure.

The *second negative rebuttal* climaxes the focusing of the debate for the negative. Like the first affirmative rebuttal, this speech must also cover the major clashes, both on the affirmative rationale for change and on the negative analysis of the affirmative proposal. In addition to covering the total argumentative ground, however, this speech must also narrow the negative attack to a focus on the crucial issues in the debate. The second negative rebuttal generally rebuilds the negative focus on the affirmative rationale for change before moving to a concluding emphasis on the negative objections to the affirmative proposal.

The *second affirmative rebuttal,* as the final speech in the debate, summarizes the debate from the affirmative point of view. While the speech must be responsive to significant negative arguments which have developed throughout the debate, it also must focus the debate on the clashes which the affirmative finds crucial to the proposition. As in the last two speeches, its consideration of negative plan objections will follow the structure established by the second negative constructive and its rebuilding of the affirmative analysis will return to the structure outlined in the first affirmative constructive speech.

The use of cross-examination time. The cross-examination format provides the advocates with a flexibility denied to them by the traditional 10–5 format. The cross-examination periods between the constructive speeches provide the advocates with an opportunity to force opposition responses to specific questions. These time periods may be used to clarify points not completely understood, to expose weaknesses in the analysis and evidence of the opposition, or to set the basis for arguments to be developed in future speeches. In general practice each cross-examination speech is used to set up the speech which follows it. If the cross-examination has been effective, the speech which follows should be filled with references to admissions gained through cross-examination. These admissions may be used in place of other forms of data. Chapter 15 will be devoted entirely to methods of handling cross-examination.

AUDIENCE DEBATE FORMATS

Many educational debate programs make an attempt to involve their students in audience debate activities as well as in interscholastic activities. Unlike interscholastic debate, however, there are no standard formats for audience debate situations. Formats for audience debating must be developed to adapt to the uniqueness of the advocacy situation involved. In the discussion of the continuum of advocacy situations we noted that public debate situations differ from academic debate situations primarily in terms of their nonspecialized audiences. When developing formats for audience debate activities, therefore, one must remember that general audiences differ from the critic judges of competitive debate in terms of their comprehension levels, in terms of their interest levels, and in terms of their propensity to allow their personal attitudes and values to influence their evaluation of the debate.

The first consideration in building formats for public debate is to adapt to audience comprehension levels. Most public audiences have difficulty following a debate which uses one of the standard interscholastic formats. In interscholastic debates there are generally too many lines of argument and too many speeches for nonspecialized audiences to follow. Formats for audience debate must be simplified and must encourage a clearer focusing of the arguments for the sake of clarity and ease of comprehension.

Second, formats for audience debating should adapt to audience interest levels. In a sense, this is closely related to the comprehension criterion, because an audience which fails to comprehend the development of arguments in a debate is likely to become disinterested in the debate. Few audiences can bear a full hour of uninterrupted debate. For this reason, consideration should be given to shortening the time limits of the format. The addition of cross-examination to the format is another way of adapting to audience interest levels. The direct give and take of cross-examination and the focusing that it permits adds elements of audience interest.

Finally, formats for public debate should permit advocate adaptation to specific audience attitudes and values. This is important because the whole reason behind placing students in audience debate situations is to remove them from the logical environment of academic debate to teach them how to deal with audiences who evaluate what they hear in terms of their own attitudes and values. While this goal can occasionally be accomplished by presurveying audience attitudes, such a mechanism is usually impractical. One way of guaranteeing audience input is to set aside a block of time within the debate for direct questions from the audience. This not only gives the advocates a chance to adapt to audience attitudes and values, but also adds an additional interest factor for the audience.

Below is outlined a sample format for use in audience debate situations. While this format is not presented as a standard audience format, it is useful in illustrating some of the changes in interscholastic formats which can be made to adapt to audience debate advocacy situations.

Sample Audience Debate Format

Affirmative Opening Statement	2 minutes
Negative Opening Statement	2 minutes
Affirmative Constructive Case	6– 8 minutes
Negative Cross-examination	2– 3 minutes
Negative Constructive Case	6– 8 minutes
Affirmative Cross-examination	2– 3 minutes
Audience Question Period	10–15 minutes
Affirmative Summary	3– 5 minutes
Negative Summary	3– 5 minutes

The format adapts to audience comprehension levels in several ways. The short opening statements permit the advocates to give the audience a summary of the case philosophy and structure before moving into detailed argument development. The shorter speeches, cross-examination, and audience question period also provide mechanisms for simplifying the debate and assisting audience comprehension.

The format adapts to audience interest levels in that it is a much faster moving format than interscholastic formats. With shorter time limits and the liveliness provided by the cross-examination periods, the debate will tend to be more interesting than a standard interscholastic debate. The fact that it is an individual format rather than a team format permits further simplification which contributes to both interest and audience comprehension.

Finally, the format gives advocates the opportunity to respond directly to audience attitudes and values. While the advocates may adapt to audience beliefs throughout the debate on the basis of prior knowledge about the audience, the direct question period adds an element of spontaneity which will test adaptation abilities.

The format above is only a sample of the many possible format alternatives available for audience debating. Half of the fun and half of the educational value of audience debating is designing formats to achieve specific situational objectives. The design of the audience debate format will provide the framework of procedures which determines the nature of the advocacy situation.

SUMMARY

The consideration of advocacy situations can be thought of as the bridge between inquiry and advocacy. This consideration is vital to the student of argumentation because the advocacy situation exerts a controlling influence over the advocate. Advocacy situations influence the advocate in that they frequently impose situational goals upon individual advocacy goals, they determine the location and extent of presumption and burden of proof, and they determine the amount and kinds of proof which he must present.

Advocacy situations may be thought of as existing on a continuum according to their goals, the nature of their procedures, and the nature of their audiences. At one end of the continuum are truth determination situations which are characterized by formal rules of procedure and highly specialized audiences. Included within this grouping are legal advocacy situations, academic debate, and parliamentary debate. In the middle of the continuum are information-seeking situations whose rules and procedures are less formal and whose audiences are generally less specialized than those of truth determination situations. This grouping includes audience-controlled forums and public debate. At the far end of the continuum are audience activation situations which are characterized by a lack of formal procedures and nonspecialized audiences. Mass persuasion, propaganda, and advertising are included within audience activation situations. Because there are no rules of procedure and because audiences are characteristically nonspecialized, the standards of argumentative inquiry are the least relevant at this end of the continuum.

Within educational debate training, students are most likely to encounter the advocacy situations of interscholastic debate and audience debate. The formats for interscholastic debate are designed for training students in logical rigor and are characterized by reasonably standardized procedures. Audience debate formats must be developed to respond to the uniqueness of the situation and to the specific educational objectives of the training program. Specifically, such formats must consider audience comprehension levels, audience interest levels, and audience beliefs.

STUDY QUESTIONS

1. What conditions might justify the classification of a committee hearing as closer to *truth determination* than information seeking?
2. Where would you place a "grand jury" on the continuum of advocacy situations?
3. Is the advocate's responsibility for conducting thorough inquiry reduced if he is preparing for advocacy in an "audience activation" situation?
4. Which of the two interscholastic debate formats outlined in this chapter do you think provides the better educational experience?

EXERCISES

1. Observe a public advocacy situation, either live or televised, and discuss the following elements of that situation:
   a. In what ways does the situational goal differ from the advocacy goals of the individual advocates?
   b. To what extent are the concepts of presumption and burden of proof relevant in this advocacy situation?
   c. What demands does this advocacy situation make in terms of the kinds of proof which the advocates must present?
   d. Where would you place this advocacy situation on the continuum outlined in this chapter? Justify your decision.
2. Observe an interscholastic debate and discuss the ways in which it falls short of the goal of truth determination.
3. Structure a format for a one-hour televised debate between two political candidates which would guarantee maximum application of the standards of reasoned inquiry. Do you think that contemporary politicians would agree to debate within this format?

11 Affirmative Approaches to Advocacy

The affirmative side of any controversy is composed of those people who support the change in policy or judgment recommended by the proposition. The affirmative side is obligated to present arguments sufficient to fulfill its burden of proof and, thus, to overcome the negative presumption. The affirmative seeks to accomplish this by providing positive responses to each of the issues.

The issues may be developed and related to one another in a number of different ways, but there are certain basic approaches which have become fairly standard. This chapter will present four basic affirmative approaches for policy propositions and two basic affirmative approaches for propositions of judgment. The identifying characteristics of each approach will be described, and the situations in which each approach would be most appropriate will be discussed.

These approaches are simply ways of developing detailed arguments into a coherent and logically adequate case. *A case may be thought of as a specific pattern of relationships used to support a proposition.* It should be noted that the formulation of a case requires the selection of certain arguments and the exclusion of others and the relating of the selected arguments in a particular way. This chapter will be concerned primarily with the logical aspects of case development. Chapter 13 will consider the strategic factors which influence case construction and presentation.

In most advocacy situations, all of the details of a case are not presented at one time. In courts of law, the prosecution or the plaintiff will typically begin a trial with an opening statement which provides a broad outline of the case which it intends to present. In the days and weeks which follow, the details of the case will be developed. In legislative debates the case in support of a bill may be worked out in a number of formal planning sessions attended by the major advocates of the bill. A prominent member of the legislative body may be selected to present an opening statement in support of the bill, and the order of speaking by other advocates and the content of their speeches may also be planned in advance. Thus, several speeches may be required before a case for a legislative bill becomes fully apparent. In academic debate, the broad outline of the affirmative case is usually presented in the first affirmative speech and additional support and refinement of the case emerge in later speeches. Even in extended public debates over national issues, careful attention is often given to the formulation of appropriate case analyses and the presentation of effective public education campaigns.

AFFIRMATIVE APPROACHES
TO POLICY QUESTIONS

The four basic approaches which may be used in developing affirmative cases for policy propositions are: (1) the traditional case, (2) the comparative advantages case, (3) the effect-oriented case, and (4) the on-balance case. These four case approaches differ from one another in terms of their levels of analysis and/or in terms of the ways in which stock issue concepts are related.

No matter which one of the four approaches an affirmative advocate uses, he is obligated to address himself—or at least, be prepared to address himself—to each of the concepts suggested by the stock issues. He must be prepared to show a significant past, present, or future problem or harm as suggested by the ill issue. He must be able to causally relate that ill to the basic philosophy of the present system as suggested by the blame issue or inherency concept. He must be prepared to outline a specific plan and demonstrate how it would solve the problem of the ill as required by the cure issue. And he must be prepared to respond to disadvantages to his proposal as indicated by the cost issue. These basic logical requirements are in no way circumvented by any of the four basic approaches.

THE TRADITIONAL CASE

The traditional approach to case analysis begins with the identification of the stated or implied goal of the proposition. Once this goal has been determined, each of the stock issues is developed in accordance with it. The analysis of the traditional case therefore occurs at the level of the proposition's goal. The ill issue of the traditional case is a direct outgrowth of the failure to achieve the suggested goal of the proposition. The existence of ills or harms is an indication both that the goal of the proposition has not been achieved and that its attainment is warranted. The blame issue argues that the basic philosophy of the present system is the *cause* of the ill, or the reason why the goal of the proposition has not been accomplished. The cure issue offers a plan based upon philosophical and structural principles consistent with the proposition but different from those of existing policies. The plan, it is claimed, will remove the cause (the philosophy of present policies) of the harms and, thus, remove the harms and accomplish the goal of the proposition.

Affirmative advocates of compulsory health insurance typically develop their arguments in accordance with the traditional approach. They generally identify the goal of compulsory health insurance to be the provision of adequate medical care to all citizens without severe economic hardship. In order to justify this goal, the ill issue is developed to demonstrate that many people receive inadequate medical care as shown by delayed treatment, incomplete treatment, and the denial of treatment. Even when treatment is received, it is claimed, the expenses incurred from a prolonged illness erode savings, create severe indebtedness, and lead to bankruptcy. Thus, the ills flow directly from the goal of the proposition. The blame issue argues that the goal of the proposition cannot be achieved through existing programs of voluntary health insurance and government assistance. Advocates of compulsory health insurance claim that the private, competitive nature of voluntary insurance means that increased insurance coverage must be reflected in higher prices. Therefore, under voluntary health insurance those who most need comprehensive protection are those who are least able to afford it. Government assistance programs, under a system of private medicine, must be limited to those in real need so that a person must first suffer severe economic hardship before he can receive government aid. As a substitute for the private, noncomprehensive, restrictive policies of the present system, advocates of compulsory health insurance offer a cure based upon the contrary philosophical concepts of public policy, comprehensiveness, and universality. By eliminating the alleged causes (the private, noncomprehensive, and restrictive nature of present programs) of the ills (inadequate care and economic hardship), compulsory health insurance would presumably eliminate the ills and achieve the goal of the proposition (adequate medical care without economic hardship).

Not all resolutions lend themselves to development according to the traditional approach. Two conditions must exist before a traditional case can be formulated: (1) the goal of the proposition must be thwarted by the principles of the present system and (2) both the ill and the cause of the ill must be capable of being eliminated by the affirmative plan. The traditional approach is thought of as the most fundamental framework for case analysis because it is based upon a single level of goal analysis and because its causal links are direct.

THE COMPARATIVE ADVANTAGES CASE

The comparative advantages case requires the determination of a secondary level of goals and the establishment of all its causal links on this secondary level. This approach to case analysis should be used when *both* the present system and the affirmative proposal are capable of achieving the primary goal of the proposition or when *neither* the present system nor the affirmative proposal are fully capable of achieving the primary goal of the proposition.

When differences do not exist at the primary goal level, then subordinate criteria must be applied in order to evaluate the two systems. These secondary goals (values, criteria) may be special qualitative factors such as speed, efficiency, fairness, or flexibility, or they may involve the application of such quantitative measures as more or less.

To develop a case based upon the comparative advantages approach, an advocate begins by selecting subgoals appropriate to the situation. The wording of his arguments should clearly reveal what those secondary goals are. The ill issue is established at the subgoal level so that the harms cited justify the subgoals rather than the primary goal of the proposition. The blame issue is also developed at the level of the subordinate goals. The principles of present policies are shown to be responsible for the harms and the reason why the subgoals have not been met. The cure issue establishes that the affirmative plan will remove the harms and establish the subgoals by eliminating the cause of the harms (the principles of the present system) and by substituting a new plan based upon the principles of the resolution.

Many city councils have recently been considering proposals to require citizens to separate their trash into different categories—newspapers, glass, cans, etc.—so that some of it can be recycled for future use. The advocates of such proposals are not concerned with the primary goal of sanitation work, that is, the removal of unwanted materials. They concede that existing systems of trash pick-up achieve this primary objective, but their concern is with such secondary objectives as the conservation of resources and the production of additional revenue. To justify a new system of trash collection, the advocates of the new system attempt to demonstrate that the failure to conserve our resources will result in future shortages (ill of the first subgoal) and that the failure to find new sources of revenue will result in less governmental services (ill of the second subgoal). The blame analysis rests on the charge that to attempt to separate the trash after its collection would be structurally impractical due to the amount of time and number of men required. The cure issue suggests that the structural impracticality of the present system is removed by having private citizens separate their own trash, and thus, the benefits of conservation and revenue production can be realized.

In the preceding illustration, *both* the conventional system of trash collection and the proposed system of trash separation could accomplish the primary goal of waste removal. A former intercollegiate debate proposition illustrates a situation in which *neither* the present system nor the affirmative proposal could fully achieve the primary goal. When college debaters argued the proposition that "law enforcement agencies should be given greater freedom in the investigation and prosecution of crime," neither side could claim that their system would fully meet the implied goal of the successful prosecution of all criminals. Affirmative debaters, therefore, offered secondary criteria as a basis for comparing the two systems. Frequently, quantitative goals such as "greater effectiveness" were selected. The ills of not having greater effectiveness were identified as rising crime rates, more violent deaths, and increasing property losses. Restrictive Supreme

Court decisions in the areas of interrogation, search and seizure, or wiretapping were blamed for the increased ills. The removal of these restrictions through the affirmative plan was suggested as the cure and the means of achieving the goal of "greater effectiveness."

THE EFFECT-ORIENTED CASE

The effect-oriented case eliminates the ills of the present system without removing the philosophical or structural cause of those ills. It treats symptoms or effects rather than causes. The effect-oriented approach should be used whenever the analysis of a proposition suggests that it would be impossible or undesirable to eliminate the basic cause of the ill.[1]

The ill and blame analysis of an effect-oriented case may be developed in terms of either a traditional or a comparative advantages approach. That is, its ill and blame analysis may occur at either the primary or secondary goal levels. The ill issue must demonstrate that because either the primary goal of the proposition or certain secondary goals have not been realized, significant harms exist. The blame issue must establish that the underlying philosophy of present programs is the inherent cause of the harms and the reason why the goals have not been met. The cure issue differs from that of earlier cases in that it does not change the philosophy of the present system (does not remove the cause of the harms). Rather, it offers a plan which, though different in principle from the present system, is capable of operating within the framework of the present system's philosophy. The affirmative plan alleviates the ills of the present system while, at the same time, permitting the cause of that ill (the philosophy of the present system) to continue.

An effect-oriented analysis was used by some intercollegiate debaters to justify a guaranteed annual income. These debaters identified the elimination of poverty as the goal of the resolution, and they described the starvation and poor health of poverty as manifestations of an ill. The cause of these continued ills was identified as the present system's philosophical assumption that a free market economy can provide an adequate job for all of those willing, able, and trained to work. By pointing out that factors such as age, geography, and changing technology make it impossible in an unplanned economy to guarantee that the right kinds of jobs will occur in the right places at the

[1]Cases built on so-called *attitudinal inherency* arguments should utilize the effect-oriented approach. Attitudinal inherency arguments identify an unchanging attitude as the cause (blame) of the ill. Since the attitude is allegedly inherent, it cannot be removed and must be circumvented.

right times, the affirmative developed its blame issue and attempted to demonstrate the inadequacy of the present system's assumption. In this way, the free market system was indicted as the cause of poverty. The affirmative presented its cure issue by offering a plan which guaranteed enough money to everyone to keep them from suffering the hardships of illness and starvation but which did not restructure the economic system of job creation. Thus, the affirmative plan only alleviated the ill of the present system (starvation and ill health) while permitting the cause of those ills (the free market economy) to continue. The affirmative chose this approach to case analysis because they believed that while the free market economy had been harmful to a specific segment of society, its overall effects upon society were beneficial.

THE ON-BALANCE CASE

The chief characteristic of the on-balance approach is its use of the cost issue as part of the affirmative's constructive warrant for change. None of the three preceding approaches to case analysis called for the presentation of the cost issue as part of the affirmative's constructive case. While affirmative teams using the earlier approaches are required to respond to cost arguments raised by the negative, they are not expected to develop the cost issue as a major part of their rationale for change. The on-balance approach is an appropriate one to use whenever the harms of the ill issue need to be maximized. Maximization may be necessary when the harms are abstract or difficult to quantify, when the harms are chance happenings rather than universal occurrences, or when the harms are future prospects rather than immediate realities.

The on-balance approach attempts to maximize the seriousness of the ill issue by comparing it to the minimum cost (slight disadvantage) of adopting the affirmative proposal. The cost issue is developed by demonstrating that present policies are either unnecessary or ineffective. Affirmatives using the on-balance approach may claim that present policies are unnecessary because the alleged benefits of them could be achieved in other ways. They may argue that present policies are ineffective because they have not achieved and cannot achieve the alleged benefits attributed to them. If, in this way, the cost of abandoning present policies can be shown to be nil, then even a relatively small or abstract ill may be sufficient reason for changing policies.

In general, the ill, blame, and cure issues of the on-balance case are developed according to either the traditional or the comparative advantages approach. If the harms of the ill issue are derived from the primary goal of the proposition, then the traditional approach would be used. If the harms result from the failure to meet secondary goals, then the comparative advantages approach would be used. It should be noted that if the harm is concerned with a chance (nonuniversal) happening, the causal link of the blame issue must be between the *unpredictable risk* of the harm and the principles of the present system rather than between the harm, itself, and the principles of the present system.

The on-balance approach has been utilized by most of those foreign policy experts who have opposed the U.S. policy of military intervention in the internal conflicts of other countries. The fundamental thesis of these experts is that, on balance, the costs of such interventions have outweighed any possible gains. They contend that the basic harm of our interventionist policy is the waste of men and resources. Every intervention is said to require some outlay of money which could be better spent on more constructive policies. Moreover, it is claimed that every intervention involves some risk to human lives and that certain interventions—notably Vietnam—have in fact resulted in the loss of many lives. The policy of intervention is inherently blamed for these ills. By its nature intervention requires the movement of men and supplies, and the movement cannot be accomplished without the expenditure of money. Every intervention is said to involve the risk of some loss of life since it is impossible to predict the exact nature and extent of the opposition's response to our military action. Balanced against these inherent harms are the allegedly minimal benefits of military intervention. The opponents of U.S. interventionist policies develop the cost issue by contending that military interventions are either unnecessary or ineffective. It is claimed that military intervention is unnecessary to stop the spread of communism because where there is a strong spirit of nationalism, communism cannot succeed. Where there is not a strong spirit of nationalism, it is contended, U.S. intervention will be ineffective. Thus, on balance, the potential harms of intervention are said to counterbalance any possible benefits.

AFFIRMATIVE APPROACHES
TO PROPOSITIONS OF JUDGMENT

There are two basic approaches which may be used in developing affirmative cases for propositions of judgment. They are: (1) the criteria establishment case and (2) the criteria application case. These two cases differ from one another in terms of the emphasis which they give to the definitional and existence frames of analysis. No matter which approach an affirmative advocate chooses, he is obligated to consider all of the relevant circumstances and to attempt to interpret them in light of the appropriate conceptual constructs.

THE CRITERIA ESTABLISHMENT CASE

The criteria establishment approach to case development considers the analytical frame of definition or criteria independently from the circumstances of the particular situation (the frame of existence of fact). This approach to developing cases for propositions of judgment should be used when the criteria to be applied are not commonly understood or when the criteria are not likely to be readily accepted.

The criteria establishment case begins with the setting forth of the criteria or definition. The nature of the criteria is described, and the relevance of those criteria to the nature of the judgment expressed in the proposition is justified. This justification may rest upon the expert opinion of an authoritative individual or group, or it may be based upon a comparison with related situations. After the nature and relevance of the criteria have been explained, the facts of the specific circumstances under consideration are examined in light of the criteria. The affirmative application of the criteria to the situation is, of course, done in such a way as to justify the acceptance of the resolution. In those circumstances where the criteria establishment case is used, the justification of the criteria usually becomes the focus of the controversy, and the application step may receive only minor consideration.

The criteria establishment approach was used by the lawyers for the plaintiff in the famous Supreme Court case of *Brown* v. *Topeka Board of Education.* This was the case which challenged the previously established doctrine that separate facilities for black students could provide equal educational opportunities. The specific charge against the Topeka Board of Education was that they had denied the constitutional rights of a black child by denying him the right to attend a school with white children. In order to establish that the black child's constitutional rights had been violated, the representatives for the plaintiff defined equal facilities as being the *same* facilities. The criterion of sameness was justified by expert testimony and sociological and psychological data which indicated that separate facilities were not equal in terms of their sociological and psychological environment and effects. Once this criterion was established the application of that criterion to the separate but similar practices of the Topeka Board of Education made it possible to establish the claim that Brown's constitutional rights had, indeed, been denied.

THE CRITERIA APPLICATION CASE

Whereas the criteria establishment approach emphasizes the *definitional or criteria frame of analysis,* the criteria application approach emphasizes the *existence of fact frame of analysis.* Cases built on this approach do not consider the criteria separately; nor do they offer much by way of justification for the criteria. With this approach the focus of concern is upon the application of the criteria to the facts of the particular situation. This approach to case development should be used when the criteria or definitions are commonly accepted ones and are not likely to be challenged.

The criteria application case does not begin with an explanation of the relevance of the criteria. Rather, it assumes that the criteria or elements of the definition are relevant and begins immediately to demonstrate that the facts of the situation conform to the criteria. The criteria are the substances whose existence must be established, and the facts of the situation are used as signs or attributes of those substances. Thus, the basic form of argument used in developing the criteria application case is the argument from sign.

The criteria application approach is used in most ordinary criminal cases. The nature of such crimes as larceny, armed robbery, and manslaughter have been fairly well defined by legislative acts and common law so that the criteria to be applied in such cases are well understood and accepted. In a first-degree murder case, for example, the prosecutor knows, based upon past experience, that he must be able to demonstrate that four criteria or conditions have been met in order to establish his case. He must prove: (1) that someone has died at the hands of another person, (2) that the defendant was responsible for the victim's loss of life, (3) that the defendant intended to kill the victim, and (4) that the defendant planned in advance to commit the murder. Since the criteria for first-degree murder are so clearly understood, the prosecution in a court case would not need to be particularly concerned with justifying the criteria or defining the specific nature of the charge. Instead, he would be expected to proceed immediately with the consideration of evidence and testimony in support of the fact that the criteria had been met. The fact that someone had died at the hands of another person might be established by a coroner's statement. The statement would indicate that the victim was dead and that there were no powder marks around the bullet hole (as would be the case if the victim shot himself). Using similar types of testimony and sign evidence, the prosecution could demonstrate each of the other issues.

SUMMARY

There are four standard approaches which affirmatives use in developing cases for policy proposition. They are (1) the traditional case, (2) the comparative advantages case, (3) the effect-oriented case, and (4) the on-balance case. No matter which of these approaches an advocate uses he is obligated to consider each of the concepts suggested by the stock issues.

The traditional case identifies the stated or implied goal of the proposition and develops each of the stock issues at that level. A traditional analysis can be used only when the goal of the proposition is thwarted by the principles of the present system and when both the ill and the cause of the ill can be removed by the affirmative proposal.

The comparative advantages case requires the identification of a secondary level of goals and the establishment of all of the stock issue concepts on the secondary level. A comparative advantages analysis should be used when *both* the present system and the affirmative proposal can accomplish the primary goal of the resolution or when *neither* can achieve the primary goal.

The effect-oriented case eliminates the ills of the present system without removing the inherent cause of those ills. It treats effects rather than causes. This approach should be used whenever it is impossible or undesirable to eliminate the basic cause of the ill.

The on-balance approach seeks to maximize the ill issue by comparing it to the minimal disadvantages of the cost issue. Maximization of the ill may be necessary when the harms are abstract or difficult to quantify, when the harms are chance happenings rather than universal experiences, or when the harms are future prospects.

Two basic approaches which may be used in formulating cases for propositions of judgment are (1) the criteria establishment case and (2) the criteria application case. Both case approaches require the advocate to consider all of the relevant circumstances and to interpret them in light of appropriate constructs.

The criteria establishment case considers the analytical frame of definition independently from the facts of the particular situation. It places emphasis on the explanation and justification of criteria. This approach should be used when the criteria to be used are not likely to be readily accepted.

The criteria application case does not consider the criteria separately from the existence of fact. It focuses concern upon the application of the criteria to the facts of the particular situation. The approach should be used when the criteria or definitions are commonly accepted ones and not likely to be challenged.

STUDY QUESTIONS

1. Some people argue that the use of a comparative advantages case reduces the affirmative's burden of proof. Do you agree?
2. In which of the stock issues frames of analysis is the effect-oriented case most different from the traditional case and the comparative advantages case?
3. Does the use of an on-balance case reduce the affirmative's burden to demonstrate that significant problems or harms exist within the present system?
4. What criteria can be used to determine whether to use a criteria establishment or a criteria application case for a proposition of judgment?

EXERCISES

1. Develop brief case outlines for each of the affirmative approaches discussed in this chapter. In each instance, select a topic which is appropriate to the type of approach to be developed.
2. Study speeches of affirmative advocacy from such sources as *Vital Speeches*, the *New York Times*, or *Representative American Speeches*. Identify the types of affirmative approaches the speakers used.
3. Listen to an academic debate and try to determine which case approach is being used by the affirmative. After the debate discuss the affirmative's approach with the team members and find out why they selected the approach they used.

12 Negative Approaches to Advocacy

The negative side of a controversy is that side which opposes the specific resolution, motion, or question. This chapter will focus on the nature of negative advocacy and will describe four approaches which negative advocates can use in opposing policy questions and two approaches which may be used to oppose propositions of judgment. Each of these approaches will be described, and an example of how each approach has been applied will be presented.

The nature of negative advocacy differs from that of affirmative advocacy in two important ways. First, the negative has the logical advantage of presumption as long as it does not advocate any alternative other than present policies or judgments. If the negative wins a single issue in the controversy, it has logically defeated the resolution. Unlike the affirmative, then, the negative is not logically bound to clash on all potential issues. While a strong negative advocate is prepared to clash in all potential areas of affirmative weakness, the application of the concepts of presumption and burden of proof permits opponents of change greater flexibility in choosing areas of clash.

Second, negative advocacy, almost by definition, is argumentation in response to an attack. Before a negative advocate can decide which specific lines of argument will be appropriate in a given situation, he must wait until an affirmative rationale or proposal has been presented. He can, however, determine in advance the general philosophical position which he will take in responding to affirmative arguments and work out a variety of possible arguments consistent with that position. In this context, therefore, negative approaches to advocacy should not be thought of as specific types of cases in the sense that affirmative approaches are. Rather, the concept of negative approaches to advocacy describes certain philosophical positions which condition the general nature of negative responses to affirmative cases.

NEGATIVE APPROACHES TO POLICY QUESTIONS

The four basic philosophical positions from which negatives may argue propositions of policy are: (1) defense of the status quo, (2) repair of the status quo, (3) straight refutation, and (4) counterproposal. These four approaches differ primarily in terms of their degree of commitment to present policies. All of these approaches may be used in opposition to any of the four affirmative policy approaches. All of them permit the negative to advance arguments under each of the stock issues, although the demands of particular advocacy situations may not require that certain issues actually be presented.

DEFENSE OF THE STATUS QUO

The defense of the status quo (or present system) approach provides the greatest philosophical commitment to present policies. This position supports both the *principles* and the *implementation* of present policies. Advocates who assume the defense of the status quo approach do not necessarily believe that present policies are the wisest and best imaginable. They do believe, however, that they are the wisest and best *possible* in light of total circumstances. The defense of the status quo should be used whenever existing policies can be shown to have met with considerable success and when alleged failures can either be denied or be shown to be temporary or unavoidable.

The defense of the status quo approach was used by many negative debate teams who argued against the withdrawal of U.S. military forces from Western Europe. In presenting the ill and blame analysis in favor of U.S. withdrawal, affirmative teams often argued that the continued presence of large U.S. military forces in Western Europe encouraged communist hostility and prevented the evolution of more harmonious East-West relations. Negative teams responded to this by denying both that harmonious relations were desirable (ill issue) and that the lack of better relations was caused by U.S. military presence (blame issue). Harmonious relations were said to be undesirable because communists view harmonious relations, not as an end in itself, but as a means of lulling the West into a false sense of security. Negatives denied that U.S. forces were the cause of poor relations. Instead, they contended that it was the communists' ideological commitment to the destruction of democratic capitalism which was the real cause. The cure issue argued that U.S. military withdrawal would not be sufficient to result in improved relations because of such other sources of antagonism as U.S.-Russian conflict of interest in Southeast Asia. The cost issue served to justify the existing policy by pointing out advantages which would be lost by U.S. withdrawal. It was argued, for example, that the U.S. presence in Europe encouraged neutral nations such as Finland and Yugoslavia to keep out of the Russian sphere of influence and that U.S. withdrawal would cause them to fall under Russian domination.

Where it can be used, the defense of the status quo approach is a strong one because it places the negative in the position of upholding a concrete policy. It is a positive approach which stands *for* something. And since both the principles and the implementation of present policies are defended, the distinction between the affirmative and the negative is sharp and clear.

REPAIR OF THE STATUS QUO

The repair of the status quo approach involves an unqualified commitment to the *fundamental principles or basic structure* of present policies, but it recognizes that the *implementation* of those principles can be improved. Advocates who use the repair position support minor administrative or mechanistic changes but oppose fundamental changes. In order to decide if a change in policy is minor or fundamental the nature of the present system must be examined in light of the proposed change of the affirmative. A repair, to be legitimate, must be different from the philosophical principle of the affirmative resolution and consistent with the essential features of the status quo. As a general rule, negative advocates tend to limit to some minimum the number and extent of repairs which they will offer, since the support of sweeping repairs may have the psychological (if not the logical) effect of compromising present principles. The repairs approach should be used when the harms of the ill issue cannot be denied but can be minimized and when the cause of those minor harms can be shown to be not inherent and, thus, repairable.

Opponents of compulsory health insurance have generally assumed the repairs position. They accept the existing philosophy of private financing and control of medical care supplemented by limited government programs, but they also recognize that the implementation of this mixed philosophy requires improvement through repairs. When supporters of compulsory health insurance have pointed to delayed care, incomplete care, and denied care as harms of the present system, opponents have generally sought to minimize the argument. In order to do this, they have referred to the overall trend towards improved care and have contended that if a person truly seeks needed care it will not be denied him. A variety of repairs have been suggested by opponents to compulsory health insurance in response to its advocates' blame analysis that under voluntary health insurance broader coverage results in higher premiums and that under limited government programs some needy will always be excluded. In 1971, for example, President Nixon offered three major repairs to the existing system in answer to such criticisms. He proposed that the federal government (1) offer legal and financial support to assist in the establishment of more Health Maintenance Organizations, (2) establish federal standards to assure more adequate coverage under voluntary health insurance and require all employers to provide insurance equal to those standards, and (3) establish a new family health insurance plan for the low-income self-employed and the unemployed. While these repairs involve considerable changes in the operation of the present system, they are all consistent with the philosophy of private financing supplemented by limited government assistance. In developing the cure issue, opponents of compulsory health insurance often argue that the proposal could not significantly improve health standards because fear and ignorance would still keep many people from seeking medical attention. The primary cost arguments raised against compulsory health insurance generally assert that the quality of care would deteriorate under a government system and that the dollar costs would be uncontrollable.

The repair position is a realistic one in that it recognizes the possibility for improvement within the system. In offering repairs, however, it is necessary to be careful not to suggest changes which are inconsistent with the cost arguments.

STRAIGHT REFUTATION

Advocates who assume the position of straight refutation make no real commitment to either the *principles* or the *mechanisms* of the present system. Any preference shown to the present system is based solely upon its existence and not upon any belief in its adequacy. The straight refutation position allows the negative to respond to the claims of the affirmative without assuming the responsibility for defending any alternate proposal or policy. Affirmative arguments are responded to in many different ways and extreme concern for consistency is often ignored. In effect, those who argue from this position are saying that they don't know what should be done, but they do know that the affirmative analysis is unsatisfactory.

The straight refutation position is useful when an advocate has not had an adequate opportunity to analyze the fundamental rationale for present policies or to formulate alternate proposals of his own. This position allows him to oppose a specific proposal for change without committing himself to any alternative.

Many of those who have opposed the legalization of marijuana have argued from the position of straight refutation. Rather than defending existing marijuana laws, these opponents of change have attacked the adequacy and significance of the legalizers' charges. They have taken the position of straight refutation by attacking the scientific accuracy of those affirmative studies which suggest only limited dangers from the use of marijuana. They have sought to minimize the significance of the loss of free choice to the marijuana user and have attempted to deny the need for anyone being subjected to severe criminal penalties. In general, they have argued that more time and more study are needed before any changes can be instituted.

The pure negativism of the straight refutation approach tends to make it a logically unsatisfactory and emotionally unappealing posture. Ultimately, problems require solutions, and those whom we seek to persuade may come to feel that even a bad solution is preferable to doing nothing. Nevertheless, the straight refutation approach may be the only honest option open to some advocates during the early stages of a controversy when they have not yet formulated a clear stand on a resolution. The straight refutation position is most appropriate as a means of delaying action in the hope that better solutions will be forthcoming.

COUNTERPROPOSAL

The counterplan negative rejects any philosophical commitment to present policies. This position admits that the present system has created serious problems which it cannot alleviate. In response to these inherent problems, the counterplan negative offers a solution which is philosophically and structurally different from *both* the present system *and* the affirmative proposal. The counterproposal is distinct from negative repairs in that it is neither a part of the present system nor is it philosophically compatible with the present system. The counterproposal is distinct from the affirmative in that it is not included within the affirmative resolution nor is it philosophically consistent with the affirmative proposition. Thus, the counterproposal negative becomes an advocate for a different kind of change rather than a defender of the status quo. Debaters who assume the obligations of a counterproposal may minimize certain of the ills cited by the affirmative or they may challenge the affirmative on the cause of the ills, but normally the cure and cost issues become the central areas of clash between affirmatives and counterplan negatives.

The counterproposal should be used when an advocate feels that there is a third approach which is better than either the present system or the affirmative proposal. The counterproposal position recognizes that our policy options are open-ended.

In the public controversy over U.S. policies in Vietnam the government's stand for military stalemate and a negotiated settlement constituted the status quo position. The major opposition to this position came from those who favored a nonnegotiated, massive, and relatively immediate U.S. withdrawal from Vietnam. Since most of the debate over U.S. policies centered on this option, the withdrawal proposals could be thought of as the primary affirmative position in the controversy. A third, less frequently considered, policy option was presented by those on the political right. This proposal called for the use of unrestrained military effort to win the war in Vietnam. This proposal was fundamentally different from existing policies since it rejected the principles of military stalemate and negotiated settlement. It was also fundamentally different from the proposals for withdrawal since it was antagonistic to the principles of immediate and massive withdrawal. The win the war position, therefore, constituted a counterproposal within this controversy.

The defenders of the win-the-war counterplan generally agreed with the ill and blame analysis of the advocates of withdrawal. Supporters of both positions believed that the policy of stalemate was responsible for excessive waste of lives and resources and for increased social division within American society. However, the win-the-war negatives charged that withdrawal would not permanently remove the ills and that the disadvantages of withdrawal outweighed any gains. They claimed that withdrawal would encourage more communist aggression and ultimately lead to the loss of even more U.S. lives and resources. On the other hand, they asserted that an all-out military effort would end the war quickly and victoriously and would discourage future aggression. They also charged that withdrawal would result in the slaughter of all those Vietnamese who had supported the United States, would encourage smaller nations to come within the communist sphere of influence, and would force medium-sized powers to develop independent nuclear forces. In this controversy, as in most debates between affirmatives and counterplan negatives, the clash largely revolved around the advantages and disadvantages of the two plans rather than around present policies.

Those negatives who assume the counterproposal approach abandon the logical advantage of presumption and assume a burden of proof equal to, but distinct from, the affirmative's burden of proof. Since the counterplan negative does not wish to see the status quo continue, it opposes presumption. Since it favors a new policy, it assumes an obligation to prove the overall desirability of that proposal.

As a general rule, those proposals which become the center of public controversy (affirmative resolutions) assume this stature because they involve acceptable and viable principles. To discover alternate policies which involve still different and equally acceptable and viable principles is often difficult. It is for this reason that good counterproposals are rare.

NEGATIVE APPROACHES
TO PROPOSITIONS OF JUDGMENT

There are two basic philosophical positions from which negatives may argue propositions of judgment. They are: (1) denial and (2) extenuating circumstances. These two approaches differ in terms of the degree of their acceptance of the affirmative analysis. Both approaches may be used against either of the affirmative approaches to propositions of judgment.

DENIAL

The denial position requires the negative to clash directly with the crucial criteria and facts upon which the affirmative case rests. This approach thus rejects the affirmative judgment as being in some way faulty. The use of the denial approach does not imply that the affirmative is lying or deliberately misrepresenting the situation. In most instances, negatives take this position because they believe that the affirmative has misanalyzed the appropriate criteria, overlooked important facts, given too much significance to certain facts, or, in other ways, drawn unwarranted conclusions from available data.

The denial approach was used by the defense lawyers for a well-known professional football player who was charged with drunken driving. The prosecution attempted to establish that the defendant was drunk by demonstrating that he had spent several hours drinking in a bar. The defense lawyer denied that drinking in a bar over a period of several hours was sufficient evidence to prove that the defendant was legally drunk (a technical matter involving a specific percentage of alcohol in the blood). The defense offered several witnesses who testified that the defendant had consumed only one glass of beer during his three hours in the bar, and it presented evidence which indicated that the alcohol content of the blood from one glass of beer would not, after three hours, be sufficient to meet that state's criteria of drunkenness. In this case the defense lawyer accepted the prosecution's criteria but denied that the factual situation conformed to those criteria.

In other cases, negative advocates may accept the factual description but deny the appropriateness of the criteria. Defense lawyers in antitrust cases, for example, often reject the government lawyers' concept of monopoly. They do this by citing various authorities from the fields of law and economics, by reference to previous court decisions, or by applying the state's definition to other situations to show its unreasonableness.

The denial approach is a strong one because it can lead to total rejection of the affirmative judgment. Only, however, when the facts of the situation or the misunderstanding of criteria warrant its use should this approach be used. Ethical advocates will avoid any temptation to distort the situation or criteria in order to maintain an unjustified denial.

EXTENUATING CIRCUMSTANCES

The extenuating circumstances position is based upon a tacit acceptance of the affirmative's criteria and description of facts. This position does not reject the affirmative's analysis as false; rather, it suggests that the affirmative's judgment is based upon a *limited perspective.* The extenuating circumstances position argues that there are unusual factors operating within the total situation which ought to be considered. If these extraordinary elements are accepted as relevant, the judgment in question must be tempered or changed.

In 1970 the U.S. Army brought charges against a number of American combat soldiers for allegedly having taken part in the mass murder of hundreds of South Vietnamese civilians. Although the details of each case varied, the lawyers for most of the defendants based their defense efforts on extenuating circumstances rather than on denial. They attempted to show that the defendants were either acting on orders from above or were suffering from extreme fatigue and severe emotional strain. Awareness of these factors did not, of course, alter past events, but they did help to explain them and temper the court's judgment of the men.

Thus, the goal of the extenuating circumstances position is not absolute rejection of the affirmative judgment but modification of it, and its method does not require direct clash but only the weighing of additional information.

SUMMARY

The negative side of a controversy is that side which opposes the specific resolution, motion, or question. The nature of negative advocacy differs from that of affirmative advocacy in two ways. First, the negative has the logical advantage of presumption as long as it does not advocate any alternative other than present policies or judgments. Second, negative advocacy is argumentation in response to an attack.

There are four basic philosophical positions from which negatives may argue propositions of policy. The *defense of the status quo* approach provides the greatest philosophical commitment to present policies by supporting both the principles and implementation of those policies. It should be used whenever existing policies can be shown to have met with considerable success and when alleged failures can either be denied or be shown to be temporary or unavoidable. The *repair of the status quo* approach involves an unqualified commitment to the fundamental principles or basic structure of present policies but recognizes that the implementation of those principles can be improved. It should be used when the harms of the ill issue cannot be denied but can be minimized and when the cause of those minor harms can be shown to be not inherent and, thus, repairable. The *straight refutation* approach makes no real commitment to either the principles or the mechanisms of the present system; it allows the negative to respond to the claims of the affirmative without assuming the responsibility for defending any alternate proposal or policy. It is most useful when an advocate has not had an adequate opportunity to analyze the fundamental rationale for present policies or to formulate alternate proposals of his own. The *counterproposal* approach rejects any philosophical commitment to present policies and presents a solution which is philosophically and structurally different from both the present system and the affirmative proposal. It should be used when an advocate feels that there is a third approach which is better than either the present system or the affirmative proposal.

There are two basic philosophical positions from which negatives may argue propositions of judgment. The *denial* position requires the negative to clash directly with the crucial criteria and facts upon which the affirmative case rests. This position should be used when the advocate believes that the affirmative has misanalyzed the appropriate criteria, overlooked important facts, given too much significance to certain facts, or, in other ways, drawn unwarranted conclusions from available data. The *extenuating circumstances* position is based upon a tacit acceptance of the affirmative's criteria and description of facts. It suggests, however, that the affirmative's judgment is based upon a limited perspective. It should be used when there are unusual factors operating within the total situation which ought to be considered.

STUDY QUESTIONS

1. When a negative adopts the "repair of the status quo" approach as opposed to the "defense of the status quo" approach, is the affirmative's burden of proof altered?
2. Why must a legitimate repair be different from the philosophical principle of the affirmative resolution and consistent with the essential features of the status quo?
3. Why is the "straight refutation" approach frequently logically unsatisfactory and emotionally unappealing?
4. Why does a negative lose the advantage of presumption when utilizing a counterproposal approach?
5. Is the "extenuating circumstances" approach logically weaker than the "denial" approach to propositions of judgment?

EXERCISES

1. Examine the newspaper accounts of two or three recent court cases and characterize the approaches taken by the defense. What factors led the lawyers to select the approaches they used?
2. Trace the account of a recent policy controversy in any of the weekly news magazines. What approach did the opponents to the policy change take? Why was this approach selected?
3. Utilizing propositions of your own choice, sketch out negative cases for each of the suggested approaches.

13 Strategic Considerations in Presentation

The two preceding chapters have described the various ways in which affirmative and negative advocates may develop the elements of their analysis into logically adequate cases. This chapter will explain how the circumstances of particular persuasive situations may influence the actual presentation of that analysis.

How much of the analysis to present at a given moment, how to make the analysis most appealing to a specific audience, how best to minimize the impact of opposing arguments—these are all factors which an advocate must consider before presenting his arguments to an audience. In this chapter the problems of presenting an analysis to a specific audience will be discussed in terms of the concept of communication strategies. The nature of communication strategies will be analyzed, and several types of strategies will be described.

THE NATURE OF COMMUNICATION STRATEGIES

Communication strategies are broad plans which determine how an advocate will adapt the presentation of his analysis to the constraints and opportunities of a particular communication situation; their aim is to heighten the persuasive impact of the analysis through alterations in perception and/or emphasis. An examination of this definition suggests that there are five primary elements to the concept.

First, *communication strategies are broad plans.* They involve overall rhetorical choices. They are concerned with how major constraints should be dealt with and how fundamental issues should be developed. The concept of strategies is not concerned with specific ways of refuting individual arguments except to the extent that the refutation of an individual argument is part of a larger strategic consideration.

Second, *communication strategies determine how an advocate will adapt the presentation of his analysis. Adapt* and *presentation* are the critical terms here. The development of an appropriate strategy does not require an advocate to abandon or alter his basic logical analysis of a proposition. What a strategy does require is that he alter, in some way, his *presentation* of that analysis. Without changing his overall position on the issues, the advocate must decide how thoroughly to develop each issue, which arguments to select in support of those issues, what order of presentation to use, and so on. The use of communication strategies ought not to imply the compromise of ethical principles or logical obligations. Rather, communication strategies simply recognize the fact that the same logical position may be articulated in various ways.

Third, *communication strategies call for adaptation to the constraints and opportunities of a particular communication situation.* In determining how to adapt his case analysis for presentation, the advocate must examine the total circumstances of his immediate communication situation. The anticipated attitudes of the specific audience toward his case and personal stature and toward his opponent's case and personal stature are important elements which must be analyzed. The nature of the occasion, specific rules of procedure, informal codes of conduct, and projected future events are additional factors which require consideration. In general, the more thoroughly the advocate understands the demands of the *total situation,* the better prepared he can be to make the *restraints of that situation* work to his advantage. Each aspect of the communication setting serves in some way to condition his choices.

Fourth, *the aim of communication strategies is to heighten the persuasive impact of the analysis.* No matter what the context, the purpose of a strategy is to increase the chances of achieving the goal in that particular situation. In military conflicts the goal of a strategy is victory over an enemy. In political contests the purpose of a strategy is to gain an advantage in terms of the number of votes cast. Since the immediate goal of communication situations is acceptance of the message, the purpose of communication strategies is to increase the chances of an advocate's ideas being accepted by an audience.

Fifth, *communication strategies seek to achieve their objective through alterations in perception and/or emphasis.* Professional photographers know how important perspective and emphasis are in making a picture interesting and meaningful. A dandelion growing through a crack in the sidewalk may not strike us as very attractive when viewed as part of a total backyard scene. But when that same dandelion is photographed against a more limited background with soft shadows forming patterns on the sidewalk, it can become an object of striking beauty and symmetry. Similarly, the impact of a given argument may be significantly increased or decreased by relating it to different values, different premises, or different conclusions. Skilled advocates, like other artists, can stimulate excitement and win responses, not by ignoring reality, but by viewing it from strikingly appropriate frames of reference.

In sum, communication strategies may be thought of as broad schemes for utilizing the limitations of a communication situation for the advantage of the advocate.

TYPES OF COMMUNICATION STRATEGIES

This section will identify a number of communication strategies which have been used in the past. They are presented, not with the intention that they will be copied and used as stock approaches, but rather to illustrate how the circumstances of communication settings may be used to achieve the goal of the advocate. What should be especially noted in the following discussion is what the constraints or opportunities of the particular situations were and how they were used to gain a persuasive advantage with no fundamental changes in the speaker's ideological positions.

Four general classes of strategies will be discussed: (1) strategies aimed at altering the perception of major aspects of the analysis, (2) strategies aimed at altering the perception of the advocates, (3) strategies aimed at gaining emphasis through adaptation to formal procedures, and (4) strategies aimed at gaining emphasis through adaptation to informal codes of conduct.

ALTERING PERCEPTION OF THE ANALYSIS

Advocates generally find themselves confronted with audiences which have some preconceptions about the topic being discussed. If these preconceptions about the topic are not compatible with the advocate's analysis, he must accommodate his presentation to that fact. He may do this in a variety of ways.

One approach to altering the audience's perception of the analysis is to absorb its antagonistic preconceptions into the speaker's own analysis. This strategy is most useful when there is a single major value upon which most opposing arguments are based. By absorbing this value into his own case and using it as a major part of his rationale, the advocate seeks to turn the audience's antagonistic preconception to his advantage.

Carl M. Moore, in his study of the Senate debate over the Full Employment Bill of 1945, identified this as the major strategy of the supporters of that bill. According to Moore's analysis, the advocates of the bill anticipated that the primary concern of those opposed to the bill or uncommitted to it was the preservation of the free enterprise system. Rather than waiting for the opponents of the bill to attack it for interfering with free enterprise, the advocates made the strengthening of free enterprise the focus of their ill analysis.

> Senator Wagner, in his opening speech, explained how S. 380 promoted and strengthened the free enterprise system. Other Senators did the same. For example, during a colloquy with Senator Radcliffe, Senator Tobey explained:
> "I think the Senator will agree with me that all through this bill, in at least a dozen places, we pay tribute to private enterprise. We put it first. We are going to stimulate it and help it and aid it. There is no question about that in the Senator's mind, is there?"[1]

Thus, the advocates of the Full Employment Bill argued that it was designed to preserve the value of the free enterprise system. They

[1]Carl M. Moore, "The Issues, Strategies and Structure of the Senate Debate over the Full Employment Bill of 1945" (Ph.D. dissertation, Wayne State University, 1972), pp. 166–67.

absorbed the value of their opponents and utilized it for their own advantage.

This strategy of absorbing the major opposition value is often utilized in academic debate. In debating the 1972–73 national high school debate proposition, *Resolved: That governmental financial support for all public elementary and secondary education in the United States should be provided exclusively by the federal government,* many high school debaters recognized that most of the objections to the proposal rested upon fear of federal control of education. They, therefore, absorbed this value into their cases and attempted to change the perception of federal control by making the need for it the basis of their rationale for change. They argued, for example, that federal financing of education would permit the federal government to reorganize the administration of elementary and secondary education and, thereby, eliminate racially imbalanced and financially impoverished local school districts.

In other situations a primary constraint upon the advocate is not the antagonistic preconceptions of the audience but rather the audience's limited view of the entire controversy. In this type of situation, advocates sometimes adopt a strategy which relates a specific problem to a set of larger, more apparent problems. By establishing a commonality with larger issues, the advocate is able to focus on the larger issue instead of the initial, narrower cause for concern. In this way, he seeks to enhance the significance of his cause.

In his study of the Conspiracy Trial of the Chicago Seven, David A. Ling describes how the defense attempted to universalize the issues of the trial. In this case, seven young radicals were charged with conspiring to incite a riot during the 1968 Chicago convention of the Democratic Party. The prosecution's aim in the trial was simply to prove the accused guilty of the stated charges. The defense, on the other hand, attempted to focus attention on the larger issue of the government's motives for undertaking the trial.

> In the case of the Conspiracy Trial, the defense argued that the trial was not simply a matter of who was responsible for the Chicago disorders of 1968. Rather, the trial was an attempt to suppress concern over legitimate social problems. In his opening statement to the jury, [defense counsel] Kunstler did not focus on the specific charges against the defendants. Instead, he attempted to discuss the motives of the government for undertaking the trial. Although he was not allowed to pursue this development, his comments set the tone for the direction the defense would take. [Defense counsel] Weinglass, at the conclusion of the trial, said that the indictments were an "act of vengeance" because the defendants dared to oppose the government's policies "on war and racism." Throughout the

trial, the defense raised three social issues (racism, war and the repression of dissent) and it argued that these existed and were what caused the trial.[2]

Thus, by viewing the issues of a controversy from a broader frame of reference, an advocate may lend universal significance to his cause.

The universalization of a problem and the adoption of antagonistic values are not, of course, the only strategies which can be used to alter the perception of an analysis. By focusing on unexpected aspects of an issue, by reordering arguments, and in numerous other ways, advocates have developed additional strategies. What is characteristic of all such strategies, however, is that they begin the presentation of the analysis at an unusual, but particularly appropriate, point.

ALTERING PERCEPTION OF THE ADVOCATE

Audiences not only have preconceptions about the analysis presented to them, but they also have preconceptions regarding the stature of the advocates who present that analysis. An audience's view of a speaker's stature may be specific to him as an individual or it may be the result of his membership in a particular group. Strategies for altering the perception of the advocate are used both to enhance the advocate's stature and to undermine the stature of the opposition. Since the willingness of an audience to consider an analysis depends, in large part, upon its view of the advocate's credibility, such strategies are extremely important.

An examination of credibility strategies used in recent presidential election campaigns provides some interesting illustrations of how alterations in the public's perceptions of political candidates have been attempted.

When George McGovern was named the Democratic nominee for president in 1972, he was seen by many Americans as a political extremist. His reported support for legalized abortion, reform of marijuana laws, and a $1,000 minimum income to all citizens suggested a marked departure from previous societal norms. Recognizing that he was being labeled a "wild-eyed radical" by his political opponents and that such a label would weaken his appeal with large segments of the voting public, McGovern adopted a strategy which sought to create an image of himself as a man who was returning America to her true traditions. This strategy is clearly revealed in the closing portion of his acceptance address:

[2]David A. Ling, "A Rhetorical Analysis of the Conspiracy Trial of the Chicago Seven" (Ph.D. dissertation, Wayne State University, 1973), pp. 46–47.

So join with me in this campaign. Lend me your strength and your support, and together we will call America home to the ideals that nourished us from the very beginning.

From secrecy and deception in high places—come home, America.

From military spending so wasteful that it weakens our nation—come home, America.

From the entrenchment of special privilege and tax favoritism, from the waste of idle hands to the joy of useful labor, from the prejudice based on race and sex, from the loneliness of the aging poor and the despair of the neglected sick—come home, America.

Come home to the affirmation that we have a dream.

Come home to the conviction that we can move our country forward.

Come home to the belief that we can seek a newer world.

And let us be joyful in the homecoming.[3]

McGovern adopted the theme of "come home, America" as his campaign slogan, and by so doing he hoped to change his public image from that of an extremist to that of a constructive reformer.

In 1968, Richard Nixon also faced an image problem. Both as senator and as vice president, Nixon had earned a reputation as a loyal party worker who engaged in hard-hitting, name-calling political campaigning. As a result, many independent and Democratic voters viewed Nixon more as a political hack than as a true statesman. Since Nixon's chances of winning the presidency rested heavily upon his ability to win over large numbers of independents and Democrats, he sought to find a way of projecting the image of a "new Nixon." Prior to 1968, Nixon delivered his speeches extemporaneously and relied upon a number of stock phrases. His characteristic style was simple and lacking in the stylistic refinement of the former Democratic president, John F. Kennedy. Nixon's adaptation to this situation, according to Ronald H. Carpenter and Robert V. Seltzer, was a change in this speaking style.

In 1968 there was a change. At times during the campaign and particularly in the Acceptance Address to the Republican Convention, the attempt to project the image of a "New Nixon" saw some unique additions to well rehearsed stylistic habits. These alterations were described by White only as an "echo" of John F. Kennedy; it may be more appropriate here to ruminate about these additions as attempts to use a style highly reminiscent of the man who won the Presidency in 1960. For momentarily, a New Nixon was Old Kennedy. . . .

Richard M. Nixon's so personally prepared Acceptance Address of 1968 is studded with the stylistic conformations associated more readily with John F. Kennedy. The speech uses some forty antitheses! Note for in-

[3]George McGovern, "1972 Acceptance Address," *New York Times,* July 14, 1972, p. 11, col. 6.

stance the antithetical "after an *era of confrontation* the time has come for an *era of negotiation*" or the more overt antithesis between "We shall *always* negotiate from *strength* and never from *weakness.*"(Perhaps this is an "echo" in form and content of Kennedy's "Let us never *negotiate out of fear.* But let us never *fear to negotiate.*") ...

Why emulate a Kennedy style in discourse? ... A possible effect of stylistic imitation would be to create an "echo" and perhaps—if style *is* the man—even evince some substance of John F. Kennedy and thus gain a measure of the admiration and support attained by the winner of 1960.[4]

As a Republican, Nixon was restrained from directly identifying with a popular Democrat, but through changes in his style of expression he was able to project a more Kennedy-like image.

The constraints which affect the image of an advocate come not only from the advocate's past record or party affiliation. They may also arise from his close identification with a particular self-interest group or from the beliefs and actions of his supporters. Whatever the restraint, a strategy appropriate to it must be devised if the advocate is to project a credible image to his audience.

EMPHASIS THROUGH FORMAL PROCEDURES

An advocate must be able to give emphasis to those aspects of his analysis which he considers most important and most persuasive. Even when adverse audience preconceptions are not a concern, the advocate must still give attention to the matter of selecting, ordering, and timing arguments for maximum impact. The utilization of certain formal procedures of the situation is one way in which such emphasis can be achieved. An examination of the rules of parliamentary debate and the formal procedures of academic debate will illustrate how the official codes of a situation may be used to the advocate's advantage.

There is danger in any clash of ideas that the really important points of disagreement will become obscured in the overall flow of words. This problem exists even in parliamentary debate with its prescribed rules of procedure. These rules do not require one speaker to respond to another. Each speaker is free to discuss a different aspect of the resolution under debate or a different reason for its adoption or rejection. As long as the discussion is relevant to the overall motion, it is acceptable, and the chairman must rule it in order. One way of forcing a group to focus on a particular issue is to offer an amendment.

Moore describes how the strategy of focusing by amendment was used by the opponents of the Full Employment Bill of 1945:

[4]Ronald H. Carpenter and Robert V. Seltzer, "On Nixon's Kennedy Style," *Speaker and Gavel 7*, no. 2 (January 1970): 42–43.

> ... the public work amendment, was offered at the start of the second day of the debate by Senator Radcliffe for Senator Taft and himself. By offering the public work amendment first and by presenting it at the earliest time an opposition amendment could have been introduced into the debate, the opponents gave prominence to the charge that the full employment bill was a deficit spending bill. From the time of the introduction of the amendment until the passage of the compromise version of the amendment on the fourth and final day, the opponents contended that the bill called for deficit spending.[5]

In this situation the purpose of the amendment was not simply to change the bill and make it more acceptable. An equally important objective of the amendment was to focus attention on a particularly offensive aspect of the proposal.

In the academic debate situation the prescribed order of speaking and the rigid time limits are major constraints upon the individual advocates. These constraints have encouraged the development of numerous strategies. One of the most common of these strategies involves the use of the *negative bloc* (the second negative constructive followed by the first negative rebuttal). This strategy calls for a division of labor between the two negative speeches and the concentration of cure-cost arguments in the second negative constructive speech. With the second negative constructive devoted to cure-cost arguments, the first negative rebuttalist is able to concentrate on the ill-blame analysis. By dividing responsibility between the two speakers in this way, the negative is able to avoid unnecessary repetition and overlapping of arguments and to develop its analysis most fully at a pivotal point in the debate. Moreover, by withholding the development of cure-cost arguments until the final constructive speech, the negative gives these arguments greater prominence and forces the affirmative to devote considerable time to them in the rebuttal periods.

Thus, the formal procedures of many advocacy situations impose certain limitations on advocates, but they also offer opportunities for the development of communication strategies which can heighten the persuasive impact of selected arguments.

EMPHASIS THROUGH INFORMAL CODES

In addition to certain prescribed procedures or formal rules, most advocacy situations also involve certain informal codes of conduct. These codes are the result, not of official rules, but of audience expectations. These expectations are a reflection of both the audience's past experiences and its sense of appropriateness. Ordinarily, an advocate

---

[5]Moore, "Senate Debate over the Full Employment Bill," pp. 176–77.

will attempt to present his case in accordance with the audience's code of conduct, but occasionally, by going counter to an audience's expectations, special emphasis can be achieved. The informal codes of the courtroom and of academic debate may be used to illustrate this class of strategies.

Defendants in courts of law are usually expected to wear relatively conservative business-type clothing and to behave in a respectful and modest manner. By rejecting these normal expectations, the defendants in the conspiracy trial of the Chicago Seven were able to dramatize the difference between their life style and that of the establishment. Ling describes the defendants' use of this particular strategy:

> Throughout the trial, the defense undertook a series of acts that were non-verbal in nature and communicated a sense of freedom from conventional norms. The most obvious of these acts was the manner of dress of the defendants. All of the defendants dressed in court as they normally dressed out of court. For David Dellinger, this included the traditional shirt, tie, and sport coat that are normally associated with a courtroom trial. However, for the other seven defendants the dress was not that which is usually worn in such a setting. Jeans, sport shirts, polo shirts, and sweat shirts were constantly in evidence at the defense table. ... Weinglass highlighted this attempt of the defendants to separate themselves from the Establishment when he contrasted the fact that the defendants present themselves "as they are," while a number of police witnesses for the prosecution appeared in suits rather than their uniforms. The effect was to create the impression of a life style unrestrained by conventional standards.[6]

An informal convention of academic debate dictates that the first negative speaker should devote his constructive speech to responding to the affirmative's rationale for change (ill and blame issues). Occasionally, however, negative teams will adopt a strategy which ignores the expected order of presentation. Instead of the first negative attacking the ill and blame analysis, he attacks the plan and presents the cure and cost issues. The ill and blame issues, then, are discussed in the second negative constructive. Generally this strategy is used when the affirmative has a particularly strong ill-blame analysis and the negative has a particularly strong cure-cost analysis. The purpose of this departure from the conventional order is to pull the affirmative team onto negative ground early in the debate and force it to debate the cure-cost arguments in greater depth.

[6]Ling, "Chicago Seven," pp. 81–82.

As the patterns of behavior in academic debate and courts of law illustrate, informal codes of conduct help to create order and predictability in communication situations. However, by calculated departures from those codes, advocates can attract attention to and give emphasis to particularly strong issues.

SUMMARY

Communication strategies are broad plans which determine how an advocate will adapt the presentation of his analysis to the constraints and opportunities of a particular communication situation; their aim is to heighten the persuasive impact of the analysis through alterations in perception and/or emphasis.

Strategies aimed at altering an audience's perception of major aspects of an analysis are useful when an audience's preconceptions are different from those of the advocate. The strategy of absorbing the audience's antagonistic value into the speaker's case and the strategy of relating a limited problem to a set of larger, more universal issues illustrate methods by which the audience's view of an analysis may be changed.

Strategies aimed at altering an audience's perception of the advocate may be used to enhance an advocate's own stature or to undermine that of his opponent. The strategies of identification with traditional values and of stylistic identification illustrate methods which speakers have used to enhance their own images.

Strategies aimed at achieving emphasis through formal procedures are derived from the official rules of the advocacy situation. By offering a perfecting amendment the rules of parliamentary procedure have been used to focus attention on a particularly offensive aspect of a resolution. By the division of labor between the two negative speakers and by the concentration of cure-cost arguments in the second negative constructive speech, the rules of academic debate have been used to give emphasis to the negative attack at a pivotal point in the debate.

Strategies aimed at achieving emphasis through informal codes of conduct are derived from the audience's expectations in that advocacy setting. In the courtroom emphasis has been achieved and an alternate code of behavior dramatized by the rejection of normal codes of dress. In academic debate emphasis has been gained by dealing with issues in an unconventional order.

STUDY QUESTIONS

1. Do communication strategies necessarily compromise the ethical criterion of truth determination?
2. Can the use of strategies be avoided?
3. Relate the concept of communication strategies to the continuum of advocacy situations outlined in Chapter 10. In what advocacy situations are communication strategies most likely to be used?

EXERCISES

1. Read an analysis of a recent political campaign and consider the campaign strategies which are identified.
   a. How does the definition of strategies used in this chapter apply to the strategies discussed in your reference source?
   b. What was the objective of each strategy?
   c. What were the constraints which influenced each strategy?
2. Listen to several interscholastic debates or read the transcripts of several academic debates; try to identify strategies used in these situations.
3. Using a proposition of your choosing, develop a communication strategy which is not discussed in this chapter. Be ready to discuss the objective of the strategy and the constraints which influenced your development of this specific approach.

14 Refutation

To this point, our discussion of the nature of advocacy has focused upon the building and maximizing of the advocate's own analysis and arguments. The advocate, however, must also be concerned with arguments and analysis forwarded by those who oppose his view. This is especially true in advocacy situations which require the presence of an opposing advocate, such as legal advocacy and academic debate. Even when an opposing advocate is not present, however, a speaker must consider what arguments will be raised in the minds of the members of his audience. When an advocate attempts to deal with arguments forwarded by those who oppose his position, he is engaging in refutation. This chapter will focus on the process of refutation. Specifically, the chapter seeks to accomplish three things: (1) to analyze the nature of refutation, (2) to outline selected methods of refutation, and (3) to discuss the mechanics of preparing for refutation.

THE NATURE OF REFUTATION

DEFINITION OF REFUTATION

Refutation can be defined as *the process of attacking the arguments of an opponent in order to weaken or destroy those arguments.* This definition suggests that refutation is essentially a *tearing down* process which begins with the arguments presented by an opposition advocate. Skill in refutation lies at the heart of reasoned advocacy because an advocate who ignores the arguments of his opposition cannot expect to win his case. The process of refutation can be compared to the defensive efforts of a football team. A football team must spend approximately half of its time warding off the offensive efforts of the opposition. Football history is filled with teams that had outstanding offensive units but failed to become champions for lack of an adequate defense. In debate, refutation is the defensive half of the game. The advocate who is skilled only in forwarding his own analysis is only half prepared to engage in debate. He must also be prepared to examine the analysis of his opponent and to understand its weaknesses, and he must also be skilled in the methods of refutation. Many football games are lost for lack of an adequate defense, and many debates are lost because an advocate was not skilled in the methods of refutation.

The term *refutation* should not be confused with the term *rebuttal;* the latter has a specialized meaning, especially in academic debate where it is used to refer to the final four speeches in most academic debate formats. Rebuttal, in this context, is the process of defending, strengthening, and rebuilding arguments after they have been attacked by an opponent. The term rebuttal, then, refers to a time period in a debate in which previously developed arguments are defended and rebuilt. Refutation, on the other hand, is the process of tearing down arguments presented by the opposition. This process may occur at any point in the debate.

SELECTIVE NATURE OF REFUTATION

It is generally impossible and usually unnecessary to refute all of the arguments presented by the opposition. In addition to engaging in refutation, each advocate has an obligation to develop his own constructive arguments. Selectivity, therefore, is necessary in order for the advocate to be able to maximize available time and in order for him to be able to focus the controversy on the most important arguments and values. Half of the job of refutation is the selection of the arguments with which to clash and the choice of the arguments upon which to spend the most time.

The basis on which this necessary selection is made will vary depending upon the nature of the advocacy situation. In many audience situations, for instance, refutative selection must be made on the basis of anticipated audience attitudes and values. In legal advocacy and academic debate situations, on the other hand, the concepts of presumption, burden of proof, and issues are more rigorously applied, making refutative selection more issue-oriented. The first step in refutative selection in these advocacy situations is to discover the issues in the given controversy. The importance of opposition arguments can only be judged in relation to the issues of the controversy.

Issue orientation in refutation is especially vital to the affirmative (or prosecution) because of the logical obligation to carry each contested issue. Only arguments which are tangential to the issues or which have no potential for establishing a clash on the issue level may be safely ignored by affirmatives. Negatives (or defense attorneys), on the other hand, have greater freedom in selecting arguments for refutation because of the logical obligation to carry only one issue. Negatives will frequently grant an issue to the affirmative in order to be able to spend more refutative time, and to focus the debate more clearly, on an issue of greater importance to the negative analysis.

Refutation, then, is selective in nature. The pressures of time and the importance of focusing the clash on the vital issues force the advocate to select areas of refutation with great care. The advocate's prior analysis must be thorough enough to permit him to judge the importance of opposition arguments in relation to the issues of the controversy. He must also be able to perceive the common premises underlying opposition arguments which permit the grouping of arguments for refutation. While refutation is essentially a tearing down process, it must take place within the framework of the advocate's total analysis of the proposition. Only within such a framework can refutation become selective in a way that will serve to focus the debate on the areas of concern which are vital to the advocate.

SPECIAL METHODS OF REFUTATION

If an advocate's analysis has been thorough, he should be in a position to anticipate the arguments which opponents are likely to forward and to judge their importance in relation to the issues of the controversy. The advocate, however, must still analyze opposition arguments in light of the various tests of data and argument and must select a method of refutation which is appropriate to the argument being considered. Previous chapters have addressed themselves to the tests of data and argument which can be used to expose the weaknesses of the argument under consideration. This section will consider the various special methods of refutation which are available to the advocate.

Many people think of refutation solely in terms of direct denial of the validity of the argument being refuted. "If you want to refute an argument," they say, "simply show that the argument isn't true." Unfortunately, refutation is generally not that simple. While the validity of some arguments can be denied directly, most opposing arguments are at least partially true and cannot be completely denied. The search for methods of refutation, therefore, leads the advocate beyond attempts to demonstrate the falsehood of opposition arguments to a consideration of methods for dealing with partially valid arguments. In this section, methods of refutation will be grouped into two broad categories: (1) methods designed to undermine the credibility of the argument and (2) methods designed to reduce the importance of the argument.

UNDERMINING THE CREDIBILITY OF THE
ARGUMENT

While most of the methods outlined in this section fall short of direct denial of the validity of the argument, they are still designed to undermine the argument's credibility by exposing weaknesses in the argument itself. This list of methods could be significantly expanded by adding the tests of data outlined in Chapter 5 and the tests of argument outlined in Chapter 8. All of these tests constitute methods for undermining the credibility of arguments. Beyond the tests of data and argument, however, there are a variety of special methods of refutation designed to undermine argument credibility. These include exposing inconsistencies, reducing arguments to absurdity, exposing fallacies of composition and division, and exposing question-begging arguments.

Exposing inconsistencies. This method of refutation suggests that an argument is not consistent with another argument previously presented by the same source. It is an attempt to undermine the credibility of an argument by questioning the adequacy of the reasoning processes or the character of the individual who presented that argument. The exposing of an inconsistency does not necessarily constitute a direct attack on the validity of the argument under consideration. Rather, if sustained, it forces the opponent to abandon or modify one of two arguments which cannot be consistently maintained.

Charges of inconsistency are a frequent tactic in American politics. Political figures search carefully for modifications in the public statements of their opponents in hopes of discovering inconsistencies which will reduce opposition credibility. The advocate who uses this method of refutation, however, must be sure of three things: (1) that the opposition's position on the two contested arguments is fairly stated, (2) that the two arguments are, in reality, inconsistent with each other, and (3) that conditions have not changed sufficiently to explain the apparent inconsistency.

Reducing the argument to absurdity. This method consists of extending an argument to a point where the conclusion is absurd or otherwise unacceptable. The method generally involves the use of an analogy in extending the argument. The argument is taken out of its situational context and extended analogically to a different set of circumstances where its application appears absurd.

Opponents of drug legalization frequently use this method of refutation in response to the argument that certain drugs should be legalized because the existing laws are difficult to enforce. In an attempt to reduce the argument to absurdity, opponents suggest that the argument implies that laws against speeding, burglary, and murder should also be repealed because of enforcement difficulties. As can be seen, this method of refutation is somewhat risky because it is so easily turned around by an opponent. If any flaw in the analogy used for the extension can be found, the link between the argument and its extension can be broken. The argument is thus stripped of its substantive base and is left with only ridicule value.

Exposing fallacies of composition and division. The fallacies of composition and division are twin fallacies in which relationships between wholes and their parts are erroneously asserted. The *fallacy of composition* consists of assuming that what is true of separate parts is necessarily true of the collective whole. The fallacy is exposed by demonstrating that the characteristics of the parts cannot logically be extended to the whole. In other words, it argues that the whole is more than the sum of its parts. A basketball team, for instance, may not necessarily be judged to be superior to another team because it has a higher percentage of all-star players. Factors of team balance, teamwork, and coaching competence must be considered. In such a situation the whole is more than the sum of its parts.

The *fallacy of division* consists of assuming that what is true of the collective whole is also true of all of the separate parts. The fallacy is exposed by demonstrating that the characteristics of the whole may not be present in all of the individual parts. A political party, for instance, may be identified as conservative as a collective whole. It does not necessarily follow, however, that all of the members and candidates of that party are also conservatives.

Exposing question begging. Question begging is a linguistic fallacy in which an advocate assumes the truth of an argument which he is purportedly proving. This is usually done by rephrasing an assertion to make a restatement of that assertion appear to be a different argument. The fallacy generally indicates a superficial analysis and superficial research, and it is exposed by showing that the supporting argument is the same as the assertion which it is designed to prove.

An example of question begging is the argument that a national health insurance plan unjustifiably fixes the wages of doctors because doctors have the right to set their own fees. The argument assumes what it sets out to prove by merely restating the original assertion in different language. The exposing of question begging reduces the credibility of an argument by demonstrating that the argument has not been supported. It also tends to reduce the credibility of the source of the argument by exposing fuzzy thinking and superficial analysis.

REDUCING THE IMPORTANCE OF THE ARGUMENT

In many instances it is difficult to undermine directly the credibility of an argument or its source. In such situations, however, methods of refutation are available despite the apparent internal validity of the argument under consideration. These methods seek to reduce the importance of the argument rather than to undermine its credibility. Among the methods of refutation in this category are minimization, denial of inherency, exposing dilemmas, exposing incomplete analysis, turning the tables, and exposing irrelevancies.

Minimization. Minimization of the significance of opposition arguments constitutes one of the most useful of all the methods of refutation. This method of refutation admits that a conclusion may be true but denies its significance in relation to other conclusions. It is particularly useful when dealing with conclusions based on statistical data. Minimization can be accomplished in a variety of ways including the demonstration of trends, the use of comparisons, and the use of factor analysis.

One method of minimizing an argument is to demonstrate that it is insignficant when viewed within the framework of a trend. Statistics which appear to be significant in isolation can be minimized by placing them in a broader framework. This method is frequently used by those who wish to minimize the significance of unemployment statistics or statistics on inflation. President Nixon used the trend method of minimization in 1972 in response to arguments that he was escalating the war in Vietnam:

> Let me begin briefly by reviewing what the situation was when I took office and what we have done since then to end American involvement in the war and to bring peace to the long-suffering people of Southeast Asia.
>
> On January 20, 1969, the American troop ceiling in Vietnam was 549,000. Our casualties were running as high as 300 a week. Thirty thousand young Americans were being drafted every month.
>
> Today, 39 months later, through our program of Vietnamization—helping the South Vietnamese develop the capability of defending themselves—the number of Americans in Vietnam by Monday, May 1, will have been reduced to 69,000.
>
> Our casualties—even during the present all-out enemy offensive—have been reduced by 95 percent. And draft calls now average fewer than 5,000 men a month and we expect to bring them to zero next year.[1]

Another method of minimization is that of comparison. An argument or a statistic may be minimized by comparing it to another argument or statistic which is considerably more significant. While the trend method generally involves the comparison of arguments and statistics within the same class, the comparison method will generally

[1]Richard M. Nixon, "The Situation in Vietnam," *Vital Speeches* 38, no. 15 (May 15, 1972): 450.

minimize through comparison of essentially different items. One frequently hears, for instance, comparisons between highway death figures and war casualty statistics in attempts either to minimize the extent of wartime casualties or to maximize the significance of highway safety problems. Another example of this method occurs when the cost of some public program is minimized by comparing that cost to the amount of money Americans spend on cosmetics or cigarettes or liquor.

A final method of minimization is factor analysis. In this method minimization is accomplished by excluding a significant element from the whole conclusion in order to achieve a desired perspective. For instance, a conclusion concerning an increase in total crime can be minimized if it can be demonstrated that a nonserious type of crime, such as minor property crimes, was the factor that accounted for the bulk of the increase in the total crime rate. Law Professor Yale Kamisar used this method of minimization in his attack on statistics on criminal conviction rates:

> For political purposes the "only one-in-eight crimes results in conviction" statistic has more than adequate gee-whiz! appeal—so long as its arrest, prosecution, and conviction components are not singled out. The lump figure may be misunderstood as meaning that only one out of every eight who are *caught* and *prosecuted* are convicted—when the primary reason for the "one-in-eight" figure is that most reported offenses *never result in an arrest or prosecution.* (Italics Kamisar's)[2]

Denial of inherency. This method of refutation responds to an opposition argument by attempting to demonstrate that it fails to identify a problem which is inherent to the structure or philosophy of the system under discussion. The denial of inherency is generally accompanied by an implied admission of the validity of the argument and a minor repair of the system under discussion. The method of refutation is designed to reduce the importance of the opposition argument by demonstrating that the argument identifies a minor and easily curable problem.

At a time when penalties for the possession and use of marijuana were generally severe, proponents of legalization of marijuana frequently argued that legalization was justified because the penalties were considerably more severe than the illegal act. Opponents typically responded that the severity of the penalties was not an inherent problem and did not, for that reason, justify legalization. The problem could be solved, they claimed, by making marijuana possession and use a misdemeanor rather than a felony, thereby reducing the penalties.

[2]Yale Kamisar, *Congressional Record,* January 19, 1972, p. E248.

Exposing dilemmas. This method of refutation reduces the opposition argument to two alternatives, neither of which is acceptable to the opponent or to the audience. To be effective, the two choices (the horns of the dilemma) must cover all of the possible alternatives and each must be damaging to the opponent's cause. If the dilemma does not exhaust the possibilities, the opponent may sustain his argument's significance by indicating an alternative which is not damaging to his cause. Also, a dilemma will not reduce the importance of an opposition argument if one of the choices can be accepted by the opponent without serious injury to his case.

Opponents of compulsory national health insurance frequently use the dilemma approach in discussing the freedom of doctors to set their own fees. On the one hand, they argue, if doctors are permitted to set their own fees as in the existing system, the cost of the national insurance plan would skyrocket and would be uncontrollable. If, on the other hand, a national health insurance plan sets maximum fees for medical services, doctors would refuse to participate in the program, fewer would go into the medical profession, and the general quality of medical service would be significantly reduced. The dilemma attempts to place proponents of national health insurance in a situation in which a choice must be made between two undesirable alternatives.

Exposing incomplete analysis. This method of refutation attempts to reduce the importance of an opposition argument by claiming that the argument does not constitute a complete analysis of the situation under consideration. The method usually involves an admission that the argument is true as far as it goes but suggests that the argument doesn't go far enough. The claim is generally accompanied by a detailing of factors which have been left out of the opposition analysis. Senator Edward Kennedy illustrated this method of refutation in 1971 when responding to the contention that the vast majority of Americans are covered by some form of health insurance. Admitting the factual validity of the argument, Senator Kennedy went on to consider the incompleteness of the analysis:

> Despite the fact that private health insurance is a giant $12 billion industry, despite more than three decades of enormous growth, despite massive sales of health insurance by thousands of private companies competing with each other for the health dollar of millions of citizens, health insurance benefits today pay only one-third of the total cost of private health care, leaving two-thirds to be paid out of pocket by the patient at the time of illness or as debt thereafter, at the very time when he can least afford it.[3]

[3]Senator Edward Kennedy, *Congressional Record,* January 25, 1971, S89.

Turning the tables. Turning the tables is a method of refutation which admits the validity of the opposition argument but claims that the argument supports the advocate's analysis rather than denying it. In other words, the reasoning or evidence of an opponent is interpreted in a manner to prove the advocate's own contention. It is a particularly useful method for dealing with the values forwarded by the opposition if those values can be demonstrated to be consistent with your analysis.

In a recent final round of the National Debate Tournament a Wayne State University debater used the method of turning the tables in arguing for a less militant U.S. policy toward Communist China:

> ... the gentleman read us a quotation saying Mr. Chen Yi said that war with the United States is inevitable. You know, that's our whole point. *Under the present system,* war with the United States is inevitable. That's why we are suggesting we remove those major barriers to U.S.-Chinese hostility.[4]

This method of refutation is dependent upon the persuasiveness of the advocate in demonstrating to the audience that his interpretation of the meaning of the argument is superior to that of his opponent.

Exposing irrelevancy. Frequently, the importance of an opposition argument can be reduced by demonstrating that the argument, while true, is simply irrelevant to the analysis at hand. This method probably ought to be used more than it is. Many advocates spend unnecessary time dealing in detail with arguments which could really be dismissed as irrelevant to the point being argued.

Many of those opposed to U.S. policy in Southeast Asia have contended that the argument that the United States must stay in Vietnam long enough to assure that the South Vietnamese government can maintain itself is an irrelevant one. They argue that the issue is not *can* we sustain a friendly government in South Vietnam but *ought* we be trying to do so.

PREPARING FOR REFUTATION

Thus far, this chapter has addressed itself to the nature of refutation and to the specific methods of refutation which are available to the advocate. This final section will consider the necessary mechanical elements involved in preparing for refutation. Thorough preparation

---

[4]"1967 National Debate Tournament Final Debate," *Journal of the American Forensic Association* 4, no. 3 (Fall 1967): 127.

of refutation is essential because of the extreme time pressures in most advocacy situations. When engaging in refutation the advocate generally has only a short period of time to record the arguments of the opposition, to select his refutative arguments and methods of refutation, to select evidence to support the refutation, and to put the refutation into a form appropriate for oral communication. To accomplish these tasks, the advocate must spend as much time carefully preparing and organizing his refutation as he does in building his constructive case for presentation. The preparation for refutation involves four processes: (1) preparation of rebuttal blocs, (2) preparation of evidence files, (3) preparation for note taking, and (4) preparation for oral presentation.

REBUTTAL BLOC PREPARATION

The skillful advocate knows in advance what method of refutation and what refutative arguments he will use in response to opposition arguments. The preparation of refutative arguments cannot be left for the moment of advocacy. Rather, considerable time must be spent prior to advocacy in efforts to anticipate opposition arguments and evidence and in efforts to work out the appropriate responses. This process is made efficient by the preparation of rebuttal blocs.

Rebuttal blocs, very simply, are outlines of the possible responses to individual opposition arguments. They are frequently recorded on index cards with a separate card for each opposition argument to facilitate filing. The accompanying sample rebuttal bloc illustrates one of the possible forms which can be used. This rebuttal bloc contains four

---

AFFIRMATIVE

Extent of Health Insurance Coverage is Exaggerated

The negative claim that 87% of the American people are covered by health insurance can be minimized by a factor analysis of that statistic (most coverage is only partial).

   A. 22% have no surgical insurance (39 million)
   B. 34% have no in-patient medical insurance (61 million)
   C. 50% have no out-patient X-ray and laboratory insurance (89 million)
   D. 57% have no insurance for doctors' office visits (120 million)
   E. 61% have no insurance for prescription drugs (108 million)
   F. 97% have no dental insurance (173 million)

Figures based on 1968 population of 180 million people under 65. (Source: Sen. Edward Kennedy, Speech in Senate, Jan. 25, 1971.)

important elements. First, it states, in complete sentence form, the argument or evidence which is being refuted. The statement of the opposition argument becomes the focal point for the organization of rebuttal blocs. Second, the bloc indicates the specific method of refutation which will be used in dealing with the argument (in this case, factor analysis). Third, the bloc outlines the specific refutative arguments which will be used in dealing with the argument. Finally, the bloc contains references to the evidence necessary to support the refutation. Academic debaters frequently clip the appropriate evidence cards to the rebuttal bloc to save time searching for the necessary evidence during the debate.

While rebuttal blocs carefully outline anticipated refutation methods, they do not necessarily constitute a speaking outline. The advocate must be prepared to respond to the uniqueness of the presentation of opposition arguments. Frequently, only a portion of a rebuttal bloc will apply to the argument as forwarded by an opposition advocate. In other cases, several opposition arguments may be grouped for a single refutative effort. A rebuttal bloc must be thorough, but the advocate must be flexible in using this thorough preparation. Rebuttal blocs constitute prethinking of refutation from which the advocate selects the elements which are appropriate in a specific advocacy situation.

The use of formal rebuttal blocs is a common practice among academic debaters. However, experienced public advocates in less structured advocacy situations may require less mechanical means for preparing refutation. Lawyers, for example, often prepare legal briefs which may serve functions roughly analogous to those of rebuttal blocs. Political advocates will often rely on their research staffs to prepare position papers which highlight significant areas of controversy and offer capsule arguments in support of the candidate's position. Other advocates may rely upon staff briefing sessions to help provide them with the specific arguments necessary for refutation. No matter what specific procedure is used—rebuttal blocs, legal briefs, position papers, or briefing sessions—advocates generally find that they need some method for thinking through refutative responses prior to actual argumentative confrontations.

EVIDENCE FILE PREPARATION

Unless the truth of the refutation is self-evident (which is rare) or unless the refutation grows out of commonly accepted premises or previously presented evidence, the advocate will have an obligation to present evidence in support of his refutative arguments. The necessary evidence must be well organized and readily available because of the time pressures of refutation in most advocacy situations. In much the same way that the analysis of the proposition must be organized into specific rebuttal blocs, the advocate's research must be systematized for easy access. This necessitates, especially in academic debate, the preparation of an evidence file.

To prepare a functional file from which the appropriate evidence can be drawn quickly and easily, the advocate must first record evidence in a form suitable for filing. A guide for this form was presented in the discussion of evidence recording in Chapter 4. Index cards, on which evidence to support a single argument is recorded, are the simplist to file and refile.

Evidence is filed by subject headings and separated from other subject headings by tabbed file guides. The methods for organizing evidence files are as numerous as are the advocates who use them. Each individual debater must find a method of organizing evidence which works for him. Some choose to organize the evidence within the general framework of the stock issues categories, subindexing by the various case approaches and proposals within a controversy. Others organize the evidence by each independent case area, using the stock issues categories as subordinate guides to more specific arguments. Whichever method is used, the primary purpose of an evidence file must always be kept in mind—to make available to the advocate the specific piece of evidence he needs in the shortest amount of time.

While advocates in nonacademic debate settings do not normally bring organized card files with them before audiences, they, nevertheless, do maintain information retrieval systems of some kind. These information systems may consist of several multiple-drawer filing cabinets, each containing systematically filed folders filled with newspaper clippings, government reports, speeches, etc. Major public figures will usually have research staffs whose primary function it is to collect such potentially useful data and to file it so that it will be readily available when needed. Although most public advocates use considerably less formal evidence in their public statements than do academic debaters, they must be able to support their claims when challenged to do so. The very nature of public advocacy, therefore, requires the maintenance of some kind of effective evidence file or information system.

The preparation of rebuttal blocs and evidence files occurs before the actual time for advocacy. The usefulness of this preparation, however, is completely dependent upon the development of adequate note-taking skills. As suggested earlier, the first step in refutation within the debate situation itself is the accurate recording of the arguments developed by the opposition advocate. The best rebuttal blocs and the most skillfully filed evidence will not help the advocate if he cannot accurately record the arguments which he wishes to refute.

A system must be worked out to facilitate adequate tracing of the arguments which have been developed, especially within the complex framework of the formats of academic debate. One method of note taking, commonly used in academic debate, is known as the *flowsheet.* This method, in more simplified forms, can also be adapted to serve the note-taking needs of most other advocacy situations. While there are a variety of flowsheet styles in use, the most basic method consists of a large rectangular sheet (such as a legal pad) which has been divided into vertical columns corresponding to the number of speeches in the debate. A sample of this style of flowsheet is illustrated in the accompanying diagram.

1 AFF.	1 NEG.	2 AFF.	2 NEG.	1 NR.	1 AR.	2 NR.	2 AR.

With this method of note taking the first affirmative constructive speech is recorded in outline form in the first column. The structure of this speech then sets the structure for the rest of the front of the flowsheet. In speeches that follow, arguments are recorded as they fit within this structure rather than as they are presented. Attacks on the affirmative plan, generally presented in the second negative constructive speech, are usually recorded on the back of the flowsheet. If the recording of arguments is thorough, this method permits the tracing of the development of arguments within the ill and blame issues on the front of the flowsheet and the tracing of the development of arguments within the cure and cost issues on the back of the flowsheet. At a glance, the advocate can see what has happened to any given argument throughout the debate.

While the flowsheet provides the debater with a form on which to take notes during the debate, it does not, obviously, tell him what to record and how to record it. Since it is impossible to record every-thing which is said in a debate, the advocate's note taking must be selective. In achieving this selectivity, the debater should remember three general guidelines for note taking: (1) take notes in outline form, (2) record exact wording, and (3) record supporting data.

It has already been suggested in the discussion of the flowsheet that the debater should take notes in *outline form.* If the debater can record the structure of the first affirmative constructive speech accu-rately, he has a framework for recording the ill and blame argumenta-tion for the rest of the debate. If he can record, in outline form, the attacks on the plan, he has a framework for recording the cure and cost argumentation. Taking notes in outline form not only helps the debater to differentiate between major and minor arguments, but it also assists him in keeping his thinking and his oral presentations well orga-nized.

A second guideline for note taking is to record the main ideas of the opposition in as close to their *exact wording* as possible. In prepara-tion for academic debates, advocates have generally taken great care in the wording of their constructive arguments. If one rewords or para-phrases the arguments of the opposition when recording them, he runs the risk of misunderstanding or misinterpreting those arguments, thereby rendering his refutative efforts inaccurate and ineffective. It is generally persuasive to an audience to be able to use the exact wording of the opposition's main arguments when you engage in refutation.

Finally, an advocate should make an attempt to record the vital elements of the *data* used to support the opposition arguments. All of the tests of data outlined in Chapter 5 constitute valuable methods of refutation for the advocate. He cannot employ these methods, however, if he does not record the data which his opponents use to support their arguments. To make a judgment on the adequacy of the data, the advo-cate should attempt to record at least the source of the data and the key phrase or phrases which link the data to the argument which they support.

While advocates other than academic debaters may find the me-chanics of the flowsheet unnecessarily detailed for their purposes, ad-vocates in any adversary setting should find its general principles to be helpful. Note taking in some form is absolutely essential if argu-ments are to be refuted. To be able to respond thoroughly and accurately advocates should strive to (1) take notes in outline form, (2) record exact wording, and (3) record supporting data.

*FORM FOR THE PRESENTATION OF
REFUTATION*

In presenting refutation to an audience, the advocate must be concerned both with the clarity of the refutation and with audience preception of the thoroughness of the refutation. To assist complete audience understanding of both the refutative effort and its impact on the analysis being forwarded, the following four-step presentation format is suggested: (1) name the argument, (2) explain the argument, (3) support the argument, and (4) conclude the argument.

The first step in the presentation of refutation is to *name both the argument being refuted and the argument used to refute it.* If the advocate fails to identify the argument being refuted, the audience may miss the impact of the refutation. Clear identification of the argument to be refuted, on the other hand, permits the audience to see the focus of the refutation in the analysis of the opposition. If the advocate fails to identify the refutative argument, he leaves the audience to figure out for itself the nature of the refutative effort—something which most audiences are unwilling to do. By clearly identifying the refutative argument, on the other hand, he greatly assists the audience in following the development of the refutation.

The second step in the form for refutation is to *explain the refutative argument.* The brief statement of the refutative argument is generally not enough to provide the audience with a full understanding of the nature of the refutation. The explanation should detail not only the specific method of refutation being employed but should also indicate the specific flaws in the argument being attacked.

The third step in the form for refutation is to *support the refutative argument.* All refutative arguments, like all constructive arguments, must be based on data. At times the support for the refutative argument may grow out of premises which have been developed and supported earlier in the debate. Occasionally, premises forwarded by the opposition may be used as data for refutation (as in the exposing of inconsistencies). In most cases, however, the advocate will have to utilize evidence to support his refutative arguments. The great majority of the methods of refutation outlined in the previous section require evidence to support the refutative effort.

The final step in the form for refutation is to *conclude the refutative argument.* This step is the one most frequently omitted by debaters in their eagerness to move on to other arguments. The conclusion of the refutative arguments goes beyond the mere restatement of the argument to indicate the importance of the refutation in the total analysis of the opposition. The individual act of refutation is thereby placed within the framework of the total refutative effort of the advocate.

SUMMARY

Refutation may be defined as the process of attacking the arguments of an opponent in order to weaken or destroy those arguments. Refutation should not be confused with rebuttal, which is the process of defending, strengthening, and rebuilding arguments after they have been attacked by an opponent.

Refutation is selective in nature. The pressures of time and the importance of focusing the clash on the vital issues force the advocate to select areas of refutation with great care. While refutation is essentially a tearing down process, it must take place within the framework of the advocate's total analysis of the proposition.

The advocate must consider the various methods of refutation which are available to him. Methods of refutation can be grouped into two broad categories: (1) methods designed to undermine the credibility of the argument and (2) methods designed to reduce the importance of the argument. The methods designed to reduce the credibility of the argument include exposing inconsistencies, reducing the argument to absurdity, exposing fallacies of composition and division, and exposing question begging. All of the tests of argument and the tests of data also constitute methods for reducing argument credibility. Methods of reducing the importance of the argument include minimization, denial of inherency, exposing dilemmas, exposing incomplete analysis, turning the tables, and exposing irrelevancy.

The advocate must also consider the necessary mechanical elements involved in preparing for refutation. Thorough preparation of refutation is essential because of the extreme time pressures in most advocacy situations. The preparation for refutation involves four processes: (1) preparation of rebuttal blocs, (2) preparation of evidence files, (3) preparation for note taking, and (4) preparation for oral presentation.

STUDY QUESTIONS

1. Is it possible to have refutation in the initial presentation by an affirmative?
2. What factors account for the fact that refutation must be selective?

3. Why is "minimization" not classified as a method of reducing the credibility of an argument?

EXERCISES

1. Read the most recent final round of the National Debate Tournament in the Summer issue of the *Journal of the American Forensic Association.* Identify the methods of refutation used in that debate.
2. Select a major ill argument of a current policy question and try to develop ways of minimizing its importance.
3. Listen to your school's varsity debate team in a practice debate and try keeping a flowsheet. After the debate compare your flowsheet with the flowsheets of the debaters and the critic of the debate.
4. Prepare two or three rebuttal blocs. Bring them to class for examination and discussion.
5. Utilizing one of the rebuttal blocs which you have prepared, orally refute a selected argument. Give special attention to the use of the four-step format for presentation of refutation.
6. Using whatever topics you desire, try to develop an argument utilizing each of the methods of refutation discussed in this chapter.

15 Cross-Examination

I. The Purposes of Cross-examination
  A. Gathering and Clarifying Information
  B. Examining Data
  C. Exposing Weaknesses in Analysis
  D. Undermining the Credibility of the Respondent
II. The Conduct of Cross-examination
  A. Substantive Aspects of Cross-examination
    1. Substantive Guides for the Questioner
      a. The questioner should first determine the appropriate method of refutation to use.
      b. Questions should be phrased to elicit factual rather than interpretative responses.
      c. Questions should be phrased so that the respondent is asked to provide the fact rather than to confirm it.
      d. Lines of questions rather than isolated questions should be prepared.
      e. Analogies and parallel situations may be used in guiding the respondent to the desired conclusion.
      f. The questioner should not seek to elicit admissions to broad, general conclusions.

    g. The questioner should be prepared to cut off a respondent if he is overqualifying an answer.

    h. The questioner should be prepared to drop a line of questioning when it isn't getting anywhere.

    i. The admissions gained through cross-examination should be used as a basis for developing arguments in the formal speeches which follow.

  2. Substantive Guides for the Respondent

    a. The respondent's answers should be consistent with his total analysis of the controversy.

    b. The respondent should be prepared to provide obvious answers.

    c. The respondent should be prepared to admit ignorance when he does not know the answer to a question.

    d. If an answer must be qualified, the respondent should qualify the answer before answering directly.

    e. The respondent should attempt to see that the questioner does not draw conclusions or make speeches during the question session.

  B. Psychological Aspects of Cross-examination

    1. Psychological Impact in Questioning

    2. Psychological Impact in Responding to Questions

III. Summary

When one uses the term "cross-examination," the tendency is to think of a lawyer questioning a witness in a courtroom or of the cross-examination situation which exists in certain academic debate formats. Certainly, these are the most common formalized uses of cross-examination. Courtroom lawyers must be skilled in cross-examination in order to succeed in their profession. Academic debaters must be able to question and respond to questions skillfully in debate formats which require cross-examination. But the skills involved in asking and answering questions are not limited in their importance to these advocacy situations. Rather, they are vital to many other advocacy situations and also have applications in many nonadvocacy situations. Audience-controlled forums, for instance, depend entirely upon the ability of the participants to question and respond to questions skillfully. Many audience debate situations involve opportunities for audience questioning of the participants. Skill in questioning and answering is also central in many classroom situations, job interviews, and counseling situations. While the focus of this chapter will be on cross-examination as it occurs in public advocacy situations, particularly academic debate, the applications of this discussion extend well beyond this limitation.

The concept of cross-examination, as it will be used in this chapter, is somewhat more specific than the mere asking and answering of questions. A cross-examination situation is composed of three essential elements: (1) a *cross-examiner or questioner* who controls the advocacy situation through the asking of questions, (2) a *respondent* or witness who is under some obligation to answer the questions posed by the cross-examiner, and (3) a *time period* which permits the questioner to ask more than one question. Situations which permit the asking of only a single question per person cannot really be considered cross-examination situations. The ability to ask a series of questions, each of which grows out of the answer to the previous question, is an essential feature of cross-examination. With this definition in mind, the remainder of this chapter will be devoted to a discussion of the purposes of cross-examination and of the techniques involved in the conduct of cross-examination. Specific applications of this discussion will be made to academic debate formats since students of argumentation encounter these situations most frequently.

THE PURPOSES
OF CROSS-EXAMINATION

The specific purpose of cross-examination will vary considerably depending upon the nature of the advocacy situation. Cross-examination can be used to achieve anything that can be accomplished through the methods of refutation outlined in the last chapter. Essentially, however, the purposes of cross-examination can be grouped into a fourfold classification: (1) to permit the gathering and clarifying of information, (2) to facilitate the examination of data, (3) to expose weaknesses in analysis, and (4) to undermine the credibility of the respondent.

GATHERING AND CLARIFYING INFORMATION

It is common to think of cross-examination as designed exclusively to destroy the arguments of the opposition. Yet, one of the most important functions of cross-examination is a pure inquiry function—the gathering and clarifying of information. In nearly every advocacy situation in which cross-examination is used there will be times when the questioner will question for the purpose of gathering information or for clarifying information which has already been presented. If a debater fails to understand completely an argument used by the opposing advocate, a portion of the cross-examination session can be used to encourage the respondent to clarify the argument so that all present may understand it fully. Questioning in congressional hearings is frequently designed to gather necessary information which is not contained in the formal statements of the witnesses. Cross-examination, then, can be used to clarify arguments and materials already presented or to gather additional information as needed.

EXAMINING DATA

A second purpose of cross-examination is to examine the data upon which opposition arguments are based. Such an examination can include analysis of both premises and evidence. Frequently, advocates do not articulate the *perceptual premises* and *value premises* upon which they base their arguments. Cross-examination can be used to examine the adequacy of the evidence which advocates use in support of their arguments. To use cross-examination to examine data, the questioner should be familiar with the various tests of data which have been outlined in Chapter 5.

EXPOSING WEAKNESSES IN ANALYSIS

A third function of cross-examination is to expose weaknesses in the analysis of a witness or an opposing advocate. Here the questioner is looking for logical flaws which may help to undermine the credibility of the analysis. Frequently, the analysis of an opposing advocate or the testimony of a witness will contain subtle logical weaknesses which are not clearly evident at first hearing. Cross-examination is uniquely suited for exposing such weaknesses because of the focusing which a carefully designed line of questioning permits. The questioner who would use cross-examination for the purpose of exposing weaknesses in analysis should be familiar with the relevant tests of reasoning outlined in Chapter 8 and the various methods of refutation outlined in Chapter 14.

UNDERMINING THE CREDIBILITY OF
THE RESPONDENT

This purpose of cross-examination is limited generally to courts of law, although it is occasionally used when questioning is part of audience activation situations, especially political situations. In courts of law, where so much depends upon the perceived credibility of the witness, major portions of cross-examination may be spent in an attempt to question the witness's character or authority. Unlike the first three purposes of cross-examination, this one does not focus on the substance of the controversy but rather on the personal credibility of the respondent.

Cross-examination, then, has a variety of purposes. The conduct of cross-examination will vary considerably depending upon the specific goal of the questioner. It is necessary, therefore, for the questioner to have a clear notion of what he is attempting to achieve through cross-examination before he begins planning his specific cross-examination methodologies.

THE CONDUCT
OF CROSS-EXAMINATION

For cross-examination to achieve its goal or goals, it must be carefully prepared and precisely conducted. A questioner must know what he wants to achieve through cross-examination and he must anticipate the behavior of the respondent. When placed in the position of answering questions, the advocate must not only be sure of his arguments—he must also anticipate the types of questions he may be asked. In considering the conduct of cross-examination, it is helpful to consider both the substantive and the psychological aspects of the cross-examination situation.

SUBSTANTIVE ASPECTS OF CROSS-EXAMINATION

Both questioner and respondent have substantive goals in cross-examination. The questioner seeks admissions and responses to specific questions which forward his analysis and focus the debate in areas advantageous to his analysis. The respondent seeks to answer questions in ways which will not damage his essential position and which will, whenever possible, clarify and strengthen his position. The following guides are designed to assist both the questioner and the respondent in achieving their substantive goals.

SUBSTANTIVE GUIDES FOR THE QUESTIONER

All cross-examination situations are designed so that the questioner maintains control of the dialogue. Whether or not the questioner is able to maintain this control, however, depends entirely upon his skill in phrasing questions, putting questions together, and anticipating the responses of the respondent. The guidelines below are designed to help the questioner control the cross-examination situation in order to achieve his substantive goals.

The questioner should first determine the appropriate method of refutation to use. Once the questioner has identified the arguments he wishes to attack through cross-examination, he should begin the preparation of specific questions by first determining the appropriate method of refutation. The method of refutation constitutes the overall approach within which the specific questions will be prepared to achieve the advocate's goal. The advocate should decide at the outset, for instance, whether he wants to attempt to undermine the credibility of an argument or attempt to reduce its importance within the controversy. If he wishes to undermine the argument's credibility, he must choose the appropriate method of refutation for achieving this goal (exposing inconsistencies, reducing the argument to absurdity, attacking the validity of the evidence, etc.). If he wishes to reduce the argument's importance within the controversy, he must also make a decision on a specific method of refutation (minimization, denial of inherency, exposing dilemmas, etc.). Once the method of refutation is chosen, the advocate can move to the preparation of specific lines of questions.

Questions should be phrased to elicit factual rather than interpretative responses. In phrasing questions for cross-examination, the questioner should always know the answer to the questions to avoid being surprised and embarrassed by an unexpected answer. This consideration suggests that questions should draw for *factual* rather than *interpretative* responses. If the cross-examiner asks a "How?" or a "Why?" question, for instance, he encourages the respondent to interpret the facts as he sees them. The response is likely to be unpredictable and time-consuming and may even result in the loss of control of the question period by the cross-examiner. Rather, questions should be phrased to force the respondent to take a precise position on limited factual matters. In questioning a respondent concerning the gaps in public assistance coverage, for instance, the question, "How do you explain the fact that many poor people are not covered under public assistance?" invites a lengthy and unpredictable answer. A more specific phrasing of the question such as, "How many Americans living below the official poverty level received no public assistance at all last year?" on the other hand, will elicit a briefer factual response.

Questions should be phrased so that the respondent is asked to provide the fact rather than to confirm it. It is generally unwise to begin a question with the phrase, "Are you aware of the fact that. . . ." Not only does such an approach give the psychological impression of arrogance, but it also may give the respondent some unnecessary assistance. In many cases the respondent may be unaware of the fact in question. By phrasing the question so that he must provide the fact, one may achieve a surprising and useful admission of ignorance. Even when the respondent knows the answer, the damaging fact becomes more credible and more persuasive when it is stated by the respondent rather than by the questioner. To illustrate, instead of asking, "Are you aware of the fact that a defense attorney may not present evidence to a grand jury?" the question should be rephrased, "Is there any mechanism within the grand jury system for a defense attorney to present evidence to a grand jury?" The change in wording is subtle, but the first question merely asks the respondent to *confirm* the question while the second wording requires him to make the *initial statement* of the answer.

Lines of questions rather than isolated questions should be prepared. It is usually difficult to accomplish any of the goals of cross-examination with a single question. For this reason, cross-examiners are given a period of time in which they are permitted to ask a variety of questions. Skillful cross-examiners will rarely move directly to the ultimate questions which they wish to ask. Rather, they will phrase several questions which lead gradually to the conclusion desired. The first questions will involve seemingly harmless factual matters, and respondents are frequently unaware of the direction of the line of questioning at this point. Each succeeding question builds upon the answer just given as the line of questions moves towards its ultimate objective. Cross-examiners should be careful not to allow the line of questioning to become too involved for fear of losing the audience in the process. The questions below illustrate the development of a line of questions.

1. You have said that there is no significant relationship between the private ownership of guns and violence, is that correct?
2. Were guns involved in the assassinations of Robert Kennedy? Martin Luther King? John F. Kennedy?
3. Can you tell me, of the 121 police officers killed in the line of duty in 1971, how many were shot with hand guns?
4. How many U.S. citizens die each year as a result of gun accidents?

5. How many robberies annually involve the use of guns?
6. In how many assault cases are guns used?
7. What is the only major nation in the world that does not control the private use of guns?
8. What nation leads the world in death by gunfire?

Analogies and parallel situations may be used in guiding the respondent to the desired conclusion. In many cross-examination situations, especially academic debate, the respondent is as thoroughly prepared to answer questions as the cross-examiner is to ask them. Within the subject matter area under consideration, therefore, respondents frequently have carefully prepared answers to anticipated questions in order to avoid being led to the desired goal of the questioner. When questions utilize analogies and parallel situations, on the other hand, the questioning is removed from the subject matter area and from the carefully prepared answers of the respondent. In responding to analogies and parallel situations the witness is forced to rethink idea relationships and frequently may be more easily led by the questioner. The following line of questioning illustrates this guideline.

1. Your position, if I understand it correctly, is that marijuana should be legalized because it is extremely difficult to enforce antimarijuana laws. Is that true?
2. Is the purpose of our laws against speeding to deter drivers from driving too fast?
3. In spite of these laws, do people sometimes speed when they are driving?
4. Are all of these speeders caught?
5. According to official estimates, has the incidence of illegal speeding increased or decreased in recent years?

The questioner should not seek to elicit admissions to broad, general conclusions. One of the greatest temptations in cross-examination is to attempt to achieve too much with a single question or with a series of questions. It must be remembered that the closer the questioner gets to the general conclusion or admission that he wants to elicit from the respondent, the more likely it is that the respondent will begin to limit and qualify his answer. One is not likely to get the desired response to a question such as, "Then you agree with my contention that grand jury procedures are contrary to the witnesses' constitutional rights?" Rather than asking broad questions such as this one which are designed to elicit important admissions, it is generally more effective to lead the respondent with a series of more specific factual questions and to stop the questioning short of the ultimate conclusion desired. This not only saves the time that would be consumed in a lengthy qualified response, but it also is generally more persuasive to allow the judge or the audience to reach the conclusion on their own. The advocate can assure that the admissions aren't overlooked by referring to them in later speeches (the lawyer in his summation or the debater in constructive speeches).

The questioner should be prepared to cut off a respondent if he is overqualifying an answer. Occasionally, respondents will attempt to qualify even the most obvious questions or will spend more time than is reasonable qualifying questions on which direct answers cannot be given. This situation arises frequently in academic debate. If the respondent has already answered the question or if the qualifications are excessive, the questioner must exercise his right to maintain control of the question session. The silencing of a respondent, however, must be handled tactfully and timed carefully. The questioner must not be hesitant or unsure, but should speak slightly over the level of the witness and move directly into the next question. If the questioner attempts to cut off the respondent too early, he will be viewed as unreasonable by the audience or judge. On the other hand, if he waits too long, he may lose complete control of the question session.

The questioner should be prepared to drop a line of questioning when it isn't getting anywhere. It is not uncommon for a line of questioning to run into some difficulty in reaching its desired goal. In some cases, the questioner may not have anticipated the answers he received and may not be able to build further questions upon these answers. In other cases, the respondent may simply refuse to provide answers to obvious questions, causing the line of questioning to bog down. In such situations it is useless to pursue the line of questioning further, and the questioner should merely drop the line of questioning and move on to another one.

The admissions gained through cross-examination should be used as a basis for developing arguments in the formal speeches which follow. Because of the give and take nature of cross-examination it is not always possible to develop ideas thoroughly or to relate ideas systematically during cross-examination. The procedures of academic debate and of courts of law, therefore, provide for formal speeches following the cross-examination periods. The purpose of these speeches is to build upon the lines of questioning developed in the cross-examination session and to relate them to the total case analysis. Statements such as: "As the witness admitted under cross-examination . . ." or "As was pointed out during the questioning period ..." or "The cross-examination revealed ..." should punctuate the following speech. Where an argument can be established through the admission of a witness no further supporting data is necessary. Failure of an advocate to refer to the cross-examination in his formal speech suggests that the cross-examination was ineffective.

SUBSTANTIVE GUIDES FOR THE RESPONDENT

Skill in asking questions constitutes only half of the cross-examination situation; the other half is skill in answering questions. If cross-examination is to function as a search for truth, the respondent must be honest and candid in responding to the questions posed to him. The respondent, however, must also be sure that he is not led to conclusions damaging to his analysis. The guides below are designed to help the respondent contribute positively to the dialogue while maintaining his basic analysis of the question under consideration.

The respondent's answers should be consistent with his total analysis of the controversy.   The respondent must attempt to understand the relevance of each question to the overall controversy. In order to answer a question in a manner which is consistent with his own analysis, the respondent must first perceive which element of that analysis is being probed by the question. This is not easy to do since questioners frequently attempt to disguise the impact of their initial questions. Once the focus of the question becomes clear, the respondent should answer the question within the basic philosophy and structure of his analysis of the controversy.

The respondent should be prepared to provide obvious answers. Many respondents, particularly in academic debate, tend to view each and every question as a threat to their analysis of the proposition. The fact is that many questions call for straightforward, obvious answers, and the respondent should provide such answers unhesitatingly. To attempt to qualify and hedge on questions with obvious answers creates unnecessary credibility problems for the respondent and destroys the whole value of cross-examination. Efforts to be evasive may also serve to emphasize the importance of a particular question or series of questions.

The respondent should be prepared to admit ignorance when he does not know the answer to a question.   Obviously, the best possible position for a respondent is to be prepared to provide the answers for all questions that are posed to him. Frequently, however, questions are asked for which the respondent simply does not know the answer. Many witnesses, afraid of admitting ignorance, will attempt to bluff their way through some sort of answer. Unfortunately, if the questioner knows the answer to the question, as he should, the respondent is frequently exposed in his bluffing attempts. While it is never a comfortable position to be asked a question for which one does not know the answer, the best possible response to this situation is to admit ignorance and make light of it.

If the answer must be qualified, the respondent should qualify the answer before answering it directly. The responses to many questions cannot be given with simple "yes" or "no" answers. When the answers to questions must be qualified, the respondent should present the qualification first and the direct answer later. The "Yes, but ..." answer is likely to be cut off by the questioner before the respondent can develop the qualification. To guarantee that the qualification is heard, it should be presented first. For example, the answer to the question, "Wouldn't cross-district bussing make it impossible for many children to participate in extracurricular activities?" might be phrased, "The extracurricular activity problem is not insurmountable, but bussing admittedly does create some difficulties in this area."

The respondent should attempt to see that the questioner does not draw conclusions or make speeches during the question session. While the questioner has the controlling role in cross-examination, that role is limited to the asking of questions. When the questioner goes beyond this limit to present speeches or to draw conclusions from answers provided by the respondent, the respondent should tactfully note this point. If, for example, the questioner during the cross-examination period attempts to state a conclusion or to make a brief speech, the witness may call attention to this fact by interrupting and asking, "Is that a question? I would like to respond to what you said." In courts of law the judges and opposition lawyers help to keep cross-examination in line, but in most other advocacy situations the respondent will have to defend himself.

PSYCHOLOGICAL ASPECTS OF CROSS-EXAMINATION

As a general rule, each participant in a cross-examination session is being evaluated by an audience, a judge, or a jury on the basis of his handling of the questioning. Each individual, therefore, must be concerned about the image he creates in his conduct of cross-examination. While the primary purposes of cross-examination deal with the substance of the controversy, the psychological impact of the ways in which questions are asked and answered cannot be ignored.

PSYCHOLOGICAL IMPACT IN QUESTIONING

Popular courtroom television shows have created an image of the cross-examiner as a hard-driving, assertive individual. In most questioning situations, however, the questioner must achieve some middle ground between being too aggressive and too weak. If his questioning becomes too aggressive, he will be perceived to be abusive and dominating by the judge or audience. Few people respond favorably to a brow-beater. If, on the other hand, the questioner is too weak in his approach, he will be perceived as unsure of himself and may, psychologically, lose control of the questioning. In attempting to strike a balance between these two poles, the questioner should appear pleasant, fair, and sure of himself. A good sense of humor and a sense of timing are also important qualities in creating the right psychological impact.

PSYCHOLOGICAL IMPACT IN RESPONDING TO QUESTIONS

The witness, as well as the questioner, must be careful to create an appropriate psychological impression. This is especially true in courtroom situations where much depends upon the perceived credibility of the witness, although respondents in all cross-examination situations will find psychological impact a crucial consideration. Like the questioner, the respondent must find the appropriate middle ground between being too evasive and too cooperative. If the respondent is too evasive he loses credibility because he will appear to be hiding something. Perceived evasiveness unnecessarily causes the question to become more important than it really is in the minds of the audience or the judge. On the other hand, if the respondent is too cooperative and answers thoughtlessly he may reveal more than is necessary, thereby weakening his position. Ideally, the respondent should appear open and honest with nothing to fear. He should create the impression that he welcomes the chance to explain his position.

SUMMARY

A cross-examination situation is composed of three essential elements: (1) a cross-examiner or questioner who controls the advocacy situation through the asking of questions, (2) a respondent or witness who is under some obligation to answer the questions posed by the cross-examiner, and (3) a time period which permits the questioner to ask more than one question.

The purposes of cross-examination are fourfold: (1) to permit the gathering and clarifying of information, (2) to facilitate the examination of data, (3) to expose weaknesses in analysis, and (4) to undermine the credibility of the respondent.

Nine guidelines assist the questioner in controlling the cross-examination situation in order to achieve his substantive goals: (1) the questioner should first determine the appropriate method of refutation to use; (2) questions should be phrased to elicit factual rather than interpretative responses; (3) questions should be phrased so that the respondent is asked to provide the fact rather than to confirm it; (4) lines of questions rather than isolated questions should be prepared; (5) analogies and parallel situations may be used in guiding the respondent to the desired conclusion; (6) the questioner should not seek to elicit admissions to broad, general conclusions; (7) the questioner should be prepared to cut off a respondent if he is overqualifying an answer; (8) the questioner should be prepared to drop a line of questioning when it isn't getting anywhere; (9) the admissions gained through cross-examination should be used as a basis for developing arguments in the formal speeches which follow.

Five guidelines assist the respondent in contributing positively to the dialogue while maintaining his basic analysis of the question under consideration: (1) the respondent's answers should be consistent with his total analysis of the controversy; (2) the respondent should be prepared to provide obvious answers; (3) the respondent should be prepared to admit ignorance when he does not know the answer to a question; (4) if the answer must be qualified, the respondent should qualify the answer before answering it directly; (5) the respondent should attempt to see that the questioner does not draw conclusions or make speeches during the question session.

While the primary purposes of cross-examination deal with the substance of the controversy, the psychological impact of the ways in which questions are asked and answered cannot be ignored. In attempting to strike a balance between being too aggressive and too weak, the questioner should appear pleasant, fair, and sure of himself. The respondent, on the other hand, should appear open and honest with nothing to fear, creating the impression that he welcomes the chance to explain his position.

STUDY QUESTIONS

1. Why is the ability to ask a series of questions essential to the nature of cross-examination?
2. To what extent is skill in cross-examination a tool of inquiry as well as a tool of advocacy?
3. To what extent are the principles of cross-examination discussed in this chapter relevant to questioning in the job-interview situation? In the counseling situation? In a legislative inquiry?

EXERCISES

1. Prepare three lines of cross-examination. Use these with a witness in class. Have the other class members evaluate your efforts.
2. Read the transcript from the Advocates television program in Appendix B. Try to identify specific examples of the methodologies suggested in this chapter.
3. Listen to one of the television interview programs such as *Meet the Press.* Compare the approach to questioning in this type of public inquiry situation with the approach used in public advocacy situations (courts of law, academic debate, the *Advocates,* etc.).
4. Have one class member present an oral argument based on an unstated value premise; attempt to expose that value premise through cross-examination.

IV A Final Comment

16 The Study of Argumentation: A Perspective

In this book, the study of argumentation has been described as a process with two primary components: an inquiry phase and an advocacy phase. Each of these two components has been further divided into subcomponents consisting of the various inquiry and advocacy disciplines which are essential to a complete understanding of argumentation theory and skills. This final chapter attempts to integrate these components, to discuss their relationships and priorities within the total study of argumentation, and to draw some implications of this study for the student of argumentation and for decision making in society.

THE RELATIONSHIP
BETWEEN INQUIRY AND ADVOCACY

A student once posed the hypothetical question, "If you had time to teach only inquiry or only advocacy in a course in argumentation, which would you teach? Rephrased, the question isolates an important value judgment concerning the nature of the study of argumentation. "Is the primary focus of the study of argumentation concerned with inquiry or advocacy?" From the perspective of this book, the study of reasoned inquiry is an essential prerequisite for the study of advocacy in argumentation. The remainder of this section constitutes a justification for this assertion.

THE PLACE OF INQUIRY IN ARGUMENTATION

Argumentation was defined in Chapter 1 as the study of the logical principles which underlie the examination and presentation of persuasive claims. Both the definition and the organization of this book suggest the primacy of inquiry in the study of argumentation. Most of the "logical principles" which underlie the examination and presentation of persuasive claims are developed in the chapters in the inquiry section. With the exception of Chapter 10, all of the chapters in the advocacy section assume the foundation of inquiry skills which are developed earlier. The chapters on affirmative and negative case construction, for example, assume an understanding of the process of analysis, the ability to gather and test data, the ability to examine reasoning, and the ability to organize ideas logically. Our consideration of communication strategies, refutation, and cross-examination all assume that thorough inquiry has taken place.

Chapter 1 outlines two reasons for studying argumentation: to help us in making personal decisions and to provide a viable means of effecting social change. The achievement of the first goal is contained entirely within the study of inquiry. Personal decision making is dependent upon the ability to analyze the facts of a situation and on the ability to evaluate conflicting values. To evaluate our own personal attitudes and beliefs and to avoid being mere sponges which simply absorb that to which we are exposed, we need the skills of reasoned inquiry to enable us to evaluate critically the ideas and influences which bombard us daily.

The second goal—effecting social change—is dependent upon the skills of both inquiry and advocacy. The study of argumentation, however, assumes that thorough inquiry, thorough investigation and testing of argument, must precede public advocacy. Argumentation assumes that the advocate's first and primary responsibility is to attempt to discover probable truth in a situation before turning to advocacy considerations.

Argumentation as an academic study, then, focuses primarily upon investigative skills, upon the skills of reasoned inquiry. This focus is based upon an important value judgment which has controlled the entire composition and development of this book. That value judgment asserts that ideas and policies which have been thoroughly investigated, analyzed, and tested are more likely to be superior ideas and policies. Without this assumption, the time and effort and mental discipline necessary for thorough inquiry would be a waste of time.

If we could teach only the skills of inquiry, we could still say that we were teaching argumentation, albeit somewhat incompletely. If we taught only advocacy skills, however, we would be teaching another course. We might call this course persuasion or studies in attitude change, but we would not call it argumentation. What makes the study of argumentation unique is its concentration on inquiry skills.

THE PLACE OF ADVOCACY IN ARGUMENTATION

Obviously, since six chapters are devoted to the skills of reasoned advocacy, we do not mean to conclude that advocacy instruction has no place in the study of argumentation. The consideration of advocacy skills in argumentation, however, occurs within a limited framework. Argumentation has been defined as focusing on "logical principles," and this focus applies to the study of advocacy as well as to the study of inquiry.

While Chapter 10 presents an analysis of situations for advocacy and Chapter 13 discusses strategic considerations in the presentation of arguments, the discussion of advocacy in this book assumes thorough inquiry and an advocate's commitment to what he has discovered to be the "probable truth." The chapters on case construction assume the relevance of the logical framework of argument outlined in Chapter 2 and of the analysis methodologies in Chapter 3. The chapters on refutation and cross-examination assume that the advocate understands the tests of data and reasoning and can apply them in refutation and cross-examination. Even the chapter on communication strategies operates on the assumption that the development of an appropriate strategy does not require an advocate to abandon or alter his basic logical analysis of a proposition.

The consideration of advocacy skills within the study of argumentation, then, is based upon the primacy of logical considerations and assumes the desire to seek probable truth through thorough investigation on the part of the advocate. For this reason the study of argumentation, even when it focuses on advocacy skills, tends to be logically oriented rather than psychologically oriented. This is not to say that motivational concepts are not important to the student of argumentation; it simply says that in-depth consideration of these concepts falls outside the framework of the study of argumentation per se. Training in argumentation may be thought of as the base upon which all other communication studies should be built. The serious student of argumentation should expand his communication studies to include the study of human motivation, attitude change, image creation, etc. But this education should be built upon a base of inquiry skills and upon an attitude that places primary value on thorough logical analysis.

THE CHALLENGE OF ARGUMENTATION IN SOCIETY

UNDERSTANDING THE NATURE OF PUBLIC DECISION MAKING

An examination of public controversy as it actually occurs reveals that the processes of decision making are not always as neat and clear as the examples used in this book might suggest. In writing this book we have attempted to make the study of argumentation clear by phrasing precise statements of propositions and by using illustrations which are simple and easy to relate to argumentation concepts. Public argumentation, on the other hand, is not nearly so clear. Any individual who examines a newspaper editorial or a public speech and analyzes the reasoning processes and the data used will find the application of the principles of reasoned inquiry extremely difficult. Three characteristics of public decision making account for this difficulty.

The first characteristic of public decision making is that existing realities are constantly changing. What constitutes the existing policy or belief today may be changed tomorrow. While we are debating large policy changes in efforts to achieve integration or inflation control or tax reform, small incremental changes in the "existing system" are taking place almost daily. This constant change, this "process reality," makes it more difficult to isolate the essence of the controversy.

A second characteristic which makes public controversy harder to analyze is the mixture of logical and extralogical factors. The necessity of adapting to the attitudes and special interests of specific decision-making groups causes public advocates to use a variety of both logical and motivational factors. For us to apply the tests of inquiry, the extralogical elements must be stripped away or converted into value premises.

A final characteristic of public controversy which contributes to the difficulty in applying the principles of argumentation is that it frequently lacks clear statements of the specific proposition under consideration. Participants in public controversy, even those engaged in face-to-face debate, rarely take adequate care to phrase a proposition which isolates the essence of their concern. The larger public controversies are often multipropositional, contributing even further to the analytical confusion.

All of these factors together make public controversy complex and not easy to analyze. If, however, we cannot identify existing realities or separate motivational from logical appeals or determine the focus of the controversy, we cannot begin to make valid judgments regarding the logical adequacy of individual arguments or of overall case analyses. Thus, the practical application of all that we have learned through the study of argumentation requires that we make the effort to overcome these difficulties. Only by argumentative analysis of public controversy can we make valid logical judgments about public policy.

INFLUENCING THE STRUCTURE OF PUBLIC DECISION MAKING

Students of argumentation have a duty not only to appraise the logical adequacy of all public statements, but also to strive to improve the structure of public advocacy situations. Public decision making must be removed, wherever possible, from audience activation situations which place no external constraints upon the advocate. To the extent that we can place public decision making in advocacy situations which guarantee a clash of ideas and critical evaluation of advocacy, we will begin to improve the quality of public advocacy.

The 1972–73 controversy over Republican bugging of the Democratic Party headquarters at Watergate provides an excellent example of what can happen to public understanding of a controversy when it is forced into a more restrictive audience situation. For nine months, all the public could discover about this controversy came through independent, unexaminable statements of individual public figures. The President and important Republican figures refused, for obvious reasons, to be questioned on this subject during the presidential campaign. It was not until after the 1972 election when Senator Ervin's Special Committee forced the issue into the open that the public began to achieve some understanding of the situation. Advocates were placed in a highly restrictive advocacy situation in which they were forced to testify under oath before trained cross-examiners in full public view.

The American public was able to see the application of the tests of reasoned inquiry in the Watergate controversy because of the change in the advocacy situation in which this controversy took place. What happened with the Watergate controversy can happen in all of public decision making if enough people are interested in guaranteeing advocacy situations which place, in one way or another, logical constraints upon public advocates.

Thus, argumentation requires of those who understand it that they work to improve both the substance and the structure of public controversies. As more members of society's audiences become skilled in the application of argumentation concepts to public statements, false and shallow thinking will be less able to prevail. And as argumentation situations are restructured to provide more opportunities for critical examination of ideas, the substance of public disputes will be more thoroughly explored.

Appendixes

A An
Intercollegiate
Debate

1973 NATIONAL DEBATE TOURNAMENT
FINAL DEBATE: SHOULD THE
FEDERAL GOVERNMENT PROVIDE A PROGRAM
OF COMPREHENSIVE MEDICAL CARE
FOR ALL UNITED STATES CITIZENS?[1]

The Twenty-Seventh National Debate Tournament sponsored by the American Forensic Association was held at the U. S. Naval Academy in Annapolis, Maryland, on April 8–11, 1973. The sixty-two participating teams debated the 1972–73 national intercollegiate debate proposition: "Resolved, that the federal government should provide a program of comprehensive medical care for all United States citizens."

Eight preliminary and four elimination rounds resulted in this final debate between Georgetown University and Northwestern University. Representing Georgetown on the affirmative were Bradley Ziff and Stewart Jay; for the negative from Northwestern were Elliott Mincberg and Ron Marmer.[2] Judges awarded the decision to the negative team from Northwestern.[3] The text of the debate follows.[4]

FIRST AFFIRMATIVE CONSTRUCTIVE:
BRADLEY ZIFF, GEORGETOWN

Ladies and gentlemen, this afternoon Mr. Jay and I will support the national debate proposition, examples of which will be provided in the following affirmative proposal.

Plank number one: All United States citizens will be legally entitled to comprehensive medical care, with the exception of cosmetic surgery, psychiatric treatment, and dental care, with no cost charged for any services rendered. Such coverage will be phased in over a three-year period, beginning with immediate coverage for all catastrophic illness.

Two: All such medical care will be a federal public service. Therefore, there will be no private practice or facilities allowed for under provisions of our plan. Wages for providers of such care will be legally set at 15 percent above specialty averages. The number of hours worked by all personnel will be governmentally set. Further upward adjustments will be allowed to compensate for relevant cost-of-living increases, shortages of technical and paramedical personnel, extensive controlled research projects, and medical treatment efficiency increments. All necessary steps, including regulation of medical schools, may be taken to ensure adequate supplies of manpower.

Three: The federal government will organize all medical workers into general health care centers. Regional service centers will be established to provide for specialized treatment. Such units will be structured in group or team fashion, utilizing models such as the Kaiser program.

Four: An independent self-perpetuating Drug Regulatory Commission will be established. Members will include Senator Gaylord Nelson, Dr. Henry Simmons, and Dr. Thomas Dunphy. Duties of the Commission will include: (1) collection, coordination, and dissemination of all relevant information on prescription drugs to all physicians through their own group practice units; (2) establishment and enforcement of complete record-keeping standards for all physicians, administered by their appropriate group practice; (3) regulation of prescription drug practices through review of all records by group practice administrators with Commission monitoring. In any complaint, the burden of proof will be on the physician to justify his prescription practices.

Five: A self-perpetuating independent Federal Regulatory Commission—commissioners with life tenure—will be established to ensure optimal levels of medical care for all citizens through extensive quality and educational controls. The Commission will be chaired and appointed by Dr. Robert McCleary of the Center for the Study of Responsive Law. In all matters relating to the use of X-ray techniques, standards will be established and directed by Dr. Karl Morgan. All other necessary staff and personnel shall be provided.

Six: Violators of the regulatory provisions of this plan will be ineligible to practice medical care as part of the federal public service. All other violations will be subject to fines and imprisonment.

Seven: Costs of the affirmative proposal will be financed through an independent trust fund, making progressive use of federal tax structures. Tax incentives will be provided employers enforcing the Occupational Health and Safety Act.

Ladies and gentlemen, Georgetown University finds warrant for adoption of this particular proposal in terms of any one of the following three independent comparative advantages.

(I) The affirmative program better provides needed medical care to more United States citizens—needed medical care to more United States citizens. We ask you to understand, first, that all too often the philosophy of our present health care system is based upon the ability to pay—the ability to pay. Senator Edward Kennedy writes: "Basically we have chosen to leave the provision of needed medical care to the cruel play of the marketplace. Certainly government has become involved, but its efforts have always been limited, categorical, and inadequate."[5]

We ask you to understand, second, that such economic factors lead to the denial of health care to millions of Americans—denial of health care to millions of Americans. There will be no reason to imply the "emptiness of rhetoric" here. Tragically, the statistics will speak for themselves as the Task Force on the Urban Coalition sets them forth: Death comes early to the poor. Their risk of dying under age twenty-five is four times the average. There is four times as much serious illness among families with low incomes. They suffer twice the number of days of restricted activity and a third longer hospitalization.[6] Thus it was that Dr. Therman Evans could recently conclude: "For poor people all over this nation, the chance of living is going down because the medical cost of living is going up."[7] But please do not be deluded into believing that if you are not black or that if you are not poor that you are safe. Senator Edward Kennedy continues: "Our current health care crisis is not just a problem of the poor. Millions of other Americans have gambled with their health in order to avoid the high cost of care they need. Millions of Americans have thus endured pain and suffering which might otherwise have been relieved."[8]

But understand, third, that while removal of these economic barriers will significantly alleviate a national health care crisis, a thorough-going restructuring of our medical care delivery system is also required—restructure the medical care delivery system. Thus major organizational changes in personnel, facilities, and efficient use of resources will be required before optimal coverage can be guaranteed. Stewart and I sadly conclude with New York Mayor John Lindsay, who writes: "Guaranteeing the financial availability of medical care to every American will not solve the whole problem. Unless our delivery structures are also radically altered, millions of Americans will still not receive the care they need."[9]

(II) Consider with us now our second independent advantage: The affirmative program will better guard against individual financial hardship—guard against individual financial hardship. Realize, first, that the costs of serious illness are both severe and extensive—severe and extensive costs. Representative Hogan testifies in January: "Catastrophic illness is any disorder from the exotic calamity to the common coronary. It is nondiscriminating to whom it attacks, where it attacks, and when it attacks. But its costs are frighteningly real. Fifty or seventy-five thousand dollars is not an uncommon charge for such a calamity."[10] The Senate Finance Committee provided the number of Americans so afflicted when they wrote in April: "More than one million American families annually incur medical expenses which will qualify as catastrophic."[11]

We ask you to note, second, that for such individuals the costs can lead to tragic hardship—tragic hardship. The Brookings Institution writes: "Even for the middle class or the wealthy the medical expenses of a health catastrophe can bring instant financial distress or even total ruin."[12] Representative Hogan of Maryland was moved to write several weeks ago that the list of catastrophic illnesses which every year financially destroy thousands of our families appears almost endless.[13]

We ask you to consider only one high-risk group, hemophiliacs—hemophiliacs. On March 28, 1973, the National Hemophilia Foundation reported that more than 100,000 persons were afflicted with the disease. The Foundation's report continued: "For the hemophiliac the only chance of a normal life lies in the daily injection of a medical device known as the clotting factor. Yet its cost is staggeringly high, often up to $22,000 a year."[14] The lack of coverage was noted by Drs. Adams, Darilich, and McIntyre in April of 1972: "The inability of hemophiliacs to purchase major medical insurance means in many instances that the bleeder is subjected to devastating medical expenses."[15] The tragic results are continued by Dr. Jane Van Eyes of the Vanderbilt Medical School: "When the hemophiliac receives adequate therapy and even full employment the consequent financial burden of the disease is an impossible one."[16] So wrote Dr. Raymond Matson of Case Western

Reserve University: "The financial burden of medical care for the hemophiliac is overwhelming."[17]

But for anyone secretly taking refuge in the mindless cliché that "it can't happen to me," we ask you to carefully consider the words of Representative Martha Griffiths in 1971: "No one is safe. Despite government programs, despite health insurance, despite savings and property, nine out of every ten Americans face financial ruin should a serious or extended illness strike them. For them there is currently no hope."[18]

(III) Consider with us now our third and final advantage: The affirmative program will ensure the highest quality of necessary medical care—highest quality of necessary medical care. In this specific advantage, Mr. Jay and I will be concerned with two very specific health problems, each and either of which could seriously affect any American citizen.

(A) Prescription drugs—prescription drugs. The *Washington Post* summarized the general evil in December of 1972: "FDA (Food and Drug Administration) data as well as extensive expert testimony has confirmed that the great majority of the medical profession is needlessly imperiling the health care and lives of millions of Americans by massive overprescription and misprescription of drugs."[19] Dr. Henry Simmons of the FDA's Bureau of Drugs discussed one such example, the misprescription of antibiotics, in testimony before the Senate Monopoly Subcommittee in December of 1972: "Today doctors are needlessly treating millions of people with antibiotics, causing thousands of deaths yearly."[20] Dr. Simmons went on to cite studies which put the number of deaths due to hospital misprescription of antibiotics at anywhere from 38,000 to 225,000 deaths yearly.[21]

(B) Medical X-rays—medical X-rays. Dr. Karl Morgan of the prestigious Tennessee Oak Ridge Laboratory writes in May of 1972: "Legal requirements for education, training, and certification of all medical personnel involved with X-ray exposures could reduce the current exposure levels by 90 percent. It would save thousands of lives each year, prevent physical and mental damage to yet unborn children, and significantly reduce many forms of cancer."[22] He writes: "As many as 30,000 malignancies, stillbirths, and spontaneous abortions will occur in future generations because of the genetic damage."[23] So also concluded the National Academy of Sciences in their Special Report of several months ago: "If current radiation exposure levels continue, upwards of 27,000 Americans will annually become afflicted with serious genetic disease. Cancer deaths will probably increase by 6,000 a year."[24] Lack of such training was noted by Dr. Morgan in May of 1972:

"Most of the X-ray equipment and machines in our country are owned and under the supervision of nonradiologists—that is, medical practitioners and others with essentially no training in the use of this equipment."[25]

In conclusion, please recognize that the affirmative proposal, by enforcing stringent legal controls in these two areas of poor-quality medicine, will seriously decrease the problem. Ladies and gentlemen, for this and each and every one of the reasons preceding, Georgetown University will ask for your concurrence in this resolution.

FIRST NEGATIVE CONSTRUCTIVE:
ELLIOTT MINCBERG, NORTHWESTERN

Two plan questions: First, how much will the federal government have to allocate to fund the plan? Second, what quality standards are used? And please be specific.

It will be the basic negative position in the debate that, to the extent that financial barriers and quality problems exist in the present system, the structures of the present system can solve them easily. However, we will suggest that the gentlemen cannot provide a causal link between the variables they isolate and the problems they cite.

Two general overviews: First, the case is not prima facie. They talk about prepaid group practice; they expand it in their plan, but give you no prima facie reason why present group practices like Kaiser could not expand to cover those who need it. That would mean of course that the case was not prima facie unless they could prove that. Second, I will suggest that the advantages do not independently warrant the resolution. Now ordinarily independent advantages stem from the same policy system or collection of plan planks. Georgetown gives you separate advantages from separate policy systems in different plan planks, the composite of which is the resolution. Thus by definition the resolution is not called for unless all advantages are carried, since each is only part of comprehensive medical care. Now, if some of you don't go along with that, think of it a different way. We would suggest a hypothetical counterplan. That is, at the end of the debate, if they don't carry all three advantages, adopt whatever ones they do carry and use the rest of the money to fund things like tax rebates, pollution control, etcetera. That, we would suggest, would be a superior policy system unless they can carry all three advantages, which is the resolution.

Now please go to (I) in terms of needed medical care; (A) they talk about ability to pay from Kennedy. Later on they talk about the middle class. Now I want them to signify and quantify the problems of the middle class and not just read you "blurb" evidence. But I will suggest it [the present system] is not marked by the ability to pay; indeed, we have a pluralistic system. First, we have private health insurance. And this, combined with people's own "out-of-pocket" expenses, means most people are all right. Dr. Gerald Dorman in 1970: "Sixty percent of all Americans already have adequate health insurance."[26] There really isn't reason for most of us. But what about the rest? Second, we have Medicaid. Robert Mayer of Social Security in 1970: "States are permitted to extend the coverage of Medicaid plans beyond recipients of public aid to all those who are medically needy—those who can get along for their normal living costs but who have and cannot pay for heavy and unusual medical expenses."[27] The Task Force on Medicaid tells us that 28 states have done so already; some [state programs] are ambitious in scope.[28]

Next, I would suggest we have comprehensive health centers. Turn to the GAO [General Accounting Office] report of November, 1972: "OEO [Office of Economic Opportunity] and PHS [Public Health Service] are funding comprehensive health centers providing continuous family-centered preventative and high-quality curative care."[29] Dr. Joseph English, who heads the program, tells us in 1968 according to *Harper's,* that they are limited only, only by the funds available.[30] Put more money in. Finally, I would suggest we have free care. *Time,* December 20, 1971: "When a patient cannot afford to pay the full price, most hospitals will not turn him away for lack of funds. They usually charge patients who have insurance what their policies allow and then write off the remainder."[31] Now they must provide for you a structural reason why these options will not work or they have no case.

But now go to (B) when they tell you that this results in denial of needed medical care. We agree that the poor are sicker. The question is, why are they sicker? The gentlemen assume that a correlation between health care and income means a causation, and that is not necessarily true. Floyd Ruch and Phillip Zimbardo in 1971: "Correlations tell nothing about what is the causal agent. The major criticism of most experimental studies is the failure to include some control group, logically necessary to prove causation and rule out alternative hypotheses."[32] Let me give you an example of why their correlation is not true. The Brookings Institution reports in 1972 that, in terms of doctor and hospital visits, actually the low-income groups see doctors and go to hospitals more than the high-income groups—the ratios are 1.07 and 1.40 to 1.[33] Now if the causal link were to finances, this should not be true; but it isn't [a causal link]. There is something wrong; what's wrong is that there are other variables. First, from Norman Cantor of Rutgers: "A multitude of factors account for the poor person not receiving sufficient services—inadequate information or knowledge, cultural attitudes, alienation, language barriers, etcetera."[34] In addition, David Mechanic of Wisconsin tells us: "Although medical care has some relation to mortality, for the most part differences reflect variations in quality of life and the environment and cannot be traced to the provision of medical services."[35] Frankly there is no reason to "buy" the causal link. Mr. Evans's evidence that you see in the first affirmative constructive is merely "off the top of his hat."

Let me talk about (C) restructuring. They provide you no reason for this restructuring or anything else. I will suggest from Dr. Mark Matsler of the VA (Veterans Administration) that the best health care can be delivered through a pluralistic system.[36] Walter McNerney of Blue Cross: "Pluralism has a greater orientation toward goals, focuses on results more, and provides adaptations to changing environments, managerial ability, etcetera."[37] I want them to tell you why we need restructuring. I give you the advantages of a pluralistic system.

Now go to (II) where they tell you about individual financial hardship (A) in terms of severe costs. Number one, I want to know the level—i. e., what is their definition of a catastrophic illness? How much does it have to be? Number two, the significance of even those who get those illnesses is a lot less than they tell you. M. M. Edwards of the Congress of County Medical Societies in 1972: "Catastrophic costs affect approximately one-seventh of 1 percent of the population to begin with."[38] That's the percent that get them (catastrophic illnesses).

Now in terms of (B), they talk about hardship. So my first question obviously is, what percentage of this one-seventh of 1 percent suffer financial hardship because of illness? They do not tell you. I will argue, secondly, that there is no such causal link. Milton Davis of USC (University of Southern California) explains in 1971: "Medical crises have even more dramatic ramifications on family finances than medical costs. Because of illness individuals are forced out of work, given inadequate workmen's compensation, etcetera. Individuals lose their savings, etcetera, simply from normal consequences of mounting bills and no income."[39] When you're sick you can't work and you're in financial trouble. Medical care itself makes no difference.

Third, let me give you a counter study. Turn to Dr. Francis Davis of the Congress of County Medical Societies in his Oklahoma study in 1972. In the study only 1 percent of hospital bills were in excess of $2,000. Of these, 84 percent were covered by a government program, 14 percent by insurance policies. The rest had ample funds to pay all their medical bills completely.[40]

But next, if someone is in trouble, he can declare bankruptcy and get out of it quite quick. George Sullivan of the Macmillan Company in 1968: "Bankruptcy works to the benefit of the debtor, granting him a legal release from what he owes plus a number of substantial benefits. In a number of instances, many individuals who have good incomes deliberately run up large debts and file a petition for bankruptcy."[41] There is no problem; you get all your debts released. Finally, of course, he can also repay them [medical bills] over a long period of time. George Sullivan again: "Almost without exception the person heavily in debt can be saved from bankruptcy under Chapter 13 of the Bankruptcy Act. Individuals pay off debts under a court-supervised payment schedule."[42] The *Duke Law Journal* in 1971 says that other techniques include formal agreements such as to cancel part of the debt or extend the time for payment.[43]

Finally, I would suggest you can get group health insurance. Turnbull and Williams of Minnesota: "Group major medical insurance is the most rapidly growing form of group insurance. It is more liberal than individual policies and all members of a group are acceptable even if they would be unable to pass individual underwriting standards."[44] Let people join groups and not group practices—but group medical insurance—and that may solve the problem. Of course we could also apply Medicaid and free care to this area as well.

In terms of hemophilia, I've "beaten" it with the arguments I've given you above. But, moreover, I would challenge the gentlemen here specifically. How many hemophiliacs die because they can't get the clotting factor? If they watch themselves and don't let themselves bleed, or if they should get a cut and quickly get treatment for it, they don't have to die. There is no reason why they should spend all this money.

Now please go to (III)in terms of quality. I will argue a number of generic arguments by which quality can be determined. The first one is voluntary controls exerted by the profession itself. Milton Roemer in 1970: "More pervasive than licensure controls of state governments are the various voluntary controls by the professions themselves. The influence [of these controls] is clearly designed to protect the patient and promote quality."[45] Three examples: First, from Washington—*Patient Care* in January, 1973: "The Washington review system, involving the Medical Association, has enjoyed enthusiastic sponsorship. When instituted in one department, average harmful delays decreased by 40 percent and cases with Apgo scores under seven decreased by over 92 percent."[46] Dr. Thomas Hayes of Santa Barbara College in 1971: "Patients for the most part are in good therapeutic hands. When doctors recognize a deficiency in prescribing drugs as a priority, they will deal with it effectively."[47] The general trend of the medical profession is good. Finally, on X-rays, Dr. George Canick of the FDA: "As a result of investigations by the AEC [Atomic Energy Commission] a new lead chromium alloy has been developed to insulate X-ray machines to make them almost foolproof even in lay hands. Regulations have been added to insure that no more than needed amounts of radiation are used."[48] We are controlling X-rays at present.

The second technique I will suggest is the use of state law. Robert Derbyshire of Johns Hopkins: "Reexamination for recertification would require no wholesale changes in medical practice law. It is within the powers of a state to require recertification, reexamination of medical personnel."[49] What I am telling you is that states have the power inherently to do everything the affirmative proposal wants to do. An example is provided by Howard Goldman in 1968: "In 1964, legislation requiring the licensure of X-ray technicians became effective in New York State."[50] The (New York) legislature set standards. Why cannot this be extended? Finally, malpractice—*Medical Economics,* September 25, 1972: "Not keeping up with medical developments could lose an MD a malpractice suit. The commission on malpractice is working on setting up standards. Once it does, the threat of malpractice suits will multiply for doctors who don't keep up."[51]

Now in terms of the specifics. One, I want to know how they determine quality standards. Two, I will suggest they cannot really link quality of doctors to what the problem is. *Internist* in May, 1971: "In general, optimal quality care varies according to the environment, social, economic, cultural, educational, and genetic factors."[52] On drugs —the World Health Organization: "Many studies have shown the complexity of adverse drug reaction, the difficulty of detecting them and relating them to a specific drug or factor. An observed increase could be an increase in reports, an increase in reporting or genetic factors and environmental factors."[53] You cannot causally link. The same is true of X-rays. He reads you "blurb" evidence that says we can reduce things significantly without ever telling you, of course, how his authorities come to that conclusion. I would love to see the studies if the gentlemen would give them to me.

It is clear on balance, then, that the gentlemen do not correlate in terms of causation on any of the three advantages. More importantly, the present system has the structure to solve the problems. And, finally, there is no reason to change.

SECOND AFFIRMATIVE CONSTRUCTIVE: STEWART JAY, GEORGETOWN

Dr. Falk of Yale University estimates the cost of the plan at about $57 billion per year, 30 percent less than the present system, including all the things we do in the affirmative plan. Number two, he asks, what are the quality standards? We tell you in the third advantage we have particular problems such as in the area of drugs, such as in the area of X-ray technology. We also indicate from our experts that they are all solvable problems. Therefore, we use these experts on the affirmative (plan) to develop standards such as will correct the problems to the extent that they have said the problems are going to be avoidable.

Number one, he tells you there is no prima facie requirement here. He does not explain to you why group practice can apply today. For all we know, there are no group practices in the United States. I indicate there are inherent barriers though. The *Harvard Law Review* in 1971: "There are a number of inherent barriers which preclude the rapid expansion of prepaid group practice plans. These include: (a) initial and operational financial barriers; (b) legal barriers in many states; (c) restrictive insurance legislation; (d) the opposition of organized medicine."[54] Kaiser himself admits that at the current rate prepaid group practice programs could remain unavailable to the majority of American people for decades to come.[55]

Number two, he operates in the area of independence. We, first, give you one policy system, which the plan clearly is—a system of comprehensive medical care. At the end of the debate you should weigh the advantages of this plan against any disadvantages which still stand. But, second, let him explain why any plank of the plan, such as the third advantage, is not independently itself a comprehensive medical care system. He does not do that for you.

Number three, in the area of his hypothetical counterplan, I first want to know what planks he intends to adopt. And show me that each plank is not comprehensive medical care. Second, if he does that, he abandons presumption. And, third, he must therefore show you some added advantage over the present system, or over the case we are presenting to you. He clearly does not do that for you.

Therefore, please go to (III), the third affirmative advantage—we ensure the highest quality necessary medical care. In the area, first, he indicates that there are voluntary controls in the present system. I don't want Mincberg's "blurbs" in the final round of nationals; I want to know about the specific problems we are talking about here.

Number one, in the area of prescription drugs, we tell you in 1973 250,000 people are dying—and that's from the FDA who conducted a national study on the problem.[56] Now if there is no problem in 1973 and your voluntary controls work, Mincberg, why are 250,000 people dying? He certainly cannot answer that question. What have the American medical profession and the federal government done? Dr. Philip Lee tells you in 1972: "The record of the American medical profession and the American government in the regulation of prescription drugs has been one of complacency, laziness, stupidity, carelessness, deceit, and greed."[57] The same source goes on to say: "Efforts of the AMA [American Medical Association] and other professional and scientific groups to control the prescription of drugs can be described as a continuing failure."[58] The ever-growing problem is increasing in the United States. I would indicate to you, therefore, you have no solution whatsoever as long as you indicate that doctors are in charge. Howard Lewis explains: "On at least one ground the typical physician can be faulted: He seldom enforces among errant colleagues the high standards of conduct he personally upholds."[59] Please note that, when he talks about the "Washington review," it is not drugs. He talks about reduction and delay. What does that have to do with quality? Two, in the area of drugs in 1971, he says, they [doctors] are recognizing their deficiency.[60] But 250,000 people are clearly dying in 1973 and the deficiencies have not been corrected. In the area of X-rays—I will deal with that below when I get to the point about X-rays in the appropriate place in the case.

Number two, he talks about state laws in the area. I want to know what state laws in the area of prescription drugs require any kind of continuing education. I indicate that state laws do not do so. The *Albany Law Review* in 1972: "The plain fact is that educational obsolescence is not viewed as a disciplinary matter by state boards. Moreover, no statute at present provides for suspension of a license for educational obsolescence."[61] Will they do it in the future? The *Journal of the National Medical Association,* 1972: "It is highly unlikely that state legislatures will enact any restrictive types of requirements for medical recertification."[62] Now what kind of education do they [doctors] get in the area of drugs? From Dr. Cluff in 1972: "Current methods of informing physicians about rational use of drugs—whether through primary or continuing education—are either unavailable or so cursory as to be completely ineffective."[63] We indicate to you, therefore, you have problems in the present system which could be solved. These [problems] are all unnecessary.

He then indicates the problem of malpractice could solve all these particular problems.[64] Number one, if malpractice was effective, then you would not have 250,000 deaths in 1973. It is not a "repair"; it is a description of the present system. But, number two, it has no effect. *Geriatrics* magazine, 1972: "There has been no empirical evidence to the effect of threatened malpractice legislation. In California where the evidence of suits is the highest, the following of prescribed procedures is less frequent than in low malpractice risk states."[65] He gives you one particular example that they could lose their license, but gives no overall impact whatsoever.

Now please go down to the area of medical X-rays. We indicate 32,000 people are dying, from the Oak Ridge Laboratory.[66] He does not dispute the source. We indicate that most of the practitioners in the country have no qualification, and I would indicate that there is no way in the present system that you can have any kind of reductions because there are no state laws in the area. Dr. Morgan explains in 1972: "In 47 of our states there are almost no certification requirements for X-ray technologists."[67] Please note that, when he talks about the machines,[68] the machines are irrelevant because we still have a 92 percent reduction below what we can do today, and we save 32,000 lives. And as long as they [X-ray technicians] are untrained, the best machines in the world will do no good. Representative Koch explains in 1972: "The most sophisticated and modern of X-ray systems cannot protect the health and safety of its patients unless the technicians operating the equipment are adequately trained and licensed."[69] Please "draw across" the fact that 32,000 people are dying.

He wants to know how quality standards are set. He gives you the *Internist* and the WHO medical organization,[70] talking about in some kinds of areas the quality standards are vague and nebulous. Make him apply this to our case. We tell you from the FDA—the guys who run the drug industry in the United States—that they know these things are occurring; they know they are needless; they know they are preventable. But 250,000 people are dying. There are quality standards available. They (the deaths) can be prevented. The same thing is true in the area of X-rays. You can have a 90 percent reduction (in deaths) if you merely add the proper kinds of training.

With that in mind, please go to (II), the second affirmative advantage—we ensure that we guard against financial hardship. He, number one, wants to know what the definition of "catastrophic cost" is. I do not know why I have to give you a definition. He [the first affirmative] indicates these costs commonly go up to $70,000.[71] The middle class cannot afford them. As a consequence, we indicate that is why they are "wiped out."

What is the significance of the problem? We tell you "one million families a year" [have catastrophic medical expenses] in the first affirmative speech from the Senate Finance Committee.[72] He does not deny that. Aetna Life and Casualty Company, 1973: "1.5 million families spend more than half of their annual income on medical and surgical bills."[73] That is April of 1973. Therefore, when he tells you about one-seventh of one percent are affected,[74] how does he explain in April of 1973—clearly updating all of Mincberg's evidence—that a million and a half families are "wiped out" by these particular kinds of bills? He in no way gives you the significance of his repairs. I would turn to

Representative Hogan in 1973: "For the average middle class American who earns too much to receive welfare, but not enough to meet large medical expenses, the result of catastrophic illness is instant poverty. The family is driven to its knees."[75] He quotes Davis about the 1 percent figure.[76] That study was from Shawnee, Oklahoma—hardly a representative study. He does not explain that is a true case around the United States. We quantify at one million people.

Next, in the area of bankruptcy which he talks about, please note, number one, that people will not declare bankruptcy because of moral stigma. *Michigan Law Review* in 1971: "Many do not seek bankruptcy because of the deterrent effect of the moral stigma attached to the bald admission of economic failure."[77] But, number two, they will be harassed by the creditors. *Ohio State Law Review* in 1971: "Debtors are frequently harassed and coerced by creditors into paying debts that may have been discharged in a bankruptcy proceeding."[78] Please note, number three, even with bankruptcy, they are "wiped out." Senator Kennedy in 1972: "In a typical medical bankruptcy the family will lose everything they own, their home, car, stove, refrigerator, even their TV set."[79] He [the first negative] talks about Chapter 13, but Linn Twinem, 1971: "The Federal Bankruptcy Act, of which Chapter 13 is a part, has jurisdiction over debts allegedly incurred as a result of loans upon false financial statements."[80] Make him apply it to the area of health care.

He then talks about insurance in the area of group health care. Mr. Pettingill of Aetna Life Insurance says in 1972: "Most Americans are covered under group health insurance. However, group plans do not provide adequate coverage for primary care or catastrophic illness or both."[81] Martha Griffiths tells you nine-tenths of the population would be "wiped out."[82] In the *Congressional Digest* of 1972, according to Senator Bennett: "Only 40 percent of our people have catastrophic insurance and the limits are up to $10,000.[83] And we tell you the costs commonly go up to $70,000.

Now he wants to know how many die from hemophilia. That's not the point. They are "wiped out"—100,000 of them; they can't get insurance. He drops it.

We therefore go to (I), the first affirmative advantage. We indicate that we provide better medical care for more United States citizens. I have a number of initial overviews before I get to the case structure. Number one, 20 million people are outside the present medical care system. Dr. Carlson explains in 1972: "More than 20 million Americans are not covered by government health programs and are still unable to pay for adequate medical care."[84] Therefore, they [the negative] must defend a policy system of expansion in the next speech, and I want to know the following things about it: Number one, how much will it cost? Two, how will you finance it? Number three, how long will it take? Number four, where will you get the manpower and facilities to pay for any of this? He does not provide that.

Number two, the philosophy of the present system is to get the government out of the area of health care. Please go to Stuart Auerbach of the *Los Angeles Times* in 1973: "The biggest cut in the 1973 budget is in the area of health services—reflecting a philosophical decision on the part of the Nixon Administration to get the federal government out of the business of providing direct health care."[85]

I would indicate to you, number three, all of the programs in the present system are poverty medicine. Julius Roth in 1969: "If the patient is on a Medicaid program, he is tabbed as "welfare" with the discriminatory behavior that goes with the label. He is likely to get relatively superficial treatment and be discouraged from becoming a regular patient."[86] Senator Kennedy in 1971: "For the average poor person current federal, state, and local programs mean pain, suffering, anguish, indignity, and humiliation."[87] And according to the American Public Health Association in 1971: "The fact is that 25 million Americans receive health care we would not let our animals endure."[88] That is what Northwestern University offers for you as a repair in the present system.

Finally, let me quantify the significance of our case. We turn to Dr. Shapiro in 1967: "After a group of Medicaid enrollees were placed in an HIP group practice in New York, there was a 14 percent decline in mortality for the members after two years. This rating takes into account differences in age, sex, country of origin, level of income, and race."[89] And, finally, I would turn to Senator Ribicoff in 1972: "Today there are many millions of Americans who go without medical care or receive inadequate care because they are poor."[90] We take care of those particular people.

Number one, he wants to know about the middle class harm. We indicate from Senator Kennedy it is millions.[91] Number two, he says 60 percent have adequate coverage. Now he admits that 40 percent of the people of the United States have inadequate coverage. Then he goes on to say, three, that Medicaid now applies to catastrophic illness. You have to be poor before you can get it, because as Congressman Fulton explains in 1970: "Under Medicaid, we have been saying, even to the self-sufficient who can clothe, house, and feed themselves, 'Spend yourselves to the point of indigency and then we can move in to help.' "[92] You have to be poor before you can get that [Medicaid]. He then goes on to talk about the general Medicaid program, but HEW explains that under Medicaid only one-third of the poverty population receives services.[93] And the *Washington Post* indicates in 1972 that there has been a month-to-month decline in the amount paid out of the Medicaid program.[94] He then talks about OEO centers. The *Washington Post* explains in 1973: "Because of state regulations OEO health centers are often limited to serving the very poor. The sizable number of "near poor" who desperately need care are legally excluded."[95] And Dr. Baker indicates the programs are being phased out under the present system.[96] Finally, he talks about free care in the hospitals and "they are not turned away."[97] But Symond Gottlieb explains in 1972: "Few hospitals have been willing to extend their services to the community for little or no charge."[98] And finally he talks about why the poor are dying. Evans explained [it is] because they can't afford it [medical care] in the first speech."[99] We quantify a 14 percent reduction [in mortality].[100] He says pluralism adds much. We indicate that's only an average; there are still millions outside the system. They [the poor] need four times more care, and what care they do get is "poverty medicine."

In short, Northwestern University offers you nothing except the same old arguments they've been using for months against this case. They do not adapt. They do not explain anything. We are the ones who have a quantified significance in this affirmative debate.

SECOND NEGATIVE CONSTRUCTIVE: RON MARMER, NORTHWESTERN

On the case, observation one: The gentlemen tell you there is a cost deterrent and tell you from Carlson in 1972 that 20 million are outside [the system].[101] But he must indicate that once you take the cost deterrent away that they will come inside. That is not the case. Klaus Roghmann, Rochester School of Medicine, in 1971: "Despite comprehensive free coverage, poor families are still more likely to receive less care, to depend more on public clinics, and to have a higher proportion of illness-related rather than preventive medical contacts."[102] I indicate once you remove the cost deterrent, you still don't provide any extra care.

Second observation: Care does not equal greater health. The gentleman gives you the HIP example,[103] but it does not apply uniformly. Shapiro, Fink, Rosenberg—directors of research at HIP—in 1972: "Results from a number of studies suggest that the health indices of the poor remain unchanged even when: (1) comprehensive medical care is available; (2) on a similar basis for all economic classes; and (3) there are no economic deterrents to its receipt."[104] Let him prove more care equals better health.

Observation three: I will argue that the quality is imprecise. The gentleman tells you these people [experts] surely must know and therefore they will be able to devise standards. That means (1) he now has the obligation of proving that they will devise standards that other people can use besides themselves, and (2) I would suggest that is unlikely. Williamson of Johns Hopkins, 1971: "While we and other investigators like Beverly Payne are convinced that peer judgment offers a practical method of setting standards, there is a paucity of data relevant to the elements of patient care. Moreover, criteria necessarily reflect individual staff values and judgments."[105] This [evidence] indicates that they [standards or criteria] are individual judgments and they need not be applied uniformly. The gentlemen must know what they have in mind, but that doesn't mean they can tell anyone else what to do in terms of enforcing the proposal.

I'll argue a fourth area of observation: The exclusion of psychiatry indicates that they can have no significant impact. One, they talk about MDs who are psychiatrists and they exclude them in the plan. That means they are "off the topic" because they are not talking about all of medical care. Two, I will argue that, to the extent they exclude them [psychiatrists], they also deny a significant area. Dr. Philip Lee, their source: "When morbidity and mortality are combined and indirect costs calculated, mental illness emerges as the single most important health problem."[106] And they do nothing about it. I would argue there is no quality that can be achieved, no health care advances possible. I will argue in the area of plan-meet-need that they cannot improve quality—they cannot improve quality.

And I will argue that education will not work. Dr. George Miller, professor of medicine at the University of Illinois, 1966: "Despite intensive educative efforts in the area of antimicrobial agents, nearly a third of the MD sample demonstrated little knowledge of the general principles involved."[107] And this was a voluntary study. They presume to impose upon doctors; let them prove they can cross that threshold and still have impact. They must do so. I will argue, secondly, to the extent they rely upon examinations, they will not work either. *Medical Tribune,* 1973: "It is not likely that someone will be able to devise realistic questions which will enable examiners to determine a practitioner's ability in his limited field. Too many factors in successful clinical work have to do with unmeasurable assets such as patience, personality, conscientiousness, and attitude."[108] I argue they cannot improve quality.

I will argue that the plan will be co-opted. To the extent I carry [this argument], I "beat" all the advantages. That is because the gentleman gives me "unmitigated pressure" evidence. He reads from Stuart Auerbach that the Nixon Administration has a philosophical commitment to get the government out of the delivery of medical care.[109] That means presumably they will do anything within their power to do so.

That means they "get rid" of the plan. Implementation does not have to take place under the plan simply because they leave to the board any type of administrative discretion they want. Members of the Nixon Administration—although the gentleman says that they will not be able to support them—can get people to exert pressure upon the local people that have to implement [the plan]. That means several things. One, they can allocate the money such that they will not provide money for enforcement. Two, they can get the "middle people" who have to enforce to argue that there is too much backlog so they "can't go it." Three, it means that every Nixon appointment to a court can simply find that they will not be able to judge in terms of the way the plan would advise. Therefore, they would not "hold up" [the plan]. And four, I will argue that they can simply frame the criteria in terms too vague to use. I give you four mechanisms by which they can circumvent [the plan], and he gives me "absolute pressure" [evidence] and that is clearly dangerous.

I will argue in the area of disadvantage (I), they deny needed primary care—they deny needed primary care. To the extent that this is true, I will argue that there is clearly a disadvantage, if you believe them up above that care is necessary for health.

(A) I will argue that this is true because they rely upon the extension of prepaid group practice across the country. That is impossible for two independent reasons. First, there is a specialist shortage. Carolynn Steinwald, Center for Health Services, 1972: "MD-population ratios for group practice plans are derived from a particular type of delivery system which is unlike the mainstream of the nation's medical care system."[110] That means that the prepaid group practice [system] works on a particular ratio mix. Do you have that in terms of specialists? No, you do not. Henry Mason, Committee on Medical Education, *JAMA,* 1972: "The question is how many specialists rather than how many MD's are needed based on the specialist-population ratios of large prepaid group plans."[111] Inspection of his [Mason's] chart reveals dermatologists, internists, obstetricians, gynecologists, orthopedists, pediatricians [are in short supply]—coming down to a total deficit of 47,700.[112] They are short close to 50,000 specialists. And that independently "beats" extension of prepaid group practice. And that means they deny primary care—it is their method of delivery.

(B) And independently, they will do so because they destroy physician selectivity—also important. I signify the level of importance. Dr. Cutting, Director of the Oakland Permanente Medical Group, in 1966: "Selection of physicians for a group can be a key factor in establishing quality when the selection is made on the basis of quality and professional competence. Among the many factors generally associated with quality, selection of physicians appears to be of utmost importance."[113] And I signify for you it is of utmost importance. What is the impact of the plan however? By definition they don't allow for any selection of physicians because everybody must be in this type [of plan]. That, by definition, destroys physician selectivity and independently renders the delivery of medical care through prepaid group practice extended across the nation impossible. That denies needed medical care to the entire country. And that is a net disadvantage.

I argue second (II), in the area of disadvantage, that it will cripple medical manpower. First (A) let me independently indicate that is true because they will increase demand to an intolerable extent. That is true, one, because of the significance of the affirmative. If you grant them any significance anywhere, that means more people will come in for care. Two, that is true because the "worried well" will flock in. Paul Ashton, President of the California Medical Guild, 1970: "National health insurance will increase the patient load ten times. There are no more really sick people—just more patients. It's human nature for people to want something free whether or not they need it."[114] Ten percent in terms of "worried well"—there is no advantage to be gained from that. John Glasgow of Connecticut in 1972: "It was reported that one result of reducing hospital stays in the Columbia plan was to increase the number of office visits. Indeed, the net effect of reduced hospital visits, use of nonprofessional personnel when appropriate, and increased office visits was about a 50 percent increase in demand on physician time.[115] They exacerbate the physician time demand by 50 percent. They have increased demand that will cripple medical delivery.

(B) Independently, however, while they have exacerbating effects on the demand side, they have even more problems in terms of supply because it will decrease. And let me give you the reason the doctors don't like it. They give it to you in terms of prepaid group practice when they quote the *Harvard Law Review*— (d) of their reason says there is an apparent organized medicine opposition to it.[116] They give you the philosophical commitment of the Nixon Administration.[117] There are a whole list of reasons. I will signify for you, however, from Cutting—previously qualified: "The realization of the full benefits of any form of medical care program requires that the participating MD's have the leading voice in all judgments affecting the availability, quality, and economy of the services they provide."[118] If this role is usurped, which they do through their fiat power, there is a real danger the plan will fail in terms of financial quality and patient satisfaction. And I give it to you at the level of the professional advocate as a motivating factor.

How will their dislike become manifest? I will give you ways. Dr. Edward Rubenstein, Senate subcommittee hearings, 1972: "There is a pressing need for over 30,000 doctors in Canada where they are afforded the highest professional status. Any attempt to force doctors against their will to accept specific salaries—which they do—or types of populations is likely to encourage doctors to relocate their practices in Canada."[119] I signify and causally relate. I will argue, second, [from] David Mechanic of Wisconsin in 1970: "There is a tremendous elasticity in the amount and quality of work a physician can do. Alienation of the physician is disruptive of the smooth functioning of a medical care program."[120] They can decrease their productivity. I will argue, third, they can go on strike. Dr. Anthony Bolthe of San Francisco in 1972: "More than half of all doctors would go on strike if necessary."[121] I signify at the level of 50 percent. But this is not idle threat; it has been done before. George Roche, consultant to the Congress of Medical Societies, in 1970 indicates that at the Lincoln Hospital in the Bronx, 27 out of 28 doctors went on strike.[122] Clearly it has been done; it is not an empty threat.

I will argue also in the area of disadvantage that (III) they destroy vital state and local programs—they destroy vital state and local programs. I will argue that is true primarily from L. L. Ecker-Racz, Professor of Economics at Hartford, in 1970: "A broad range of public services have become dependent on state and local borrowing to finance capital expenditures. Schools, public utilities, and water and sewage systems are highly dependent on bond sales."[123] Realize that this is critical in terms of bond sales. The *Report of the Ad Hoc Committee on School Finance,* 1971: "Voting on bond referendums is virtually the only remaining chance for the electorate to express direct control over public finance. When taxes increase, voters take out their anger and frustration by rejecting needed bond referendums."[124] This indicates several things. They tell you the position of the Nixon Administration is to get out of the [direct medical care delivery] system. This means that the people aren't going to like it. Two, it tells you that tax increases always result from this. And he tells you he's going to increase taxes by $37 billion—not the savings, which is relevant, but the taxes and allocating mechanism and perceptions and scenario it sets in motion. Therefore, I indicate to you they will reject bonds, and the impact of that I will quantify for you now. United States President's Commission on School Finance in 1971: "At the local level, the electorate is voting down school finance proposals with increasing frequency. Any further increase in bond rejections is likely to cripple innumerable school districts."[125] Adopt their plan and you cripple school districts. The Department of Interior in 1968: "Modern sanitation systems for the 1970's, employing latest techniques of tertiary treatment, will be funded largely at the whim of taxpayers. If citizens do not approve bonds for sanitation systems, cities will be in a position where they can neither improve existing systems nor keep up with the future. They will risk disease such as typhoid and dysentery, long thought to be eradicated in the United States."[126] I indicate that you will have these massive diseases running rampant.

I will argue, finally, that (IV) they will increase the use of dangerous blood—they will increase the use of dangerous blood. This is true because they no longer provide an incentive to use private donors. They will use commercial blood. Dr. Balatille, President of the American Association of Blood Banks, indicates to the Committee on Ways and Means, 1971: "Providing payment for blood under any proposed NHI [National Health Insurance] plan will result in the increased use of commercial blood and the associated risk of increased hepatitis."[127] I want to quantify for you, however, the reasonable range of increase in hepatitis from this blood. The *New York Times,* March 3, 1972: "Various medical authorities have estimated that a person receiving a transfusion from a pint of commercially obtained blood runs 10 to 70 times the risk of developing hepatitis as the risk from the pint of blood that has not been donated for profit."[128] Now at this point I will signify for you this—I give you a 10 to 70 percent incremental, additive disadvantage because of the use of commercial blood. That is a reasonable range. The mitigating factors the gentlemen will ask be taken into account, I submit are taken account of in that range as well. Most teams will stand before you and quote 70 percent and hope by the end of the round you'll cling to 10 [percent]; I will start with the 10 to 70 [percent] and hope you will move between them. Finally, let me argue that the only possible solution would be if you had a screening mechanism. Regrettably, the most hopeful mechanism has not been that successful. *Science,* March, 1972, page 1344: "The Australian antigen test developed a few years ago is now almost universally used, but the test detects hepatitis in only 25 percent of affected blood."[129] Clearly that is not the level we need.

I will argue, therefore, in terms of disadvantages, that in terms of denying needed primary care to most Americans, they cut off effectively all primary care to all people because the system they rely upon for delivery cannot be effected. In terms of crippling medical manpower, they have exacerbated the demand and they are going to diminish the supply. That means, in combination or independently, you do cripple medical manpower, and that is reason to reject as well. You also can set in motion a bonding scenario that results in schools closing and sanitation departments closing across the country, and that is not desirable either. And finally, you increase the use of dangerous blood. Now you're supposed to weigh that against whatever level of significance comes out in terms of the affirmative case. And when they tell you that we do not "extend" or use new materials, I leave that for your judgment, because, while Elliott and I may not be the two finest debaters you will see in your lives, we hope there is still justification for presumption for this [present] system.

FIRST NEGATIVE REBUTTAL:
ELLIOTT MINCBERG, NORTHWESTERN

On independence, the additive advantage will be all the other things that we could do with the money we wouldn't have to spend on the rest of the Georgetown proposal. But he suggests that each of these [plan planks] would be a separate proposal. He defines the resolution operationally as this proposal. Each of these is only a part of comprehensive medical care. By definition, needed medical care is only part—that is, only one section of it. The second part is only catastrophic. The third part is only regulation of quality. None is a total program of comprehensive medical care and that is why the independence program carries.

Now, in terms of the ability to pay of the middle class, he does not signify but merely reasserts his "blurb." In terms of his general analysis, the 20 million "outsiders" is merely descriptive and not inherent —I'll get to it later. Costs-financing-manpower: I've "beaten" the 20 million already. It will all be the same as his plan or we can finance it if we want to.

Third, he says the present system is on the "way out." *American Medical News* says no, that even Weinberger admits it.[130] The Special Analysis of the Budget says that 11 million more people will want the federal health programs.[131] And besides, it's "should-would." He gives you no inherent reason why this is true.

Then, fourth, he says it's poverty medicine. First, he does not indicate that's true in terms of CHC [Community Health Centers], Medicaid, and free care specifically. But, moreover, Handler and Hollingsworth of Wisconsin tell us: "Data indicated that those who felt stigmatized were not less likely to use services. On the contrary, they demanded what was due them and used them more—use of medical care was pronounced."[132] In other words, there is an advantage to the stigma policy system.

And in terms of HIP, Merwyn Greenlick, who works for Kaiser, says in 1972: "There is no evidence that medical care in any form affects health status. The HIP study is dated, narrowly focused, and not definitive."[133] He gives you "millions" again without specifics. I tell you that 60 percent can afford [health insurance]. Now what about the other 40 percent? First, we have Medicaid. He says that "we do bad things to the poor." There is nothing about that in the law; that is an opinion of a Tennessee congressman,[134] and he doesn't tell you what he is talking about specifically. Then in terms of the one-third and the cutback: The 1972 *Catalog of Federal Domestic Assistance* tells us that actually the number of recipients in 1971 was 18.2 million; in 1973 it was estimated it will be 23.5 million—a 5 million increase; in 1974 the estimate is 27.2 million.[135] And there is no inherency in that anyway. He does not tell you why.

Now in terms of OEO, he says it's only for the very poor. Dr. Robert Van Hoek tells us in 1972 that the eligibility [requirement] has been eliminated.[136] He [the affirmative speaker] says they [OEO-CHC's] are being phased out. *American Medical News* says there will be increased funding in 1973.[137] I can refer to [evidence] cards just as well as he can. Then in terms of free care, he says that few [hospitals] will increase [services],[138] without ever indicating to you why this is true. And I tell you that they will not turn them away. Make him prove people are turned away.

And then—in overtime—he gets to all my causal link arguments. Pull everyone through, and I will not bother you with repeating them. I win them cold. There is no causal link.

Please go to (II). In terms of up to $70,000,[139] I want to know the minimum level. Why? So we can find out how many people suffer. And he won't tell you. You have no criteria. All you have is his "one-half" [evidence] card.[140] And my one-seventh of 1 percent [evidence] is talking about an income level of $2,000.[141] His [evidence] does not say that the people suffer, only that they spend half of their income. Maybe they spent nothing the year before and half the next year. We don't know that they are suffering from that cost, and that of course is what we are talking about. There is no causal relationship. The USC-Davis [evidence] card[142]—remember that—pull it through.

In terms of significance, the Shawnee, Oklahoma [study][143] is old and poor people, so that's probably even less biased against the negative —which is good for us, I think. In terms of the repayment, I'll give him bankruptcy, but I want to take a look at that Chapter 13. You may see the Xerox [copy] of the statute if you want; it says nothing about the limitations he talks about. His [evidence] card does not say "only."[144]

You may see it [the Xerox copy of Chapter 13 of the Bankruptcy Act], and we win that one cold. We also have other mechanisms besides Chapter 13.

Insurance, he says, is not adequate, but he gives you no inherency for that at all. Pull through Medicaid and free care. And in terms of the hemophiliacs, if the people can afford it they can get the clotting factor. If they can't afford it, they should watch out not to cut themselves or go to hospitals when they do. Where's the problem? I don't know.

Now go to quality. He says, we have atrocities—your repairs aren't working. Maybe the reason for the atrocities is my alternate causal hypothesis—genetic, environmental, etcetera factors. Do not let him get away with quoting atrocities at you if I carry that causal link argument. Now on self-review, the Washington [review system] gives you an example of that.[145] He doesn't tell you why it could not be applied to drugs. I gave you the drugs evidence.[146] I can show you further evidence from Dr. Eric Martin, who tells us in July of 1972 that hospitalization for adverse [drug] reactions is on the way down.[147] And X-rays: If we had the standards, why cannot we apply them [presently]?

Now on the states—and this is the critical inherency argument—he says that there is no law that they do it [certify X-ray technologists] and 47 states don't.[148] Why, I ask, is this inherent? And he does not tell you. Why can't the states do it? What is the structural barrier? I asked that at the beginning, and I ask them every time we debate them, and I still don't know.

Now on malpractice. He says, in effect, that there are no deaths. That, of course, I've refuted above. Empirical evidence: Turn to *Trial* magazine of March/April, 1973, which gives the statistics on how doctors change their practices as a direct result of malpractice.[149] Look at the evidence if you want to.

Now on the causal link, he wants me to apply it to the case. On the drugs evidence, I read you stuff from the World Health Organization that says there are loads of other factors.[150] Dr. Modell tells us: "There are always certain patients in whom a drug produces odd, unpredictable reactions."[151] You do not correlate that to doctor quality. The same is true of X-rays. What he is relying on in his third advantage is merely authority. He says, because the FDA says so and because Oak Ridge Laboratory says so, why it must be so. Now I don't believe that. I want to know what the studies are and how they got the conclusions, because I have raised prima facie methodological challenges and—unless he is willing to give me that kind of evidence—I don't think you can "buy" the causal links and jumps that Georgetown wants you to.

FIRST AFFIRMATIVE REBUTTAL:
STEWART JAY, GEORGETOWN

Number one, 20 million people don't come under the system. He proves that below when he says [there was] a 50 percent increase in the Columbia plan study.[152] Number two, we decrease the death rate 14 percent in the HIP study.[153] His evidence indicates it [the HIP study] is limited in scope, etcetera.[154] He does not explain why. The Medicaid population was put into the [HIP] service; they got 14 percent lower [mortality]. And why does the 1967 date make it [the evidence] outdated? I'll give you another study then. The *American Journal of Public Health,* 1972: "In a fully controlled comparative study between similar populations using HMO's [Health Maintenance Organizations] and traditional delivery modes, the HMO's were found to reduce nonwhite infant mortality by 23 percent; white infant mortality by 16 percent; premature deaths were reduced 20 percent; and elderly mortality was down 11 percent."[155] It clearly will happen.

Two, in the HIP example, he points to another authority saying in other parts of the system their habits will be unchanged.[156] That might be because there is poor quality care in the other parts of the system—charity care, etcetera.

Three, in the area of quality, he indicates there are no quality standards, etcetera, because these are individual value judgments. Make him prove that applies to the area of drugs. We repeatedly tell you—back in the first affirmative constructive, in the second affirmative constructive—we do know what is wrong in all these cases. They were unnecessary and they were preventable. *Trial* magazine—their own source—explains in 1973 from HEW: "These cases are well documented and predictable and preventable."[157] Senator Kennedy says: "80 percent of all adverse drug reactions are preventable. They are simply due to physician negligence and misinformation."[158] Finally, we indicate from Ralph Nader, 1971: "Drs. Stapleton and Zwerneman in their two-year study of over 1100 cases concluded that stimulation in training programs is a valuable source that improves patient care."[159] We give them a continuing education. We indicate the quality will be high.

He therefore goes on to say, number four, [that we provide] exclusion of psychiatric illness. Number one, that might be covered under the present system. Prove there is inadequacy there. That is why we do not include it in the plan. Number two, we decrease physical illness with the affirmative plan by 14 percent.

In the area of education, I have already indicated above the education programs, when designed properly, can be effective. But, number two, he indicates that some educational programs have been ineffective. That is because I prove to you back on the case that there are bad educational programs. I give you the Nader evidence[160] indicating we have good educational programs. You can solve the problem. And it is logical because they are all avoidable errors.

Point six, in the area of circumvention, he says the board will circumvent, etcetera. Number one, we appoint all officials in the agencies, even the state and local agencies if necessary, to ensure high-quality care. Two, we "deal out" all the money; therefore, there can be no cuts whatsoever. Three, show that [President] Nixon can corrupt all the courts by finding enough people who are willing to be corruptable around the United States; show the number of judges who can be corrupted by the Nixon Administration. Four, what criteria are vague in the affirmative plan? He does not tell you.

[In the area of disadvantages], number one (I), denial of primary care: Please, number one, this is not a disadvantage; it is a plan-meet-need argument. But (A), he talks about a problem of speciality-mix today and how there is a problem if you increase prepaid group practice —you aren't going to have enough specialists. I've seen this [evidence] card[161] all year; it is talking about the shortage in prepaid group practice. I tell you the reason for that is because doctors do not go into the system. I indicate to you there will be no problem because as Leonard Woodcock explains in 1972: "A doctor in a group can treat twice as many patients as a physician practicing alone."[162] Therefore, we increase the number of doctors in the United States by two times. And the *Harvard Law Review* explains in 1971: "Those in prepaid group practice plans have half as many common surgeries as the general population."[163] This indicates in that particular case you only have to have one-half of the doctors.

(B) He says you destroy selectivity. Number one, it only says that it is one check in a particular area; it does not say this is the only check available. Number two, we introduce quality checks in the affirmative plan which take care of this particular kind of problem—to make sure everybody is at the same high quality. And, three, we have continuing education to raise the quality.

Two (II), [the affirmative plan will] cripple manpower because (A) the "worried well" are going to come into the system. He gives no significance whatsoever. Senator Kennedy says in 1971: "Should the financial barrier to medical care be removed, we should expect no great overutilization of health facilities for frivolous or psychological reasons. All of our experience to date, both with the Army and prepaid group practice, indicates that substantial overutilization is not a problem."[164] But, number two, we have a 14 percent decline in mortality.

Next (B), the doctors will not like the system. He, number one, talks about Canada. They are under a national health insurance system. Why would it be any different? Number two, they said they'll lower the quality, the efficiency. We have quality and efficiency checks. Three, he says they'll strike, they'll leave the system, etcetera. I will indicate to you that will not happen. Please turn to the fact that, number one, money will overcome any barriers. Dr. Glen Garrison explains, 1972: "It is well known that physician opposition to restrictive regulations markedly diminishes when money is distributed."[165] We increase the [doctors'] salaries by 15 percent. Listen to Drs. Peterson and Meyer in 1973 [stating] that doctors will not leave the system: "American doctors will not go on strike. By withholding patient care health would be jeopardized; no action ever taken by physicians will abrogate the solemn responsibility of doctors to safeguard the health and well-being of their patients."[166] I will indicate to you, finally, it's only a threat. Look at the British example, *AMA Journal* of 1970: "Although socialized medicine was introduced against the opposition of 95 percent of the British medical profession, 98 percent of the doctors quickly joined it."[167] Make him show the example abroad, how long the strike was, and what its actual result was.

Three (III), cripple vital services: Number one, you can channel federal money in there. He does not give you a reason why you cannot do this. But, number two, he does not prove that sanitation [referendums] will be passed in the future at all. Number three, we spend less for the affirmative plan. The GAO study explains in 1972: "Exhaustive studies of group practice plans reveal that subscribers receive high quality medical care for 20 to 30 percent less than the cost of comparable care outside the plan."[168] Therefore, we serve more; we can increase taxes; the taxpayers will not mind.

Number four (IV), in the area of blood shortages: Number one, why would they not donate blood if they knew they were going to get hepatitis (from commercially obtained blood)? Number two, his text is from March of 1972.[169] I indicate in 1972—later than that—we have discovered a test which is effective: Tufts University investigators have developed a process for filtering practically all of the hepatitis-associated antigen from blood, according to the AMA.[170] Number three, there is no reason why we can't have a voluntary blood system. *The American Medical News* in 1973: "Even in the largest cities in the United States, the trend is inescapable. All-volunteer blood programs are the wave of the future."[171]

With that in mind, please go to his observations. Number one, we give you one policy system. Number two, he does not explain why any particular plank of the case is not comprehensive medical care. He merely reasserts that. Please go to the third affirmative advantage. He talks about genetic factors. We indicate all these drug deaths are avoidable. He talks about review and how the hospitalization is down. That is 1972 evidence.[172] We indicate in 1973 from the FDA that the [drug] reactions are going up.[173] He talks about the states. You cannot change state laws, Mincberg, that are already in existence. He drops malpractice when I indicate it has absolutely no effects in the area of drugs. Quite obviously the quality standards are derived by experts, the FDA —and also, in the area of X-rays, by the Oak Ridge Laboratories, which he does not dispute the quality standards of whatsoever. In short, we have thousands of lives still left in the third advantage. The significance of (I) and (II) [the second and third advantages] will be extended by Brad. But on balance, our policy system, when weighed against those "zilch" disadvantages, certainly warrants your ballot.

SECOND NEGATIVE REBUTTAL:
RON MARMER, NORTHWESTERN

They tell you they have one policy [system], but that is not true because separate [plan] planks call for it. Therefore, if all things together equal comprehensive medical care, individually they do not if you don't have a warrant for it. Two, we have an additive advantage because you spend whatever money you don't have to spend on the plan elsewhere, and that's clearly better. Secondly, we say each [plan plank] separates and therefore is only a part. He has no response.

(I, A) There is no significance. He is dropping entirely. He has no response anywhere on (I); therefore, I will abbreviate. Clearly there is no inherency in terms of the 20 million. We tell you—the *American Medical News,* Weinberger—all indicate that 11 million are increasing.[174] We tell you there is a double "should-would" standard. We talk about CHC, Medicaid, and free care. Hollingsworth says there is demonstration that they are moving in this direction.[175] Then we move to HIP; Greenlick says there is no evidence that it worked,[176] that there was any translation into the case; and he [the affirmative speaker] has no denial. Private insurance can deal with 60 percent; Medicare care takes care of the rest. They give you a Tennessee congressman,[177] and we tell you that is not in the law itself. Catastrophic: We give you the *Catalog of Federal Assistance* saying that you have increased [the number of recipients of federal health programs] by 5 million to 27.2 [million] in 1974.[178] OEO: Van Hock says eligibility has been removed and the *American Medical News* in 1972 says it's expanding.[179] Free care: He never proves they'll be turned away. Into overtime, he never gets to the causal links anywhere. Draw through all of that. And, critically, draw through two things: One, the advantages to stigma; and, two, the advantages to pluralism from McNerney and Matsler.[180] Now you've got to weigh whatever advantage is going to be "pulled out" against these "disads" [disadvantages]. I'll carry in the reasons for spending $180 billion or whatever against the advantage to stigma and the advantage to pluralism until they are refuted.

Now (II, A) How many suffer? You still don't know. One-half of 1 percent under $2,000.[181] We defend the study; he doesn't answer. We only spend one-half of income.[182] Do they suffer? He gives you no answer. (II, B): No causality: No answer. The Davis of USC quotation indicating that this never occurs: There is no answer. The old and poor people in Oklahoma only exacerbate it, and the evidence is for the negative: No answer. We give them bankruptcy, but we said they can pay back over time and Chapter 13 [of the Bankruptcy Act]: We ask you to inspect; he has no response. Group health insurance can do it and there is no inherent barrier to expanding it: No response. Free care, Medicare is there. Bleeding: In terms of that, let them be careful. He has no response. Again, subtract whatever it is and warrant whether you want to spend that much money for it. How much significance remains for Georgetown?

(III) In terms of voluntary controls: All he does is tell you atrocities persist, but does not indicate how that is true. He says that all are available—and now the gentleman is in overtime at this point; I hope you did not "flow" it. We say it may be due to an alternate causal hypothesis. That's why atrocities are not valid. He has nothing now to defend it. Examples only: We say why not apply them to the evidence we give you. In terms of the Martin 1972 [evidence], [183] we say it [the evidence] denies that it [hospitalization for adverse drug reactions] is down. We say apply X-rays as a standard; he has no response. Critically on the states, he says—in overtime—you can't change the laws. We say, what's inherent about that? He admits that three states do [certify X-ray technicians] and we give you the New York example where they did.[184] You've got states already that have done it. And we give you the Derbyshire quotation[185] saying it's well within the range [for states to require medical recertification]. He has no response at this point.

In terms of malpractice, we say in 1973 [evidence] that the statistics are available to indicate its use [threats of malpractice suits] also changes physician activity.[186] He has no response. He said that we dropped malpractice threats. I will reclaim it for us in that the threat or perception is what is essential, and he talks only about manifestations. The threat is before that and is therefore valid.

In terms of drugs, we gave you the World Health Organization saying it [adverse drug reaction] is due to other factors,[187] and he is not defeating the alternate causal hypothesis. And we talk about Dr. Modell who said you can have "unpredictable reactions."[188] Turn to X-rays: We say apply [our arguments] from up above. And now you must ask yourself again what significance persists for Georgetown when all they do is give you "atrocities" and do not explain alternate causal hypotheses.

Observation one on the plan. He says [we will have a] 50 percent increase [in doctors].[189] That is a "time" statement; it is not evidence in terms of increases. He is distorting.

Observation two, care is not equal to health: He gives you three other examples, but what they do not do is tell you that there is no equivocal result. I tell you that sometimes you get it, sometimes you don't. You have no clear warrant, therefore, if any doubt persists and, for these reasons, he does not, I hope, indict [the argument].

Observation three, he says that quality is imprecise and apply to his case: First, you don't know what the hell he is going to use in all his responses. Group them, because he does not tell you that once they [quality standards] are developed, they can be used by the people who must enforce them. That is what [conclusion] I draw.

Observation four, he says it [psychiatric care] could be coordinated now, but he doesn't deny that he is "off the topic." And in terms of psychiatrists, he does not indicate that that is important. In terms of "cannot improve the quality," he says education won't work. He says some do, but I tell you with compulsion versus voluntary [methods]. He does not draw the distinction. Draw it through. In terms of testing won't work, he does not respond at all. Draw through testing—it wins cold.

Circumvention: He says that they proved they can appoint all [agency officials], that all they have to do is appoint the local guy and "write him off." And I give you the philosophical indication they tell you that is clearly warranted for it.

(I) Deny needed medical care—specialization: Note that is disclaiming need if they deny medical care to anybody. That's disadvantageous. He says, regarding the shortages in the present system, they [doctors] will go in [group practices] and you can increase doctors. Increasing doctors is irrelevant to an increase in specialists. That is unresponsive; 50,000 [specialists short] persists independently. Independently, physician selectivity: He says that they [doctors] will go in [group practice] because they like it, and they will have twice as many [doctors under the affirmative plan]. That does not indicate that they will not by definition include everyone and destroy the motivation. And quality checks do not appropriate themselves to attitudes in that area. Therefore, his other responses are irrelevant.

(II) Cripple medical care: He says there is no significance from Kennedy.[190] If that's true, then where is his advantage on (I), where he tells you people should be "flocking in?" Two, in terms of the 10 percent increase, he does not indicate that the cost barrier does not affect it. In terms of supply, therefore, what is the professional ethic? It was undenied that that was the motivation. Therefore, consider the manifestations. He says, what about Canada? I tie [the argument] to professional ethics—you may inspect [your flow sheet]. Efficiency: I talk about elasticity; efficiency checks are irrelevant. The number of [doctors] who come in: I indicate they can't do it because of professional ethics and tie practicality. In terms of threat: I tell you they [doctors] have done it [gone on strike]. And he says, what is the result of that? The government capitulated—that was the result in the Bronx.

(III) Destroy vital state and local programs: He says the federal [government] can do it, but does not indicate to you that they will. I tell you that you destroy the level of funding right now. He says they [bond referendums] can be passed in the future. I indicate that you are exacerbating [the problem]. He says, spend less. And I talk about the perceptions. He is unresponsive.

(IV) Increase the use of [dangerous] blood: He says, why not if they have the antigen test? It [getting hepatitis from commercial blood] is viewed as a remote chance. He says later in 1972 [a better hepatitis test was developed].[191] It is the same test. Make him prove it is different. The *American Medical News* says it is doubtful [that commercially obtained blood will be used much in the future].[192] I give you a reasonable range.[193]

Now you must ask yourselves in terms of the impact of these disadvantages whether the significance we have "whittled away" on each of these advantages still gives you compelling warrant to spend the amount of money this team will with unnecessary portions of its plan intact for reasons which will remain a mystery to all of you.

SECOND AFFIRMATIVE REBUTTAL: BRADLEY ZIFF, GEORGETOWN

On the PO's [plan objections], number one, increase the time: He indicates that we do not indicate that they will be better. We indicate, number two, the 14 percent study we defend.[194] We also defend an up to 23 percent decrease in mortality.[195] We claim we will have a comparative advantage in terms of the affirmative proposal.

Observation number two depends on that, and go on to observation three—quality is going to be subverted: He says, what kind of [quality] checks are you going to provide? And we indicate, number one, we have continuing education, and, two, we have quality checks. *Trial* magazine, 1973, says they [misprescription of drug cases] can be prevented.[196] Senator Kennedy says 80 percent [of adverse drug reactions] can be prevented,[197] and Nader says that in 1,100 cases training increases the quality of care.[198] Please causally link. I refer you to advantage number three—we will carry the debate on the basis of it.

On observation number four, psychiatric limitation: He does not indicate it is bad under the present system. We do not have to indict something that is good presently now.

On the PMN's [plan-meet-need arguments], number one, quality of medical care: Number one, he indicates it is going to be compulsory versus voluntary. We indicate, number one, this proves that the present programs under the present system are bad in terms of continuing education. Two, we provide for the quality checks under the affirmative proposal. They have to mandate the care. There is no reason the education cannot work. And we prove, up above, from Nader that in 1,100 cases it is effective. Two, the plan will be co-opted: He says they will "drive off." We appoint all the people at the state and local level that are necessary. It is an independent board. And, number two, he does not tell you what the vague standards are.

On "disad" [disadvantage] number one (I), deny necessary medical care: Please note, one, he says this is an increase of doctor specialists. We said, for the second time, that there are shortages of specialists under the status quo. We indicate from Woodcock, that you can save half the doctor's time;[199] therefore, they can treat twice as many patients. Two, we indicate from the *Harvard Law Review* that it [group practice] takes half as many surgeries.[200] Those are very clearly specialists if that is surgery. You can save half the doctors time over the present system; there is no reason you cannot. Physician selectivity: We indicate we have quality checks under the present system and continuing education can be effective.

Two (II), cripple medical manpower: He indicates that we do not have a significant advantage. No, the Kennedy [evidence] card said there is no overutilization for psychological reasons.[201] We indicate from HIP and HMO[202] that you can have a 14 percent to 23 percent reduction of mortality if you can get the poor to come in, and we indicate they will. In terms of harm to other programs, he indicates, number one, the elasticity of the program. Number one, we indicate that that proves they are going to have less service under the present system. Under the present system that is true. But under the affirmative proposal, we provide for the elasticity because of the quality checks under the plan. Two, he asks, will they [doctors] go on strike? We quote from Garrison who says that money absolutely makes the difference.[203] They will not strike. Two, we quote from Meyer of the AMA, who says the doctors will not go on strike because they do not want to hurt the people.[204] Third, we gave you the example of Britain where 98 percent [of doctors] decided to participate in the system.[205] There is no significance to Northwestern's "disads."

Third (III), in terms of vital state and local programs: One, we indicate that you can utilize federal money in terms of grants and aids. He gives you no reason to the contrary. Two, we indicated sanitation [referendums] will be passed. He has the burden of proof in rejoinder and he does not assume it. Third, in his response to "perceptions," we indicate it will be 30 percent less under the affirmative proposal. We save $27 billion. There is no reason you cannot fund them [vital state and local programs].

Fourth (IV), in the area of blood, he said it is the same [antigen] test. No, the Tufts test is better. We indicate you can do it there. And, two, we indicate all the cities are switching to voluntary blood.

We will ask you now, ladies and gentlemen, to please go to the justification argument at the top of the flow [sheet]. One, we indicate to you that he does not tell you why separate planks in the plan cannot be comprehensive medical care. He gives you no reason to believe that is true. Two, we give you absolutely one policy system—any advantage justifies that [policy system]. There is no response from Northwestern. Third, he does not tell you what his counterplan is; he does not tell you what these additive advantages are. And, four, he gives up presumption in totality.

I would suggest that we go to advantage three (III), the critical distinction: Number one, he says there are alternate reasons why the drugs could be bad. Now Mr. Jay indicates from the FDA that 250,000 people are dying because of misprescription or overprescription of drugs.[206] And we say, from Kennedy, we can save 80 percent of these people.[207] That is misinformation. Two, he says the [drug] reactions are down. No, we disproved that in 1973—250,000 lives are saved. Third, he says all year he has been asking for inherency. And all year he has gotten inherency—and lost both times—because we indicate from the *Albany Law Review* that there are no statutes on the books of 47 states.[208] That is the inherency in this particular affirmative case, that is why you cannot have continuing education or laws. Fourth, he talks about malpractice. We indicate to you in California in 1972 there is absolutely no deterrence.[209] If the harm exists, clearly there is no deterrence. Next, he goes to alternative factors. We have defeated that. X-rays: We will claim 30,000 lives. There are no reasons to the contrary.

On advantage number two (II), individual financial hardship: He asks, number one, can you provide for the criteria? We have indicated, number one, [medical bills can run] up to $75,000 a year. Two, he asks, can you offer the causal link? Yes, we indicate from Hogan in the first affirmative speech that thousands of families are "wiped out,"[210] and Hogan in the second affirmative, who says it is "instant poverty."[211]

That is 1.5 million people who spend half of their income on medical bills.[212] Shawnee, Oklahoma: He does not show it is a nationwide center. We have faith in 1973. Third, he gives us bankruptcy. Fourth, he says they can pay at their own limits in terms of Chapter 13. Mr. Jay indicates that Chapter 13 only provides for false (financial) statements. He does not show you that people have taken advantage of this. Clearly it is quite a viable alternative. Next, he talks about group insurance. But, we indicate from Mr. Pettingill that it cannot be expanded.[213] In the area of free care and Medicaid, we will deal with that on advantage number one, but it cannot be expanded. In the area of hemophiliacs, he says "be careful." Being careful doesn't do them any good because we indicate, even if they are careful, the cost of it (the clotting factor) is $22,000 and 100,000 are "wiped out." That is significance to weigh against the "disads" [disadvantages].

In terms of (I) the first advantage, I've already covered that. Twenty million people, we've indicated are shunted out of the system automatically. There is no inherency because of the Medicaid. Two, he indicates that the present system is expanding. But he does not prove it to you, because we indicate in 1973 there is no good charity medical care. He indicates that HIP is good care, but we indicate to you in 1973, on balance, Kennedy says that there is "pain and suffering."[214] We indicate, number two, in terms of medical costs, millions of people are "pressed out" of the market. On the Medicaid example, he said it is expanding to 24 million, but we indicate there are eligibility limits which are basic. We carry at least two and one-half significant comparative advantages in the debate, ladies and gentlemen, and there are absolutely no [disadvantages to] weigh against them—warrant enough for Georgetown in the debate.

[1]Stanley G. Rives, ed., "1973 National Debate Tournament Final Debate," *Journal of the American Forensic Association* 10, no. 1 (Summer 1973): 16–45. Reprinted by permission of The American Forensic Association and Stanley G. Rives.

[2]The debate was held in Mahan Hall Auditorium at the U.S. Naval Academy on April 11, 1973. The coaches of the two teams were Professors James Unger of Georgetown and David Zarefsky of Northwestern. The tournament director was Professor Merwyn Hayes of Wake Forest University and the tournament hosts were Professors Philip Warken and Lt. Patrick Miller of the U.S. Naval Academy.

[3]Judges for the debate were Professors Mark Arnold, Harvard University; Mary Alice Baker, Lamar University; David Dunlap, Wooster College; Dixie Howell, University of California–Los Angeles; Steve Hunt, University of Massachusetts; J. W. Patterson, University of Kentucky; and Jack Rhodes, University of Utah. The decision was 4–3 for the negative.

[4]The debate was edited from a tape recording. Except for the correction of obviously unintended errors, this is as close to a verbatim transcript as was possible to obtain from the recording. Sources of evidence used in the debate were provided by the participating debaters as indicated in the footnotes.

[5]Testimony of Senator Edward Kennedy on January 26, 1971, Hearings of Subcommittee on Health, Senate Committee on Labor and Public Welfare, *Health Care Crisis in America, 1971.*

[6]National Urban Coalition, *Report of the Task Force on Health,* 1970. Copy available from: Urban Coalition, 2100 M Street NW, Washington, D.C.

[7]Testimony of Therman Evans, Executive Secretary of the Student National Medical Association, Hearings of Senate Labor and Public Welfare Committee, September 24, 1970.

[8]Testimony of Senator Edward Kennedy, Hearings of Subcommittee on Health, Senate Committee on Labor and Public Welfare, *Health Care Crisis in America, 1971.*

[9]Testimony of Mayor John Lindsay on April 7, 1971, Hearings of Subcommittee on Health, Senate Committee on Labor and Public Welfare, *Health Care Crisis in America, 1971,* Part 6, pp. 1238 and 1240.

[10]Statement of Representative Lawrence Hogan on January 27, 1971, *Congressional Record,* Volume 117, Part 1, p. 532.

[11]Report of the Senate Committee on Finance cited in *National Health Insurance,* Hearings of Senate Committee on Finance, April 26–28, 1971, p. 280.

[12]Brookings Institution, *Setting National Priorities: The 1973 Budget,* 1972, p. 214.

[13]Statement of Representative Lawrence Hogan on March 14, 1973, *Congressional Record,* p. H1745 of daily edition.

[14]*Report of the National Hemophilia Foundation* (Fact Sheet), March 28, 1973. Copy available from: National Hemophilia Foundation, Washington Chapter, 1346 Connecticut Avenue, Washington, D.C.

[15]*American Journal of Public Health,* April, 1972.

[16]*Journal of the Tennessee Medical Association,* May, 1971.

[17]*Bibliotheca Hematologica,* 1970, p. 89.

[18]Statement of Representative Martha Griffiths, *Congressional Record,* Volume 116, Part 3, p. 2783.

[19]*Washington Post,* December 8, 1972.

[20]Cited from *Trial* magazine, March/April, 1973 issue.

[21]Testimony of Dr. Henry Simmons, December 5, 1972, *Advertising of Proprietary Medicines,* Hearings of Subcommittee on Monopoly, Senate Select Committee on Small Business, Part 3, pp. 1042–43. The affirmative team supplied the following analysis of Dr. Simmons's testimony leading to the conclusion cited: Each year there are approximately 32 million hospital patients; one out of every three of these patients receives an antibiotic; 60 percent of these prescriptions are for antibiotics not needed by the patient; 2 to 7 percent of these patients receiving antibiotics develop superinfections; and 30 to 50 percent of such hospital superinfections are fatal. Hence: One-third of 32 million equals 10.7 million patients receiving antibiotics; 60 percent of that total equals 6.42 million patients who do not need the antibiotics; 2 to 7 percent of that figure equals˙128,400 to 449,400 patients who develop superinfections; and 30 to 50 percent of that figure equals a low of 38,520 patients to a high of 224,700 patients who die each year due to superinfections caused by misprescribed antibiotics.

[22]Testimony of Dr. Karl Morgan, May 15, 1972, *Physician Training Facilities and Health Maintenance Organizations,* Hearings of Subcommittee on Health, Senate Committee on Labor and Public Welfare, Part 5, pp. 2168 ff.

[23]Same source as footnote 22.

[24]*The Effects on Populations of Exposure to Low Levels of Ionizing Radiation,* Report of the Advisory Committee on the Biological Effects of Ionizing Radiations, Division of Medical Sciences, National Academy of Sciences, National Research Council, November, 1972, pp. 1–3.

[25]Same source as footnote 22.

[26]*Fortune,* January, 1970.

[27]Robert Mayer, *Medicare and Medicaid Coverage,* 1970, pp. 266 and 269.

[28]Department of Health, Education and Welfare, *Report of Task Force on Medicaid and Related Programs, 1970* (#12596 in 1970 *Monthly Catalog of United States Government Publications),* pp. 11–12.

[29]United States General Accounting Office, *Report to the Congress: Study of Health Facilities Construction Costs,* Enclosure C—Means by which Construction Costs

Could be Reduced by Reducing Demand for Health Facilities, November, 1972, pp. 31–33.

[30]Marion K. Sanders, "The Doctors Meet the People," *Harper's,* January, 1968, p. 62.

[31]"Survival for $25,000," *Time,* December 20, 1971, p. 57.

[32]*Psychology and Life,* 1971, pp. 120 and 125.

[33]Brookings Institution, *Setting National Priorities,* 1972, pp. 224–25.

[34]Norman L. Cantor, "The Law and Poor People's Access to Health Care," *Law and Contemporary Problems,* Autumn, 1970, p. 901.

[35]David Mechanic, "Problems in the Future Organization of Medical Practice," *Law and Contemporary Problems,* Spring, 1970, p. 248.

[36]*Family Practice News,* October 15, 1972, p. 4.

[37]Walter J. McNerney, "Health Care Financing and Delivery in the Decade Ahead," *Journal of the American Medical Association,* November 27, 1972, pp. 1153–54.

[38]*Private Practice,* October, 1972, p. 44.

[39]Hearings of Subcommittee on Health, Senate Committee on Labor and Public Welfare, *Health Care Crisis in America, 1971,* p. 38.

[40]*Private Practice,* April, 1972, p. 4.

[41]George Sullivan, *The Boom Is Going Bust: The Threat of a National Scandal in Common Bankruptcy,* 1968, pp. 17, 55, 63, 64, 70, 71, 96.

[42]Same source as footnote 41, pp. 71–72, 74, 84.

[43]Melvin G. Shimm, "The Impact of State Laws on Bankruptcy," *Duke Law Journal,* December, 1971, p. 881.

[44]John G. Turnbull, C. Arthur Williams, and Earl F. Cheitt, *Economic and Social Security,* 1967, pp. 181 and 426–27.

[45]Milton I. Roemer, "Controlling and Promoting Quality in Medical Care," *Law and Contemporary Problems,* Spring, 1970, p. 228.

[46]*Patient Care,* January 1, 1973, pp. 52–53.

[47]*Modern Medicine,* November 29, 1971, p. 75.

[48]Dr. George Canick, *AECH,* September 21, 1971, p. 63.

[49]Robert C. Derbyshire, *Medical Licensure and Discipline in the United States,* 1969, p. 16.

[50]Howard L. Goldman and Alan R. Cohen, "State Licensure of X-Ray Technicians: The Experience of New York State," *American Journal of Public Health,* March, 1968, p. 529.

[51]*Medical Economics,* September 25, 1972, p. 47.

[52]*Internist,* May, 1971, p. 3.

[53]World Health Organization, *Health Hazards of the Human Environment,* 1972, pp. 303–5.

[54]*Harvard Law Review,* February, 1971.

[55]Edgar F. Kaiser and Clifford H. Keene, *Group Health and Welfare News,* September, 1970.

[56]See footnote 21 in first affirmative constructive.

[57]Testimony of Dr. Philip Lee, December 7, 1972, *Advertising of Proprietary Medicines,* Hearings of Subcommittee on Monopoly, Senate Select Committee on Small Business, pp. 1142–43.

[58]Same source as footnote 57, p. 1158.

[59]Howard Lewis, "The Problem Doctors," *New York Times,* December 19, 1970, p. 27.

[60]See footnote 47 in first negative constructive.

[61]*Albany Law Review,* Spring, 1972, p. 503.

[62]*Journal of the National Medical Association,* May, 1972, p. 263.

[63]Testimony of Dr. Leighton Cluff, December 8, 1972, *Advertising of Proprietary Medicines,* Hearings of Subcommittee on Monopoly, Senate Select Committee on Small Business, p. 1205 and following.

[64]See footnote 51 in first negative constructive.

[65]*Geriatrics,* September, 1972, p. 128.

[66]See footnote 24 in first affirmative constructive.

[67]Testimony of Dr. Karl Morgan, May, 1972, *Physician Training Facilities and Health Maintenance Organizations,* Hearings of Subcommittee on Health, Senate Committee on Labor and Public Welfare.

[68]See footnote 48 in first negative constructive.

[69]*Congressional Record,* August 17, 1972.

[70]See footnotes 52 and 53 in first negative constructive.

[71]See footnote 10 in first affirmative constructive.

[72]See footnote 11 in first affirmative constructive.

[73]"Aetna's Med-Major," a flyer describing the company's major medical insurance plan supplied to the editor by Georgetown.

[74]See footnote 38 in first negative constructive.

[75]Representative Lawrence Hogan, *Congressional Record,* March 14, 1973.

[76]See footnote 40 in first negative constructive.

[77]*Michigan Law Review,* June, 1971, p. 1350.

[78]"Dischargeability: A New Perspective," *Ohio State Law Journal,* Fall, 1971, p. 891.

[79]*The New Physician* (Journal of the Student American Medical Association), July, 1972.

[80]Linn K. Twinem, "Determination of Dischargeability of Debts in Bankruptcy Proceedings," *Banking Law Journal,* July, 1971, p. 592.

[81]Daniel Pettingill, *Best's Review,* July, 1972.

[82]See footnote 18 in first affirmative constructive.

[83]Wallace F. Bennett, *Congressional Digest,* February, 1972, p. 54.

[84]"MDs Back Subsidy for Health," *Milwaukee Journal,* December 20, 1972, Part 2, pp. 1-2.

[85]Stuart Auerbach, "Nixon to Seek Big Cuts in U.S. Health Services," *Los Angeles Times,* January 5, 1973, p. 7.

[86]Julius Roth, *Poverty and Health,* 1969.

[87]Testimony of Senator Edward Kennedy, Hearings of Subcommittee on Health, Senate Committee on Labor and Public Welfare, *Health Care Crisis in America, 1971.*

[88]*Report of the American Public Health Association,* 1971.

[89]Sam Shapiro, Josephine Williams, Alonzo S. Yerby, Paul Densen, and Henry Rosner, "Patterns of Medical Care by the Indigent Aged Under Two Systems of Medical Care," *American Journal of Public Health,* May, 1967, pp. 786-87.

[90]Abraham Ribicoff, *American Medical Machine,* 1972.

[91]See footnote 8 in first affirmative constructive.

[92]Representative Richard Fulton, *Congressional Record,* Volume 116, Part 19, p. 25306.

[93]Secretary Richardson, Senate Health, Education and Welfare Hearings, February 22, 1971.

[94]*Washington Post,* November 26, 1972.

[95]"Healing the Poor of Beaufort-Jasper," *Washington Post,* February 25, 1973, p. C-2.

[96]Leslie Baker, *Journal of the National Medical Association,* November, 1971, p. 489.

[97]See footnote 31 in first negative constructive.

[98]Symond Gottlieb, *Hospitals,* October 1, 1972.

[99]See footnote 7 in first affirmative constructive.

[100]See footnote 89 in this speech.

[101]See footnote 84 in second affirmative constructive.

[102]Dr. Klaus Roghmann, *New England Journal of Medicine,* November 4, 1971, p. 1053.

[103]See footnote 89 in second affirmative constructive.

[104]*Medical Care,* June, 1972, p. 208.

[105]Dr. John Williamson, *Journal of the American Medical Association,* October 25, 1971, pp. 565 and 569.

[106]Philip R. Lee, "Health and Well-Being," *Annals of the American Academy of Political and Social Science,* September, 1967, p. 200.

[107]Leslie J. De Groot, Ed. *Medical Care: Social and Organizational Aspects,* 1966, pp. 102 and 103–4.

[108]*Medical Tribune,* January 17, 1973, p. 32.

[109]See footnote 85 in second affirmative constructive.

[110]Carolynn Steinwald, "A Critique of 'Manpower Needs by Specialty,'" *Journal of the American Medical Association,* December 11, 1972, p. 1411.

[111]*Journal of the American Medical Association,* March 20, 1972, pp. 1621 and 1624–25.

[112]Same source as footnote 111.

[113]*Medical Care,* 1966, p. 258.

[114]Paul Ashton, "The Health Security Program: Medicine in the Free Enterprise System," *Vital Speeches,* December 1, 1970, p. 101.

[115]*Inquiry,* March, 1972, p. 5.

[116]See footnote 54 in second affirmative constructive.

[117]See footnote 85 in second affirmative constructive.

[118]*Medical Care,* 1966, p. 262.

[119]Hearings of Subcommittee on Health, Senate Labor and Public Welfare Committee, 1972, p. 78.

[120]David Mechanic, "Problems in the Future Organization of Medical Practice," *Law and Contemporary Problems,* Spring, 1970, p. 250.

[121]*Medical Opinion and Review,* July, 1972, p. 23.

[122]*Private Practice,* November, 1970, p. 68.

[123]L. L. Ecker-Racz, *The Politics and Economics of State-Local Finance,* 1970, pp. 117 and 125.

[124]*Report of the Ad Hoc Committee on School Finance,* Hearings of the Senate Select Committee on Education, 1971, Appendix Volume, p. 8386.

[125]President's Commission on School Finance, *State and Local Revenue Systems and Educational Finance,* 1971, Chapter V, p. 7.

[126]U.S. Department of Interior, 1968, p. 57.

[127]National Health Insurance Hearings, Committee on Ways and Means, October 28, 1971.

[128]"Blood Bank Study Ordered by Nixon," *New York Times,* March 3, 1972, p. 24.

[129]*Science,* March, 1972, p. 1344.

[130]*American Medical News,* March 12, 1973, pp. 4 and 8.

[131]Special Analysis, U.S. Budget, 1974, pp. 135, 148, and 151.

[132]Joel F. Handler and Ellen Jane Hollingsworth, *The 'Deserving Poor': A Study of Welfare Administration,* 1971, pp. 174–75.

[133]Merwyn R. Greenlick, "The Impact of Prepaid Group Practice on American Medical Care: A Critical Evaluation," *Annals of the American Academy of Political and Social Science,* January, 1972, p. 104.

[134]See footnote 92 in second affirmative constructive. Representative Fulton is from Tennessee.

[135]*1972 Catalog of Federal Domestic Assistance,* p. 333.

[136]Testimony of Dr. Robert Van Hoek, April 19, 1972, Hearings of Senate Committee on Appropriations, *Departments of Labor and Health, Education, and Welfare and Related Agencies Appropriation for Fiscal Year 1973,* Part 2, p. 1927.

[137]*American Medical News,* March 19, 1973, pp. 1 and 3.

[138]See footnote 98 in second affirmative constructive.

[139]See footnote 71 in second affirmative constructive.

[140]See footnote 73 in second affirmative constructive.

[141]See footnote 38 in first negative constructive.

[142]See footnote 39 in first negative constructive.

[143]See footnote 40 in first negative constructive.

[144]See footnote 80 in second affirmative constructive. The negative speaker produced a copy of Chapter 13 of the Bankruptcy Act to which he refers.

[145]See footnote 46 in first negative constructive.

[146]See footnote 47 in first negative constructive.

[147] *Private Practice News,* July 15, 1972, p. 28.
[148] See footnote 67 in second affirmative constructive.
[149] *Trial,* March/April, 1973, p. 12.
[150] See footnote 53 in first negative constructive.
[151] *Illinois Medical Journal,* July, 1972, pp. 9–10.
[152] See footnote 115 in second negative constructive.
[153] See footnote 89 in second affirmative constructive.
[154] See footnote 133 in first negative rebuttal.
[155] "American Journal of Public Health Study," May 1, 1972, *Physician Training Facilities and Health Maintenance Organizations,* Hearings of Subcommittee on Health, Senate Committee on Labor and Public Welfare, p. 1842.
[156] See footnote 104 in second negative constructive.
[157] *Trial, March/April, 1973.*
[158] "Kennedy Expands Concern to Include Medicine Misuse," *Washington Post,* December 17, 1972, p. A14.
[159] Robert S. McLeery, Louise T. Keelty, Mimi Lam, Russell E. Phillips, and Terrence M. Quirin, *One Life—One Physician: An Inquiry Into the Medical Profession's Performance in Self-Regulation—A Report to the Center of Responsive Law,* 1971, p. 18.
[160] See footnote 159.
[161] See footnote 112 in second negative constructive.
[162] "Health Security Program," a position paper published by the UAW, 1972, p. 10. Copy available from: United Auto Workers, 1126 16th Street, NW, Washington, D.C.
[163] *Harvard Law Review,* February, 1971, p. 923.
[164] Edward Kennedy, April 7, 1971, Hearings of Subcommittee on Health, Senate Committee on Labor and Public Welfare, *Health Care Crisis in America, 1971,* p. 5745.
[165] Editorial, *Medical Times,* April, 1972, pp. 21–22.
[166] *Medical World News,* February 16, 1973.
[167] *Journal of the American Medical Association,* 1970.
[168] General Accounting Office, *Report to the Congress,* Comptroller General of the United States, Enclosure C, Study of Health Facilities Construction Costs B-164031 (3), November 20, 1972, pp. 75–90.
[169] See footnote 128 in second negative constructive.
[170] "Filtering Process 'Cleans' Blood of Hepatitis Antigen," *Journal of the American Medical Association,* October 2, 1972, p. 13.
[171] *American Medical News,* February 12, 1973.
[172] See footnote 147 in first negative rebuttal.
[173] See footnote 19 in first affirmative constructive.
[174] See footnotes 130 and 131 in first negative rebuttal.
[175] See footnote 132 in first negative rebuttal.
[176] See footnote 133 in first negative rebuttal.
[177] See footnote 92 in second affirmative constructive.
[178] See footnote 135 in first negative rebuttal.
[179] See footnotes 136 and 137 in first negative rebuttal.
[180] See footnotes 37 and 36 in the first negative constructive.
[181] See footnote 40 in first negative constructive.
[182] See footnote 73 in second affirmative constructive.
[183] See footnote 147 in first negative rebuttal.
[184] See footnote 50 in first negative constructive.
[185] See footnote 49 in first negative constructive.
[186] See footnote 149 in first negative rebuttal.
[187] See footnote 53 in first negative constructive.
[188] See footnote 151 in first negative rebuttal.
[189] See footnote 162 in first affirmative rebuttal.

[190]See footnote 164 in first affirmative rebuttal.
[191]See footnote 170 in first affirmative rebuttal.
[192]See footnote 171 in first affirmative rebuttal.
[193]See footnote 128 in second negative constructive.
[194]See footnote 89 in second affirmative constructive.
[195]See footnote 155 in first affirmative rebuttal.
[196]See footnote 157 in first affirmative constructive.
[197]See footnote 158 in first affirmative constructive.
[198]See footnote 159 in first affirmative constructive.
[199]See footnote 162 in first affirmative constructive.
[200]See footnote 163 in first affirmative constructive.
[201]See footnote 164 in first affirmative rebuttal.
[202]See footnotes 89 in second affirmative constructive and 155 in first affirmative rebuttal.
[203]See footnote 165 in first affirmative rebuttal.
[204]See footnote 166 in first affirmative rebuttal.
[205]See footnote 167 in first affirmative rebuttal.
[206]See footnote 21 in first affirmative constructive.
[207]See footnote 158 in first affirmative rebuttal.
[208]See footnote 61 in second affirmative constructive.
[209]See footnote 65 in second affirmative constructive.
[210]See footnote 13 in first affirmative constructive.
[211]See footnote 75 in second affirmative constructive.
[212]See footnote 73 in second affirmative constructive.
[213]See footnote 81 in second affirmative constructive.
[214]See footnote 8 in first affirmative constructive.

B A
Public Debate:
Should
Gambling
be Legalized

The debate presented here is an unedited transcript of the January 18, 1972, broadcast of *The Advocates.* This Public Broadcasting Service program originated at KCET, Los Angeles.[1]

Topic:	Should Gambling be Legalized?
Moderator:	*MICHAEL DUKAKIS*
Participants:	*Advocate JACK COLE (Pro)*

Mary Manoni, Ph.D.
Research Director
Policy Sciences Center, New York City

Jimmy "The Greek" Snyder
Las Vegas Oddsmaker

Michael Armstrong
Chief Counsel to the Knapp Commission, N.Y.C.

[1]"Should Gambling Be Legalized," *The Advocates* (WGBH Boston—KCET Los Angeles), January 18, 1972.

Advocate HOWARD MILLER (Con)

Prof. Arthur Rosett
Former Associate Director
President's Crime Commission

Tom Harmon
Former Heisman Trophy Winner

Jack Danahy
Director of Security
National Football League

Aaron M. Kohn
Director, Metropolitan Crime Commission
New Orleans

ANNOUNCER: Tonight, from Los Angeles, THE ADVOCATES. Jack Cole. (applause) Howard Miller. (applause) And the moderator, Michael Dukakis. (applause)

DUKAKIS: Good evening and welcome to THE ADVOCATES. Every week at this time we look at an important public issue in terms of a practical choice. Tonight, in the midst of the biggest and the most bet upon sporting events of the year, we consider gambling. And specifically our question is this: Should gambling be legalized? Advocate Jack Cole says yes.

COLE: The overwhelming majority of the human race regards gambling as fun and always has. Laws against it are unenforceable. Not only that, they breed corruption and disrespect for the law itself. With us tonight to tell us why and how we must bring gambling into the open where it can be enjoyed and regulated and taxed are Dr. Mary Manoni, a social scientist who just might be the leading authority on the game we call numbers; Jimmy "The Greek," whose point spreads are the morning line in virtually every newspaper in the country; and Mr. Michael Armstrong, Chief Counsel for the Knapp Commission investigating police corruption in New York City. (applause)

DUKAKIS: Advocate Howard Miller says no.

MILLER: Tonight's proposal is for organized legal gambling. It will strengthen, not weaken, organized crime. And for the first time it will legally entice millions to place their bet with the syndicate. With me tonight to oppose this organized, legal gambling are: Arthur Rosett, professor of law at UCLA; Tom Harmon, former Heisman Trophy winner; Jack Danahy, Director of Security for the National Football League; and Aaron Kohn, Managing Director of the New Orleans Crime Commission. (applause)

DUKAKIS: Thank you gentlemen. It is a difference of opinion, as Mark Twain once observed, that makes a horse race. And so, to gamble, simply put, is to bet a sum of money on an event whose outcome appears uncertain.

(film)

DUKAKIS: While in the American tradition gambling has generally been disapproved of, 34 states permit some form of gambling. Nevada allows casinos; New York, off-track betting on horses; 3 states operate lotteries; 13 permit bingo; and 31 allow on-track betting on horses or dogs. But the great bulk of gambling in the United States, at least $20 billion a year, is done illegally. Gambling on sporting events is universally practiced. Football, basketball, baseball, hockey—professional and amateur sports of all kinds—are the object of wagers. And almost every major newspaper in the country publishes the odds or point spreads that originate from Las Vegas and other cities. In the urban ghettos the game is policy or, as it is commonly referred to, the numbers. It is a bet on a totally unpredictable number, such as the last two or three digits of the day's take at a designated race track. Bets are usually small, less than 50¢; the odds against winning are great; and the payoffs are big, if infrequent. In the ghetto, nearly everyone plays the numbers.

(end of film)

DUKAKIS: Recently, state and local governments, faced with mounting budgets, have been eyeing the huge, illegal, untaxed and untaxable betting operations as a source of possible new revenue. New Hampshire started with a lottery, New York and New Jersey followed, and so too soon will Pennsylvania, Connecticut, and Massachusetts. And New York has gone to off-track betting. And so, piecemeal, traditional barriers against gambling have been breeched. Tonight we consider a proposal to legalize under government regulation all currently illegal forms of gambling commonly practiced. For the purposes of our discussion these will be understood to include all gambling now done on sporting events as well as policy or the numbers game which is popular in so many American cities. Mr. Cole, tell us why we should legalize gambling.

COLE: Almost everybody gambles. We think nothing of a little Friday night poker or bridge at a tenth of a cent a point or a bet on a ball game.

Governors do it. They get their pictures in the paper—a crate of oranges, maybe, versus a Michigan ham on the Rose Bowl. But did you know that's against the law—a federal law at that—if the governor crosses a state line or makes a phone call. Now, nobody enforces those laws, and it would be pretty silly if they did, but there's the problem. Because when you pin a badge on a man and ask him to enforce some laws, sometimes, against some people, you're asking for trouble. People are going to gamble. Now they do it illegally mostly, and the underworld rakes off an estimated $50 billion a year from the action. Wouldn't it be better to have it out in the open and regulated? Some years ago Great Britain said yes.

(film)

SIR STANLEY RAYMOND (Chairman, Gaming Board for Great Britain): We decided in this country that there was so much illegal gambling going on that the law enforcement agencies could not cope with it, and therefore we had a situation in which the law was breaking down, the criminal elements were taking command, and that was bad from the social point of view, and therefore our legislation has directed itself to remedying the fault socially. We were not concerned with raising revenue. We were concerned with deciding what should or should not be allowed, and what should be legal and what the circumstances should be of that legality. We in this country decided that it is better to have rules under which gambling can take place legally than to have an unenforceable, illegal situation. And the result has been plain and clear for everyone to see. I think we can say that the danger that there was that international criminal elements should take over in this country in large sectors of illegal gambling has been averted by strong social legislation.

BETTOR #1: I don't think it's done England any harm, as I say, if kept in moderation, to within one's own personal pocket. It's like any kind of entertainment. If you like going to the cinema you spend so much a week, if you want to go to the theater, you spend so much. If you enjoy gambling and the fun and excitement of it, then fine, spend whatever you feel you can reasonably afford.

BETTOR #2: Betting shops are a very good thing, they should have them in America.

SHOP MANAGER: In a democratic society, people should have the free choice to go in or stay out.

BETTOR #3: People will still gamble, because if they want to gamble, they will gamble and nothing will stop them from gambling whatsoever. If you want to have a bet you'll come and you have a bet and if you don't, you don't. But you will.

BETTOR #2: If you have a wager in a betting shop, it's legalized, it's taxed, the government gets a benefit out of it and everything is hunky-dory. It's not bad, it's good.

BETTOR #4: I find it's very good relaxation and I enjoy doing it . . . completely harmless . . . provided you're not losing all the time. (laugh)

SIR STANLEY: But it's a mugs game whatever way you look at it and the punter in the end is going to lose because the odds are always against him. But if he loses in a way that he has not lost twice, because of criminal organization, then that is surely better for the social fiber of the country and better for the country all around.

(end of film)

COLE: You know, one argument that you hear against legalized gambling is that it is really an unfair tax on the poor. "They'll gamble away their welfare checks. They'll never learn what we all know so well—that you can't get something for nothing." Well that's patronizing hogwash. It just doesn't make it in the ghetto where nothing is exactly what they've got. Our first witness is a social scientist who learned so much about the policy racket in Bedford-Stuyvesant that she was asked to become a consultant by a syndicate boss. She declined. She's Dr. Mary Manoni. (applause)

DUKAKIS: Welcome to THE ADVOCATES Dr. Manoni.

MANONI: Thank you.

COLE: Dr. Manoni, on the basis of your copious study of gambling in Bedford-Stuyvesant, would you describe for us briefly the role that it plays.

MANONI: Well, it plays a multiple role, but largely in the economic and social spheres. There are 1,200 businesses in an area that is slightly more than 2 square miles, 800 of them, I believe, would be out of business like that if it were not for policy. This is what keeps them in business. But socially it is not under any opprobrium. The policy collector is something like the matchmaker, the overall village gossip, if you will.

COLE: You mean he's a man of some reputation then?

MANONI: He is a man of considerable reputation. If you lived in the ghetto and you had some difficulty he'd be the person you'd go to.

COLE: Could you quickly explain for us how the numbers racket works?

MANONI: Well, as the screen previously indicated, it is on a completely unpredictable number dealing with horse race policy. It's usually three digits, sometimes one or two. It's based on adding up win, place and show in a number of races at the local race track.

COLE: How much of the take leaves the community?

MANONI: Roughly 30 percent.

COLE: Where does that go?

MANONI: That goes to the members of organized crime.

COLE: Dr. Manoni, now as a social scientist, what do you think is wrong with the laws that there now are against gambling and policy in particular?

MANONI: I think not simply that they are unenforceable, Mr. Cole, they're not viable. The laws are supposed to respond to the self needs of a community, whether the community is geographical or bound by a common characteristic. These do not. And, for example, if you even attempted to enforce them in New York City and arrested all known collectors you'd have 17,000 persons arrested and the state itself can only accommodate 3,500 in its jails.

COLE: There is some attempt being made now, is there not Doctor? What is the cost of enforcement based on your study?

MANONI: The costs of enforcement are roughly 15 working days for a five-man team for a cost of $3,500 to the police department, exclusive of clerical expense, for what is popularly referred to as a single bust or a single arrest of a bank. And this will take in at least two persons and, normally speaking, the individual who is arrested is out almost before he's in. In the last ten years in this small area 356 arrests were made, almost 200 of them, as I indicated, were dismissed. It was just like coming in one door and going right out the other. The few that were fined, the average fine was $117 and one person in the entire ten-year period went to prison for one year and one day.

DUKAKIS: Dr. Manoni, let me break in at this point. The small area is Bedford-Stuyvesant?

MANONI: Yes.

DUKAKIS: And that is where?

MANONI: That is in the borough of Brooklyn in the city of New York.

DUKAKIS: And it's a neighborhood in that particular borough?

MANONI: It is a neighborhood that could be compared to Watts here in Los Angeles or Hyde Park in Chicago, or central Harlem, South Bronx for areas which might be better known.

DUKAKIS: Fine. Mr. Miller wants to ask some questions about Bedford-Stuyvesant and other things.

MILLER: Dr. Manoni, your study was in Bedford-Stuyvesant, do you favor legalizing gambling all across the United States in all communities?

MANONI: Yes, I favor the legalization of gambling.

MILLER: Well, let's talk about a community that now doesn't have the policy or, as Mr. Cole calls it, numbers racket.

MANONI: Then we're talking about a small town I assume.

MILLER: No, a small town or there are large cities in which there's no widespread policy to the extent there is in Bedford-Stuyvesant. Certainly in Los Angeles and San Francisco.

MANONI: Widespread is a relative term. What would you mean by this?

MILLER: There is no substantial numbers in Los Angeles or San Francisco.

MANONI: On what are you basing your information?

MILLER: We will have testimony to that effect. But certainly to the extent that there is, and there is no substantial amount, it's in limited parts of the city, there's no widespread policy in many parts of major metropolitan cities is there? Are you saying every major metropolitan area in the United States has a numbers racket?

MANONI: I would say that every major metropolitan area in the United States has numbers, I'll use your relative term, to some extent.

MILLER: To some extent. And you would favor legalizing it in areas where a third of the people live in rural areas, those parts of middle class metropolitan areas. . . .

MANONI: Yes, because despite the fact that, shall we say a third of the people live in one type of an area, and obviously the other two-thirds of the people live someplace else. I do not feel that the legalization of it is instantly going to attract the other two-thirds so they're going to go wildly racing into the ghetto area.

MILLER: But no, no, the question is, is that something we ought to encourage. Do you think that a community that doesn't now have the numbers racket ought to have it?

MANONI: No, but I don't think legalizing it is going to bring it in. Frankly, I think it's simply going to bring it out into the open.

MILLER: But if it's profitable, of course it's going to bring it in, if there's money to be made in it.

MANONI: But the same way I think there's a certain person who gambles. All right, if it were to be legalized you have someone try it on for size, shall we say. And in the first couple of weeks, the first couple of months, six months perhaps, but after that, if the individual is not a gambler by nature he or she would not gamble I suspect.

MILLER: By nature, let's look at that. In fact in New York a study of the Off-Track Betting systems shows that 60 percent of those who place bets in the Off-Track Betting system have never before placed a bet with a bookie.

MANONI: Yes, but I rather suspect that that survey is something like the Kinsey Report, that they're given back the kind of answers that they expected to receive.

MILLER: But what about the English survey that Mr. Peterson reports that we'll hear more about that indicates that after gambling was legalized in England there was a fourfold increase in the amount of gambling that was done through the bookie.

MANONI: I would question the validity of these mythical numbers, because you're relating something that now you can legally survey with what were you doing before. It's a rare individual, if he knew that what he were doing say two years ago, last month or whatever, was unlawful is about to say, 'Oh sure, I did that.'

MILLER: Suppose these studies were accurate. Suppose we have a fourfold increase as we had in England, that we have a substantial two-and-a-half times as in Off-Track Betting in New York. Do you think it would be good for the country to increase the number of people who play the numbers game?

MANONI: I really don't think it would increase the number of people.

MILLER: But if it did, would that be something to put on the balance?

MANONI: But you're dealing in the area of supposition and I'm afraid I'm always dealing in the area of facts that are codifiable.

MILLER: But I'm always dealing in the area of suppositions which happen to be supported by studies in England and New York. Let me ask you, but very much your position is based on your assumption there would be no substantial increase, you're just dealing with those who gamble by nature.

MANONI: No, other than the initial one that I spoke of for anything that is new.

DUKAKIS: Thank you very much Dr. Manoni for being with us. (applause) Mr. Cole.

COLE: The point about numbers, of policy if you will, is that it is the recreational form of gambling in the ghetto. The middle class is not, in the suburbs or in the cities, into numbers to anywhere near the same extent. The form of gambling most prevalent there is, I guess, the bridge game for a few pennies a point or less, maybe betting on a ball game, as to which there are a lot of football widows who think a wide receiver is probably some kind of stereo set. Until, that is, their husbands start betting on pro games. Then they care who wins, and who loses. Sometimes they even get to like the game. My next witness knows all about that—you can bet on it. You know him as Jimmy "The Greek." (applause)

DUKAKIS: Welcome to THE ADVOCATES James.

SNYDER: Nice to be here.

COLE: Jimmy, you don't mind if I call you Jimmy do you?

SNYDER: Everybody else does.

COLE: Jimmy, I think everybody in the country knows that you used to be, at least, one of the most important, one of the biggest gamblers of all time. The Off-Track Betting Corp. in the state of New York knows that, they have asked you to be a consultant, and I understand you're probably going to testify before the state legislature in Albany on ways of improving that system.

SYNDER: Yes, we're making a proposal up for them now.

COLE: Well then, let me ask you, as a genuine expert on the subject of gambling, if you were called upon by, let's say the Congress of the United States to testify on the subject of gambling and it was said to you, "We're going to wipe all the laws off the books, Jimmy, and we're going to let you recommend to us some ways to restructure them," where would you begin?

SNYDER: I would legalize the part of betting on professional sports.

COLE: How would you do that?

SNYDER: Well it could be done in two ways similar to the race track operation where the money goes into a pool, a commission is taken out by the race track, the commission would be taken out by the state, and then what is left would be divided among the winners and, of course, the losing money is lost.

COLE: You mentioned two ways, what's the other one.

SNYDER: The second way would be to capitalize on the fact where, similar to the laws of Nevada, where an applicant would come in and apply for a license.

COLE: Sort of a regulated private enterprise?

SNYDER: Right.

COLE: Jimmy, what would you do about policy, about the numbers game?

SNYDER: If policy were legalized, actually, the government or whoever legalized it—the community that legalized it because I think it should be up to the community itself—they would automatically knock them out of business regardless of what anybody else says.

COLE: Knock the syndicate who is now running the policy racket out of business, is that what you mean?

SNYDER: Well, whoever is running it, let's put it that way.

COLE: A final question, Jim, what would you do about a private bet that, well, Mr. Miller, who went to Pepperdine College, and I, who went to the University of Virginia, might make on a ball game between our two schools? Would you make that illegal as it is now or not?

SNYDER: I don't think so. Everybody loves some sort of a challenge and I'm sure Mr. Miller likes to bet on his school on occasions.

COLE: Maybe we'll find out.

DUKAKIS: Mr. Miller, how about it?

MILLER: Of course we're not talking about that kind of private bet, we're talking about an organized system of betting. You mentioned you would favor legalizing gambling on professional sports. Why not college sports?

SNYDER: Well, professional sports are more exposed and I don't see any reason why you should legalize it on college sports when it's only a local game in a local community.

MILLER: The Rose Bowl is a local game?

SNYDER: That happens once a year.

MILLER: The games that settle college championships? Games between the midwestern schools and the coast? Those are local games? You think that the difference in college and pros, the college are local games?

SNYDER: Professional games are more exposed. They're on television every week. I am not of the opinion that sports should be legalized on college.

MILLER: Tell me why? Is it only because they're local, do you consider bowl games, national championships, etcetera, local or are there other reasons as well. Are there risks?

SNYDER: For the same reason, Mr. Miller, that a young person can't walk into a bar and have a drink.

MILLER: We're not talking about the players betting, although presumably they might be able to.

SNYDER: It's a regulation. It's an age regulation.

MILLER: Are you afraid that gambling on college sports might lead to corruption of college athletes?

SNYDER: In the same way I'm afraid that certain movies would hurt my child at a certain age and in the same way that the laws of the liquors ...

MILLER: But you think, then, there would be a risk of corruption in college sports and you don't favor organized gambling on college sports. You wouldn't favor organized gambling on the Rose Bowl?

SNYDER: I don't favor amateur gambling on amateur events. No I don't.

MILLER: You talk about the age limit. What about professional baseball where in the minor leagues and in many major leagues many of the players are the same age as in colleges?

SNYDER: The percentage of that, Mr. Miller, is very trivial.

MILLER: But not in the minor leagues. In the minor leagues most fellows go in when they're eighteen.

SNYDER: But there won't be any betting on minor leagues. We're talking about betting on professional sports—the NFL, the AFC, professional hockey.

MILLER: We're talking about betting on college basketball, college football as well.

SNYDER: No I'm not saying that, Mr. Miller.

MILLER: But we are tonight.

DUKAKIS: Mr. Miller, I think that Mr. Snyder's made his point clear that he doesn't favor it on amateur sports.

SNYDER: And he continues sticking on that same point. I'm in favor of legalizing gaming on professional sports and professional sports only, and that's it.

MILLER: But the proposal tonight as I understand it includes college as well, that's why I'm sticking.

DUKAKIS: Mr. Snyder doesn't agree to that extent with it.

SNYDER: I agree with you on that end of it.

MILLER: Now the question I'm asking is why. Why is there a risk of corruption for the 23-year-old red-shirt all-American football player and no risk of corruption for the NFL quarterback who's also 23 years old.

SNYDER: Let me ask you one question. When you were 18 were you as smart as you are at 23 or 24 that you are now.

MILLER: Well, and then at 30, you know, it keeps going up and presumably you, in this area, are somewhat smarter than I am, but let's talk about the specific case now. You say the 23-year-old football players are subject to corruption and the 23-year-old NFL quarterback is not.

SNYDER: It's a matter of economics, Mr. Miller. A kid in school gets $50 a month and room and board. A professional football player gets a bonus to sign, he gets anywhere from $15,000 up to $150,000 a year to play. He has fringe benefits. He has retirement policy. It's impossible for him to think of doing anything wrong.

MILLER: It's your assumption that the wealthy cannot be corrupted?

SNYDER: That's a matter of a situation. . . .

MILLER: Is that your own experience. . . .

DUKAKIS: I have to break in. Clearly there's a difference of opinion. Jimmy, thank you very much for being with THE ADVOCATES. Thank you. (applause)

COLE: Mr. Dukakis, I certainly agree with Mr. Miller that there is great potential for corruption so long as making book, that is to say accepting wagers, on professional football, college football, is done by people who are operating under the table, who are operating outside of the law. But I submit that most if not all of that would be removed were we to have the state or a regulated body, licensed by the state, make the book, accept the wagers, as is done in the United Kingdom and I think it's some 84 other civilized countries around the world. And as to numbers, it strikes me as highly hypocritical for us to allow ourselves to play poker and bridge and to gamble in the ways that we do, betting on football games as you know is a common practice. Jimmy "The Greek's" point spread's in every paper in the country, and that's not by accident. It's because people do bet privately on football games. And yet we pass laws and we enforce the laws to some degree, done at great expense, against policy, against numbers, which is just recreational gambling in the ghetto. I think that's inconsistent. I think that's undemocratic.

DUKAKIS: Thank you Mr. Cole, we'll be back to you later for your rebuttal argument. Mr. Miller, why shouldn't gambling be legalized?

MILLER: Gambling shouldn't be legalized because the government shouldn't get into the business of promoting gambling. That's what we're talking about. No one is concerned about the private bet. Those laws are not enforced and no one here proposes that they be. We're talking about government organization of gambling. Now why should it be? One of the reasons that is given sometimes is to raise revenue for the state, but that reason simply doesn't hold up. There is no magical source of revenue by taxing legalized gambling. In fact, no witness tonight has put that forth as a reason for legalizing gambling and there's good reason. It doesn't stand up. Why then should the government get into this business? To drive out organized crime, as has been suggested? People will bet legally rather than illegally? But you see, the legal operation can never compete with the illegal operation, because the illegal winnings are not taxed, because the syndicate gives credit, because there's secrecy. The legal operation can never drive out the illegal operation. All it does is strengthen the illegal operation and that's the history of whatever has happened where this has been tried.

So why, then, should the government sponsor it? Do we really want a society where the government is in a business of encouraging people to gamble and increasing the number who do eventually go to illegal gambling? Let's find out. Our first witness to oppose this proposal is Arthur Rosett. (applause)

DUKAKIS: Welcome to THE ADVOCATES Mr. Rosett.

ROSETT: Thank you.

MILLER: Arthur Rosett is a criminologist and professor of law at UCLA. Mr. Rosett, should we simply repeal all laws relating to gambling and let anyone form any organization he wants to to gamble?

ROSETT: That seems unthinkable. It would just legitimatize the syndicate as it now exists, give them an absolute free hand to do whatever they want in the community. We're having enough trouble with them as it is.

MILLER: But what about a system of regulation where government sponsored regulated gambling business?

ROSETT: Well, I think that would incur very heavy costs and would probably not have the benefits that have been suggested that it would have. I doubt that it would produce much in the way of tax revenue and in New York and in other places it's produced less than 5 percent. It's a very expensive way to collect taxes. In the New York experience, again, is that the tax collection costs run 35 percent on the gambling tax. That's 35 percent of what's collected whereas other taxes run 1 to 2 percent at most. Thirdly it's a very unwise tax. It's a tax on the poor. It's a regressive tax. It's the kind of tax we're resisting in other areas. It's a tax that tends to hit most heavily those who are least able to carry it.

MILLER: Well, let's focus on the problem of the poor, the Bedford-Stuyvesant example has been given. Why shouldn't we legalize policy in Bedford-Stuyvesant?

ROSETT: Well, it's been suggested that it would somehow create economic development, although I must say I am unable to see at all how it would add any money at all to the community. At best all it can be is a redistribution of money within the community. As a redistribution which, instead of being on some rational basis to meet people's needs and to award productivity and to produce goods, will be just redistribution on the basis of chance. I think the key element, though, is to ask if we did it in Bedford-Stuyvesant, who would run the racket there?

Who would run the operation? And there I think we have a lot of experience. We've experienced in Las Vegas, we've experienced in the Bahamas, we've experienced in the London casinos, we've experienced in other South American and Caribbean places, and in every single situation when organized gambling activities are legalized the people who run it are the people who know how to run it and that's the very syndicate which is running it now.

MILLER: But doesn't legalization help drive out the syndicate? People bet legally instead of illegally, isn't that the way it works?

ROSETT: No it doesn't. I think that again we can look at the Las Vegas experience for some light there. Legalized gambling can't really compete with the syndicate's operation for two reasons. First of all, a major benefit of illegal gambling as it now stands, is that they've got a tremendous tax benefit. They exist on the basis of avoiding taxation. Secondly, they can extend credit.

MILLER: Tell me, aside from being unable to compete, are there any harms that would be caused by putting government in this business?

ROSETT: Well, there's a lot of encouragement of a very bad activity and I think you can best see it in the sort of things that are going on now in New York where, on the back of city buses, there are signs which read "winners ride in limosines and bet Off-Track Betting." Radio commercials say, "start your morning with coffee, a donut, and the daily double."

MILLER: Is that the kind of society we want to encourage?

ROSETT: I don't think so at all, Mr. Miller.

DUKAKIS: All right, Mr. Cole.

COLE: Professor, if you don't want to encourage gambling, would you want to go one step beyond and enforce those laws which are now on the books which prohibit private bets between you and me?

ROSETT: No, not at all.

COLE: So you're not that concerned about gambling?

ROSETT: No, I think there's a tremendous need to revise our legal codes, to bring them up to date, to make them realistic. I'm against organized gambling.

COLE: Would you do away with the OTB, with Off-Track Betting in New York?

ROSETT: I'd have to know more about that. I certainly think that it's a very questionable proposition which isn't paying off as well as it was claimed to be.

COLE: Well, would you in terms of its driving some bookies out of business, because there's some indication of that's happening is there not?

ROSETT: I think that's a very unlikely thing since Off-Track Betting handles only about 15 to 20 percent of a bookie's business anyhow, I doubt that they would be driven off the streets, if that happened. And since six out of ten people who are going to the OTB shops are people who didn't used to go to bookies.

COLE: Well, Dr. Manoni is not terribly sure about that testimony, neither am I. Let's talk about something you've said about taxation. Is there any reason in your mind why the federal government could not exempt gambling winnings from taxation and instead get its rake-off, as it were, as Jimmy "The Greek" has suggested by getting it out of the handle rather than by getting it from the winner? Is there any reason why that couldn't be done?

ROSETT: Certainly. I think it is absolutely immoral, however one feels about whether gambling itself is immoral, to treat one's earnings from gambling as being exempt from taxation and only tax earned income. In other words you would tax people who worked for a living for the money they make by working. . . .

COLE: So you want to use the internal revenue code to enforce your idea of morality, is that right?

ROSETT: Oh no, I didn't say that at all.

COLE: Let's get to this matter of extending credit, which you said again could not be done by the state or by a licensed bookmaker. Why not? I mean, why can't we set it up if, for example, I the state license you to be a bookmaker, why can't I say you can extend credit if you want, Professor, if you lose it's your loss not mine. Why can't I do that?

ROSETT: Because I don't think the state or you would be willing to extend the kinds of collection methods that the syndicate now depends upon to make their debt collection and credit enforcement much more effective than you can get from the courts or civil collection of debts.

COLE: Well certainly you're not talking about that type of collection in terms of the ghetto. I mean, as Dr. Manoni has testified, the numbers racket is a very accepted thing there and there is no indication there of people busting heads over that, is there?

ROSETT: I didn't understand Dr. Manoni. . . .

DUKAKIS: Gentlemen, I think I'll have to break in at this point, I'm sorry. Thank you very much Prof. Rosett. (applause) Mr. Miller.

MILLER: Aside from increasing the number of those who gamble there's a very real risk that more widespread gambling even of so-called legalized would increase the risk of corruption in sports. Here to talk to us about that, I've asked to join us tonight ex-Heisman Trophy winner, Tom Harmon. (applause)

DUKAKIS: Welcome to THE ADVOCATES Mr. Harmon.

HARMON: Thank you.

MILLER: Mr. Harmon, what is the importance of sports and the integrity of sports today in our country?

HARMON: Well, of course, that's a personal opinion, but in my opinion, in my experience I think that this country of ours is sadly in need of heroes. I think that we have perhaps destroyed most of our national images. And I think the youngsters of this country don't have very much to look up to. And I think the one area in which they do have an admiration for a man or somebody they may not know, they see on television or know by reputation through newspapers, is in the sports field. And the basis of sports has always been clean living, good sportsmanship, play hard—play tough, but play honest, give your opponent the even break, yet win.

MILLER: Do you think that legalizing gambling would have the risk of corruption of sports, of tainting the integrity·of sports?

HARMON: I don't think that any man can avoid the risk of somebody being an idiot enough to attempt to bribe an athlete. You have to understand, Mr. Miller, that the people who are not knowing, those who are on the outside, are those who feel that sports can be fixed. And even today I think that you'll find many people who feel that the closeness of games was planned. And it's absolutely impossible and it's a ridiculous statement. Nonetheless the feeling exists and I think that the minute you tempt anyone in this area then you question the integrity of a sport.

MILLER: Is there a special risk in the college area?

HARMON: I think again, as Jimmy said, it's a question of age more than anything else. Plus the fact, here's a boy who perhaps never made more than $50 to $75 a week in his life and all of a sudden somebody comes up and offers him $5,000. If he is a boy who perhaps might have a very big need for that $5,000 he might listen.

MILLER: Thank you.

DUKAKIS: Mr. Cole, you have some questions for Mr. Harmon.

COLE: Mr. Harmon, I guess for tonight's purposes I shouldn't call you Lucky. Excuse me for that. Mr. Harmon, were you offered bets, the chance to throw a game when you were a football player? You won the Heisman Trophy, you were obviously a key player, not only in college, but for the L.A. Rams. Were you ever offered a chance to throw a game for a large sum of money?

HARMON: No.

COLE: Did no one ever bet, then, on the games in which you played?

HARMON: I would have no idea, I assume they did.

COLE: Well, what's the difference now?

HARMON: Well the only thing you're talking about is legalizing it. You're bringing it out into the open where you're going to obviously make it much larger than it is today.

COLE: Why obviously?

HARMON: Well, because as you just said, there would be four to one the number of people who bet today that would bet if it were legalized.

COLE: I didn't say that. No. I think that was said by somebody, but I didn't say that.

HARMON: Some statistics, then, we'll say that.

COLE: Well, some statistics. . . .

DUKAKIS: Mr. Harmon, do you think it would encourage people to bet?

HARMON: Do I think it would hurt people to bet?

DUKAKIS: No, do you think it would encourage people to bet?

HARMON: Absolutely. I think anytime you make anything easier for anybody they're going to take a shot at it. Let me make one point very clear—I think anybody who bets on a football game's an idiot. And that's because I know the game.

COLE: You never bet on a football game?

HARMON: No.

COLE: Never in your life?

HARMON: No, well with friends who when they're talking about my particular team, as you say the $5 bet. No, not going to a bookie or betting in a legalized gambling place.

COLE: Well, okay, I mean, the proposal is not that we make gambling compulsory, only that we make it allowable, right? So, you're concerned about the bookie and I'm concerned about the bookie. I don't like the fact that now the fellow who's going to make a bet who doesn't have a friend and he wants to make a bet has to go to a bookie. And I'm concerned about the fact that the rake-off goes not to the public where it belongs, I think at least. It goes to the bookie and it goes to the syndicate and I think that's wrong. There's an aura of illegality about it. That's the kind of thing it seems to me that casts a bad image about sports.

HARMON: You feel, Mr. Cole, that everything in Las Vegas is legal?

COLE: I don't, well let's see, gambling is legal in Las Vegas.

HARMON: Do you think there's never been a case of where "skimming," as they say, did not quite reach the legal authorities in terms of taxation?

COLE: Mr. Harmon, I looked into that because of something that will be said a little later tonight. It's interesting, there are a couple of indictments pending right now about skimming, but if you really want to talk about Las Vegas, you realize that you're talking about the people who own those casinos and those are some of the major corporations in the United States whose stock is traded publicly, so you're making some pretty heavy accusations. Now, it does come up from time to time, but I know a lot of politicians who've been indicted for a lot of things worse than skimming and I don't think we ought to make politics illegal, do you?

DUKAKIS: Gentlemen, if this goes much further I'm going to have you switch roles.

HARMON: I think I'd have to place that in the right category. I think that a lot of politicians, some that I've met and heard about, I think could be included in with some of the folks who are running the mafia.

COLE: On that, sir we agree.

DUKAKIS: Thank you very much, Mr. Harmon, for being with us. (applause) Mr. Miller, perhaps with your next witness you could define what skimming is for some of us who don't understand those terms.

MILLER: What skimming is and the other real risks as well, the real risks of integrity to professional and college sports, and to talk to that point, I've asked to join us tonight Mr. Jack Danahy, Chief of Security for the National Football League. (applause)

DUKAKIS: Welcome to THE ADVOCATES Mr. Danahy.

MILLER: Mr. Danahy also is the former supervising officer in the New York office for the Organized Crime Strike Force. Mr. Danahy, what is skimming?

DANAHY: Skimming is a process that was regularly utilized when the casinos in Las Vegas were under the control of hoodlum elements whereby the proceeds of the casino, on the way to the counting room, were skimmed off, they weren't reported to the Gaming Commission of the State of Nevada and no taxes were paid on them.

MILLER: And that went on regularly despite the fact that gambling was legal?

DANAHY: It most certainly did.

MILLER: Tell me, switching to the problem of sports, how do all the commissioners and coaches and all the professional leagues, you know —football, basketball, baseball—how do they stand on the question of legalized gambling?

DANAHY: They're all vehemently opposed to the legalization of gambling on professional sports.

MILLER: Why?

DANAHY: Because of the influences that can result by the expansion of the availability of betting to the public. We will create a completely new group of fans who will not be fans of professional sports per se. They will be fans solely for the purpose of winning bets and this will have a bad influence on professional sports.

MILLER: Is there a real security problem, though, in terms of tampering?

DANAHY: There is always a security problem and we're very well aware of it. We've taken elaborate precautions to protect our professional athletes in all professional sports. But where you enlarge the number of people who are engaged in gambling operations and bettors themselves, you're going to enlarge the possibility of someone attempting to fix a game.

MILLER: But what about the problem we've heard that somehow if you legalize it we'll cut out illegal gambling. You've followed gambling as Chief of Security for years. Can legal gambling in any way compete with the illegal gambling operation?

DANAHY: It will be impossible to compete with them for the sole purpose of the tax-free benefits that are obtained illegally.

DUKAKIS: Mr. Cole, some questions for Mr. Danahy.

COLE: Again, Mr. Danahy, I know of no reason and I wonder if you do why we can't simply exempt gambling winnings from the internal revenue code sweep, if we take the rake-off from the handle, if, that is, we tax the winnings at the source. Do you?

DANAHY: No, I would repeat the same answer that was given before. You still are not. . . .

COLE: Well, let's not do that, okay.

DANAHY: Very well, I think it was made perfectly clear, though.

COLE: Mr. Danahy, do you remember, I guess it was a couple years ago, there was some problem with the Kansas City Chiefs, particularly one very important member of the backfield of that team. As I recall, it was said that he was in some form of association with a gambler, that is to say, a man who operated outside the law and who made book on football games. Do you remember that?

DANAHY: I wasn't Director of Security at the time, but I think you're confused on your facts. There was a problem with the Kansas City Chiefs in the year before I became Director of Security wherein the game had been taken off the board. There was a complete investigation done by the Security Department of the National Football League. Two of the players volunteered to take lie detector tests, polygraph examinations, and they were cleared.

COLE: But wasn't the allegation, though, that there was an association between this particular individual and an illegal gambler?

DANAHY: I did not hear of any such allegation whatsoever.

COLE: O boy I did. Well, let's go on beyond that. You've said that were gambling to be legalized you'd be afraid of the aura of badness, I guess is the only word I could come up with, which would surround sports. Now, gambling is lawful in the United Kingdom and they play soccer, they call it football over there. Is that a corrupt sport in the United Kingdom or elsewhere in the world, Brazil where it's played?

DANAHY: I don't have any knowledge of that.

COLE: Well, don't you make studies? Your job must have a counterpart with reference to the National Football League in the United Kingdom does it not?

DANAHY: I don't know that they have any security problem over there at all. I don't know that they have a director of security. I frankly can't answer your question. I'd like to revert to your previous question. Were you referring to Lenny Dawson?

COLE: I was.

DANAHY: The instance of Lenny Dawson supposedly having an association occurred several years after the problem of the Kansas City Chiefs. This was a question two years ago, just prior. . . .

COLE: Wasn't he the quarterback for the Kansas City Chiefs?

DANAHY: He was the quarterback for the Kansas City Chiefs and I personally conducted that investigation and I learned that Lenny Dawson had a very innocent involvement with a man that he didn't know. . . .

COLE: I agree. I'm not saying that he had any kind of an association. I'm saying that the allegation was, that's the reason the game was taken off the boards and that Jimmy "The Greek" wouldn't quote point spreads on it.

DUKAKIS: Gentlemen, I have to break in at this point whether it's the Kansas City Chiefs or anybody else. Thank you very much, Mr. Danahy, for being with us. (applause) Mr. Miller, you have a witness.

MILLER: Legalized gambling, in fact, feeds illegalized gambling. It in fact will strengthen, not weaken, the syndicate. To talk to that point I've asked to join us tonite Mr. Aaron Kohn. (applause)

DUKAKIS: Welcome to THE ADVOCATES Mr. Kohn.

KOHN: Thank you very much.

MILLER: Aaron Kohn is Managing Director of the New Orleans Crime Commission. Mr. Kohn, should the government get in the business of encouraging gambling?

KOHN: Only if we desire the kind of society in which a government teaches its people that it's perfectly acceptable to utilize their funds to try and acquire from others monies they didn't earn, without producing anything of value in exchange.

MILLER: Tell me about the British experience we've heard so much about it. Is that a successful experience—legalized gambling in Great Britain?

KOHN: Mr. Carlino, who headed the New York State Assembly, had a very thorough study made of that experience and I would think some very serious conclusions must be drawn from it as would affect the rest of our nation as a whole if we adopt the London practice. One significant thing was the fact that most of the bookie shops opened in the substandard income areas where they were getting most of the income from low-income people who then were unable to pay bills at the grocers or drug stores and there was a 25 percent increase in difficulty in collecting accounts in these small businesses. I think another very important consequence that for the first time after they legalized gambling they knew the invasion of the American organized crime syndicate.

MILLER: In other words, illegal crime followed the legalization of gambling?

KOHN: That's their thrust.

MILLER: But tell me, what about the problem of police corruption? Talking about the syndicate, it's said that if we get rid of illegal gambling that feeds police corruption that'll cure the problem of police corruption.

KOHN: Well, corruption among police and other public officials did not begin with gambling. Organized crime merely took advantage of it. We've never come face to face with the realities of our responsibility to suppress corruption. Corruption in public office is a crime, like burglary, robbery, or any other. We have somehow or other evaded the necessity for suppressing crime in public office.

MILLER: Well tell me, we've all heard that we all gamble a bit, that gambling is natural. It's quite a different thing from saying organized gambling, whether organized crime or state sanction is natural. Do you think it's possible, if we enforced the laws, to end organized criminal gambling?

KOHN: Of course, it's been done in this country. I can mention New Orleans as an experience. I can mention the city that we're in today—Los Angeles, which had organized gambling and widespread police corruption some 25 years or more ago and by instituting professionalization in the police department, introducing management which was effective and competent, and creating a buffer between politics and police management it was possible to create instead one of the most respected police agencies in the country in a city in which, for a large city, has a minimal organized crime problem.

DUKAKIS: Thank you Mr. Kohn. Mr. Cole.

COLE: Mr. Kohn, is it your testimony that there is effectively no numbers racket in Watts here in Los Angeles?

KOHN: Oh, no, no.

COLE: I'd say there's some. Is there a lot? How much would you say there is?

KOHN: They still have a problem, but I'd like to point out. . . .

COLE: Why do they have a problem, sir? Why do they have a problem, particularly with that? The LAPD is a pretty uncorrupt, as you've said, police department. Why do they have a problem with that do you suppose?

KOHN: All right, we get down to what I believe is the most vulnerable and correctable level of criminal justice in suppressing popular vice in gambling—that's our courts. It's the tradition of our courts, and one of your witnesses well expressed statistics to support it, of somehow or other taking a very tolerant attitude about an offense in which we invest a great deal of police energy and effort.

COLE: Well let's explore that. You've used the word offense, and you're right, it's a crime, it's on the statute books. And you're also right that a great many judges don't think it is. A great many judges also don't think that private betting is a crime, although it is. I can show it to you in the California Criminal Code, Michigan, Illinois, state after state, it's a crime for you and I to make a bet on the Rose Bowl or on any other thing, the outcome of which is uncertain. Do you think those laws ought to be enforced? The judges are throwing those cases out too.

KOHN: Well, for example, we do not have such a law in Louisiana. In Louisiana it must be a business before it's a crime. I don't consider gambling between peer groups, friends, associates, family to be a social problem.

COLE: What's wrong with the kind of thing that goes on in the ghetto with reference to the numbers racket?

KOHN: Because that is a society-wide, community-wide problem. It does affect total community. It's not just the decision of the individuals who privately, in their homes or with their friends, gamble.

COLE: Well I wish you'd make clear the distinction to me between my going into a drug store or policy shop of some other kind and placing a quarter bet along with the 500,000 other people on the outcome of three different races which is totally unpredictable and my sitting down with six other people around the poker table and playing for a penny a shot. What's the difference?

KOHN: A number of differences.

COLE: Well, what are they?

KOHN: When you're playing with your friends, all the money you bet comes back to you. When you play into an organized. . . .

COLE: I certainly agree, and I would take the 30 percent. . . .

DUKAKIS: Mr. Cole, you're going to have to let Mr. Kohn answer this question.

KOHN: The money does not come back to the players. Now, whether it's business of organized crime or the government, they want to skim off the investment of the players and withhold it.

DUKAKIS: Gentlemen, I'm going to have to break in at this point, I'm sorry Mr. Cole. Mr. Kohn, thank you very very much for being with us. (applause) Mr. Miller.

MILLER: Well you see where the proposal leads. Of course, if the returns from illegal gambling are not taxed and the returns from legalized gambling are taxed as income tax, that means legalized gambling can't compete so that we have the further proposal which has been advanced tonight that gambling winnings be made nontaxable. That means if you earn $100 a week you're going to have to pay your 15-20-25 percent tax on that hard-earned money. The man who wins it in legal or illegal gambling will not have to pay an income tax. Mr. Cole says you're using the internal revenue code to enforce your moral strictures. No, the principle is that all income should be taxed. Why exempt the gambling winnings? That's what's being done, enforcing that morality. Do you think gambling winnings should be exempt when earned income is not? There can be no competition here with organized crime, there can simply be a government-sponsored increase in betting by everyone and a greater harm to everyone.

DUKAKIS: Thank you Mr. Miller. All right, Mr. Cole, it's time for your rebuttal argument in favor of legalizing gambling.

COLE: Not only can there be competition with organized crime, I would argue very strongly that there must be competition with organized crime, that it can be done. We can make gambling income exempt from ordinary income tax by the simple device of taxing the money at its source. That's the way it's done in the United Kingdom. There are all kinds of ways to do it and I know of no particular reason why we can't do it here. There are all kinds of reasons why we should do it—one of the most important of them being that when you pass a law that nobody believes in, what you're doing is pinning a badge on a man and asking him to enforce it sometimes against some people. That breeds corruption. My next witness has a great deal to say about that. We are very fortunate to have with us the Chief Counsel to the Knapp Commission which is investigating police corruption in the city of New York, Mr. Michael Armstrong. (applause)

DUKAKIS: Welcome to THE ADVOCATES Mr. Armstrong.

COLE: Mr. Armstrong, very briefly now, from your experience as Chief Counsel to the Knapp Commission, what happens in connection with the fact that gambling is illegal in New York City?

ARMSTRONG: Gambling plays a very central part in the findings that we have come up with with respect to corruption in that the average police officer we've found comes on the job with a great deal of idealism and wants to do a good job. He runs into a level of petty graft when he first comes onto the force and then gambling enters the picture. And when he gets into plain-clothes duty, which is responsible for enforcing gambling, that's where we've found the most organized and most systematic levels of corruption. Police officers can get $1,100 to $1,200 a month on an organized basis and it helps to create an attitude in the department which is, I think, very destructive which can lead to more serious corruption perhaps in the narcotics area when such police officers go onto narcotics duty.

COLE: Outside of the police department, now, what does this kind of thing do to respect for the law as an institution?

ARMSTRONG: In the ghetto, particularly, with respect to the numbers game, as testimony before, you talk to the people up there and it's a situation that they accept and they see nothing wrong with the numbers, they don't see anything wrong with doing their thing and they certainly don't have any respect for police officers who are being corrupted and who are being paid off in that area and who are expected to enforce the law in others.

COLE: Now you had a great deal to do with a great many police officers in connection with your work, what do they think about legalizing gambling?

ARMSTRONG: The district attorney in one county in New York and the police department, I understand the official police department of the City of New York now, as well as the former police commissioner and other high police officers who have testified before us, seem to take the position that in one way or another gambling should be legalized.

DUKAKIS: Mr. Miller, your opportunity to ask a question.

MILLER: To the extent that you're proposing a solution, Mr. Armstrong, is it for New York or the country? Do you think we ought to allow this throughout every city in the country where there may or may not be the same kind of corruption as in New York?

ARMSTRONG: Well, I have to make a couple of disclaimers. First of all, my expertise is very much limited to New York, and secondly, I am not really free to make broad recommendations on social changes because I work for a commission and the commissioners are going to make whatever recommendations they want and I don't think they'll go into the broad questions. The area that we've looked into and that I can testify about is the effect of gambling upon corruption in New York in the police department. I would suspect that it is the same in other areas.

MILLER: Your factual investigation very much is based on what's occurred inside the City of New York.

ARMSTRONG: Very much so.

MILLER: Tell me about whether you think if gambling were legalized in New York the amount of gambling would increase. Would there be areas where there is not now substantial gambling that there would be?

ARMSTRONG: Again this is really out of the area of my expertise. Certainly in the ghetto I don't think there'd be much of an increase because right now it's an institution.

MILLER: What about outside the ghetto?

ARMSTRONG: I really don't know. Personally it wouldn't bother me.

MILLER: Do you think there ought to be any regulation at all if the government were to legalize gambling? Would you allow anyone to set up a gambling enterprise or ought there to be regulation?

ARMSTRONG: As Mr. Rosett said, the problem once you start regulating you get additional problems of corruption because you always have people who want to operate outside the regulations.

MILLER: That's clear.

ARMSTRONG: However, if you didn't go as far as licensing, if you regulated the way you regulate other industries, I think the corruption problem would be minimal.

MILLER: The way we regulate other industries, in other words you'd basically allow anyone who wanted to to set up a gambling operation whether or not he was now a gambler, whether he was running an existing organization, you'd simply allow any group to sell shares on the New York Stock Exchange, raise money, borrow money and set up the gambling operation?

ARMSTRONG: I see nothing wrong, for instance with legalizing the kind of people who are now running the numbers games in Harlem where they're doing it anyway and the only reason they're criminals is because the law has said that the policy game in Harlem and Bed-Sty. . . .

MILLER: Legalizing those who run bookie operations on sports, those same people?

ARMSTRONG: Well, again, it gets out of the area of our study, although sports betting is one that does affect police corruption.

MILLER: What about slot machines on principle, would you favor legalized slot machines in New York City?

ARMSTRONG: That's just my own personal opinion and it's very uninstructive of it. I have no problem with slot machines.

MILLER: You have no problems, so you're pretty much wide open on gambling. What about burglary, the police department in New York and other parts of the country where burglary is a substantial source of police corruption. On the burglary detail police officers take bribes, cases are known. Would you, in those cities where burglary is a substantial source of police corruption, legalize burglary?

ARMSTRONG: No, I'm against burglary.

MILLER: Well why? (laughter) You're telling us that gambling is healthy and that burglary is not. Burglary represents a community response. . . .

ARMSTRONG: I'm saying as a personal matter to me it doesn't bother me if people gamble and it does bother me if somebody burgles my house.

MILLER: Burgles your house, so the question then is do you find the gambling, even if sponsored by the government, inoffensive? You don't think there's any harm in encouraging people to gamble.

ARMSTRONG: I don't think there's any harm in allowing people to decide if they want to gamble and I do find it. . . .

MILLER: Or for people to run advertising, for an advertising, you know, daily double for breakfast, Madison Avenue on gambling, that's all okay with you.

DUKAKIS: Gentlemen, I'll have to cut in at this point. Thank you very much Mr. Armstrong for being with us. Thank you. (applause) Now, Mr. Cole, you have one quick minute in which to summarize your case.

COLE: Thank you Mr. Dukakis. You've heard a number of reasons why gambling should be legalized tonight. You have just heard that the illegality of gambling breeds a great deal of police corruption, more, I submit, than even burglary. It breeds, worse than that, disrespect for the law as an institution. And I guess, really, it ought to, because there are laws now against you and I having private games of chance. They are not enforced, nor should they be enforced, that the same kind of activity which goes on, recreational gambling in the ghetto, is proscribed and those proscriptions are enforced to some degree, to the degree that police corruption doesn't prevent them from being enforced. Moreover the money which is raked right off the top of that now goes to the syndicate. I don't think that's too good an idea. I think that that money ought to be kept in the community, used for the public good. But you may not think that gambling is good for you. I happen not to agree with you if that's what you think, but remember—the proposal tonight is not to make gambling mandatory, just legal.

DUKAKIS: Thank you Mr. Cole. Mr. Miller, you also have one rapid minute to summarize.

MILLER: What have we got here? Those of you interested in legalizing gambling will notice that no one who favors the proposal has put forth the suggestion that it is a revenue-raising measure that would be successful enough to justify its institution. We can put that to one side. Well, if it doesn't raise revenue, if it doesn't lower the tax burden, then why in the world should we allow the gambling? Becuase it will drive out organized crime? But it has been said, in order to compete with organized crime you have to have tax-free gambling earnings. Now saying tax at the source doesn't change anything. You either have to tax it, in which case the return is less and you can't compete, or you don't tax it, in which case you're saying to the man who earns money he gets taxed, the man who earns on gambling he does not get taxed. Is that the extent we want to go? Even Jimmy "The Greek" is afraid of legalized gambling on college sports, and for good reason. With some thought he and we all could see that it would apply to professional sports as well. What kind of society do we want? Do we want a society where our government sponsors, encourages, permits advertising for gambling that may eventually go to illegal gambling? Or do we want a society that recognizes gambling as a fact, seeks to channel and control it as best we can?

Index